Mobility

*A New Urban Design and Transport Planning
Philosophy for a Sustainable Future*

By John Whitelegg

Mobility

Published by Createspace Independent Publishing Platform, 2016.

ISBN-13: 978-1530227877.
ISBN-10: 1530227879.

Acknowledgements

I have been very fortunate indeed to receive support and encouragement from many splendid people. They include Per Homann Jespersen, Jeff Kenworthy, Gordon Clark, Robert Poole and Helmut Holzapfel. I am also indebted to all those individuals I met during a formative period of employment in the Ministry of Urban Development, Housing and Traffic in Düsseldorf in the late 1980s. That was a long time ago but it brought about a major paradigm shift in my own thinking which has resulted in this book. In a similar way I benefitted enormously from discussions with splendid people in Australia especially Paul Tranter in Canberra and the late Paul Mees in Melbourne. My project work in India and China has had a huge impact on my thinking about mobility and global trends and that experience has also fed into this book. It is impossible to walk around Kolkata (Calcutta) without reflecting on the consequences of year-on-year growth in mobility. I owe a special thanks to Mark Tanner in Lancaster who with great patience and kindness has steered me through the alien world of producing an e-book and without whom I could not have got this far. As always in spite of the wonderful support and first class advice there will be errors and when they occur they are entirely my fault. Any serious errors will be corrected in a subsequent edition.

John Whitelegg, Järna, Sweden

Dedication

This book is dedicated to 8 children who will have to sort out the mess created by those of us who were children in the 1950s and 60s. They are Jacob, Teo, Lauren, Fynn, Kilian, Rebecca, Henry and Hedda.

Contents

Introduction

In the 1950s as a primary school child in Oldham (UK) I had very limited mobility measured in terms of the number of miles I ranged over each week. Life was intensely focused on the locality, intense contact with other children who lived within 500metres of my home, and intense outdoor play for as many hours as my parents would allow (usually more than they would allow). We children decided when to go out, where to go, with whom and what to play and from an early age acquired a great deal of proficiency in negotiation skills, dispute resolution and independent decision-taking. Life was very good, full and rich and the low level of mobility contributed to that richness. Time that might have been spent in a car being taken to organized "things" was put to good use in ways we decided. We did not need to roam very far from home and we enjoyed our local streets, second world war air-raid shelters (dark, dirty and mysterious) and large amounts of untidy urban space.

Daily activities included digging in clay pits to release ground water, playing on "the woods" (large structures of substantial planking erected to support an unstable wall on a public building) and playing in derelict homes scheduled for demolition in the massive "slum clearance" fetish of the late 1950s and early 1960s in Oldham. As an aside they were not really slums but that is another story about the destruction of traditional urban communities and the compulsory relocation of thousands of residents to remote outer areas which then necessitated more travel to do anything i.e. more mobility.

Mobility measured crudely in terms of how many kilometres we move around every day has nothing whatsoever has to do with quality of life, rich human interaction, satisfaction, happiness and a detailed knowledge and familiarity with places and the things we chose to do in those places. I would go further and say that the limited mobility we experienced actually contributed to the development of self-confidence, spatial ability and relationship skills.

It is fashionable in an age of high mobility to dismiss these views as another example of looking through "rose-tinted spectacles" or even worse as the ramblings of older people reminiscing about a golden age or signing up to the "things were better in my youth than now" perspective. These dismissive comments should be dismissed. The reality of those years in the 1950s is documented in many oral histories and contemporary documentaries and is rich in corroboration.

The importance of these personal stories lies in their ability to question the centrality of the mobility paradigm that grew in strength through the decades after 1960 and continued to grow in strength in the first two decades of the 21st century. Whatever high levels of mobility have brought to enrich the lives of children or improve the quality of life of all of us, and the balance sheet is far from positive, it is clear that low mobility was associated with high level of satisfaction, enjoyment and developmental significance.

The low mobility world of the 1950s was embedded in a wider life style and societal context that has been largely swept away in so-called developed societies or post-industrial societies. The Oldham of my childhood in the 1950s was character-ised by large numbers of local shops within walking distance, a vigorous and enormous open air market and indoor market (Tommyfield) again within walking distance, local parks, a local library, a local swimming pool (Robin Hill Baths) and perhaps even more surprisingly a public wash house where my mother took the family washing and joined in with many other women to do the washing in an enormous, steamy room full of washing and drying facilities (and from the point of view of a 6 year old boy, full of very scary women). This was less than 500m from my home and on the way to my primary school (Dunbar St infants).

At some point in time around the age of 10 or 11 the world got bigger as we children roamed even further afield but once again under our own steam, control and decision-taking responsibility. We used the number 9 bus to travel approximately 8kms to a huge countryside park (Tandle Hills) and played all day in wooded areas with numerous paths and byways. We discovered the train and went to Manchester, 12kms away on a line now closed and replaced by a tram system from Oldham Werneth station to Manchester Victoria. We then wandered aimlessly and slowly around the centre of Manchester and then went home.

Fast forwarding to the year 2015 we find a lively discussion amongst architects, urban planners and transport experts about compact cities, sustainable cities and "children's independent mobility" (CIM). We are told that increasing urban density is a good thing, that we should increase the amount of walking and cycling and that we should reduce car use. These are all laudable aims but surely it is necessary to try and understand why these things were the norm in the 1950s in many parts of Britain and were then swept away by decades of thoughtless road building, tearing down the kind of densely populated streets we are now trying to reinvent and encouraging car use even for very short journeys.

Just as stories about life in the 1950s reveal the emptiness and sham of stories around the wonderful things that flow from higher mobility so the same stories tell us that there are many examples of sustainable cities and child friendly cities and they did exist and we did destroy them. If we really do want to restore this kind of world with all its benefits we can only do so if we redefine our love affair with mobility, redefine it as an historical blip, show how lower mobility produces magnified benefits and embed 21st century "new" urban thinking in a strong low mobility context. That is the objective of this book.

During the development of these ideas in the next 14 chapters it will be important to keep uppermost in our minds the very clear implication of "low mobility". Low mobility is a decoupling concept. This book argues that we must decouple mobility from its association with progress, happiness and quality of life. The consumption of ever-increasing amounts of distance does not increase happiness or improve quality of life and is associated with a growing list of negative consequences. Low mobility quite simply suggest that we can all benefit enormously from reduced levels of physical travel and an intensification of what we do within smaller geographical areas. This will not "sit well" with the world view of most of us in 2015 but the point of this book is to demonstrate that a low mobility world has a great deal to offer and its opposite is a logical impossibility. We cannot accommodate an annual average percentage increase in distance travelled for all 7 billion of us so we may as well start explaining, designing and delivering a low mobility alternative.

It could not be clearer that most governmental statements in the UK about new urban design or so-called "active" transport (this means walking and cycling) are meaningless unless we engineer this paradigm shift from high mobility to low mobility. Such a paradigm shift also involves a shift in language. The phrase "low mobility" whilst accurately describing a world characterized by fewer kilometres travelled per person per annum fails to convey the richness of a world characterised by many more destinations opportunities within a much smaller physical area and a world where enormous amounts of time and money (and pollution) are not devoted to the business of accessing distant places. This is a world where we can do far more "things" within walking and cycling distance of our homes than is now the case. It is a world that can be described as "the city of short distances" for those who live in urban areas and it is a world where accessibility has replaced mobility as a key policy objective.

Mobility is a very slippery concept and for a word and an ideology that is used to support much of the contemporary rhetoric about progress, economic growth and modernity this is rather odd. Mobility is associated with more wealth, more social mobility, opportunity and more happiness and all these notions are untested and cannot be corroborated by reference to an evidence base. The attentive reader will struggle in vain to find a convincing argument based on evidence that higher levels of mobility equates to higher levels of quality of life, happiness, social justice or health.

At the risk of labouring the point (but it is necessary to labour the point given the paucity of clear thinking on mobility) let us imagine a report from a CEO to the annual general meeting of shareholders who announces with great pleasure that the company has had a very successful year:

"In the past 12 months we have moved all our outward freight shipments twice as far as in the previous 12 months and we have achieved an increase in the daily commuting distance for all our staff from 20kms per day to 50kms per day. More significantly as a sign of our commitment to expansion and innovation the inputs into our manufacturing process now come twice as far as in the previous 12 months and the food in our excellent staff restaurants now travels on average 1200kms for one lunch sitting compared to 800kms 12 months ago."

Is this a very successful company? Whether it is successful or not the company has fully embraced the ideology of mobility. Everything that can move, now moves much more than it did in a previous accounting period so if we are to celebrate mobility and encourage higher level of mobility (which we do most of the time) it follows that we must congratulate this company on its success.

The reality, however, is different. The CEO's annual report will strike most people as rather odd. There is something not quite right about it and the thing that is not quite right about it is that mobility is problematic. It is not an unalloyed good thing. It is not praiseworthy if we increase levels of mobility. It could signal the opposite of success if we choose to source inputs into our manufacturing process that originate thousands of kilometres away and en route pass nearer sources. Boege (1995) revealed the depth of this inefficiency in her classic yoghurt study which we return to in a later chapter. For now we note that the substitution of far for near is illogical and perverse. It generates extra kilometres of movement. It is a sham.

The CEO's report could be replicated with an average family living in urban England. If that family has to double its kilometres of travel to go shopping, go to school or attend a hospital appointment is that a good thing? If we think mobility is a good thing then these increases in mobility are a good thing but they are not. It rarely attracts the interest and excitement of urban and transport planners that we routinely create the city of longer distances by closing post offices, closing smaller primary schools and centralizing hospitals at ever-more remote locations, all of which add to the amount of time that must be allocated to our journeys, and then put time savings at the centre of our decisions making and appraisal when we come to look at look at ways of prioritizing spending on transport projects. This is clearly illogical and self-defeating but most professionals seem to be content with managing policies that directly contradict each other.

If we want to set out to increase mobility it is rather easy to do. We can start by closing local hospitals as Plymouth (SW England) did in the 1970s. If we close local hospitals and build a new one that is many miles away from where people live we force users to travel the extra miles and increase mobility. Derriford hospital (the new one that replaced 3 closed hospitals) was the subject of a major transport study in 1995 that revealed a car-trip generation of 3 million pa. This added many problems of congestion and delay to the highways system and forced people to travel further. Mobility went up but the so did the difficulties associated with accessing health care and so did expenditure on highway "improvements" (i.e. extra road space) to cope with increased demand. Higher mobility also added to inequality. Those with cars could access the new hospital relatively easily but those without cars could not. Increased mobility comes with very serious consequences which is a redistribution of costs and difficulty to penalise poorer groups in society.

In Oldham in the 1950s it was not necessary to consume so much distance each day. Shops, schools, markets, health care, libraries and swimming pools were all within easy reach. We accomplished all our daily travel purposes on foot, within a very short time budget and at a very low cost and in a curious kind of way contemporary urban and transport planning tries to recreate this mixture but on the back of higher mobility. This was clearly demonstrated by Illich in his 1974 publication "Energy and Equity":

"Beyond a certain speed, motorised vehicles create remoteness which they alone can shrink. They create distances for all and shrink them for only a few" Illich (1974), page 42."

The Derriford Hospital example is a clear example of decision-making creating remoteness, increasing distances to be travelled and penalising those who do not have the means to overcome the barriers of longer distances.

Holzapfel (2012) has shed a considerable amount of light into the dark corners of the mobility debate. He makes very clear links between mobility, accessibility, urban design and quality of life through two accounts of daily life and travel choices in German localities:

"If I'm going to be talking about mobility today, I should start with two fictitious everyday scenarios, which illustrate people's situations: Mr Branger lives some-where small near Kassel called Kleinalmerode. He works in a large factory approximately 50km away. As far as shopping goes, of course, there's nothing left in Kleinalmerode. But Mr Branger has an estate car, and regularly drives to a supermarket 10-15km away. If he can't do it, then his wife does, in her small second car, which she also uses to take the children to kindergarten and school, as Kleinalmerode doesn't have a school or kindergarten any more. As a result the Branger family has built a lovely, big and low-cost detached home on an inexpensive plot of land, with lots of space round about outside.

The second everyday scenario shows the Kebberich family, who live in a terraced house in the old part of Tübingen. He or she – let's leave that open for the moment – cycles to work at the university; the other half has a part-time job, let's say, in a fashion boutique nearby. The children go to a nearby school. They can get to this school on foot. The family's small car is parked little-used in a communal garage nearby. The Kebberichs use the small space in front of the house as a garden. The couple regularly discuss whether it wouldn't make sense to get rid of the car, because the mileage is very low, and when necessary sign up to a car sharing scheme.

Which family is more mobile? The Kebberichs in Tübingen or the Branger family in Kleinalmerode with their detached home – whose adjoining double garage already has space reserved for the children, so that perhaps they too can have wheels later on. Who lives better? Where's the better place to be living? In the detached house in the open countryside or in Tübingen?"

It is clear from these two accounts that a high quality of life with a large number of associated benefits for public policy and expenditure can be the result of lower mobility. The task for all of us is to elevate this rather obvious story line into a clear policy imperative and one that can replace the dangerous, outmoded and perverse "mobility is good" paradigm.

In the remainder of this book I will attempt to demonstrate that mobility is a chaotic concept already in a state of collapse as a result of internal contradictions. The elevation of mobility to a central position in political, economic, architectural and planning discourse represents a significant error in those areas and social science discourse in general. The time is now right to correct that error. Mobility as a goal or a central organising principle is irrelevant and should be deleted from the transport and urban planning lexicon. Other things matter much more including time budgets, fiscal prudence, equality, accessibility, and health and all these dimensions of everyday life can be enriched within a low mobility framework and will remain unobtainable if we continue to pursue high mobility goals.

Chapter 1
How mobile are we and how did we get here?

The mobility growth paradigm

Mobility is most commonly measured, if at all, as total distance travelled per annum per capita in kilometres and/or total distance travelled per day per capita. There are other important dimensions e.g. number of trips made per day or number of destinations that can be accessed by different modes of transport in a defined unit of time but these are not generally measured in a systematic way or included in data sets. Usually mobility is not defined. It has become a rather vague concept associated with quality of life or progress and it is invoked as a "good thing" and something that should be increased. This is very clear in most national transport policies and at the European level where major transport policies and funding mechanisms are increasingly framed.

A recent EU research and development document (European Commission 2013a) begins with the main heading "Mobility for growth." It does not define mobility. The document is an undiluted manifesto accepting and promoting the growth of mobility and advocating the importance of this growth for the success of wider economic policy objectives, asserting the unquestioned importance of endless economic growth and ignoring the voluminous literature on the impossibility of endless economic growth and of ecological and resource limits to growth (Douthwaite, 1992, Schneidewind, 2014). The European Commission document contains no recognition whatsoever of the well-developed sustainable transport discourse with its emphasis on traffic reduction, demand management, urban planning in favour of the "city of short distances" and modal shift from the car to walking, cycling and public transport or from the aircraft to electronic substitution e.g. videoconferencing. Similarly it airbrushes out of the picture the need to de-carbonise transport and link something called "mobility for growth" to the urgent need to reduce greenhouse gas emissions in the transport sector. There is no suggestion that spatial planning has a role to play. We could, for example, plan for the tripling of rail capacity in the UK on the West Coast Main Line (WCML) or we could plan for a step change in the importance and functionality of Liverpool and Manchester so that we do not "need" to get on a train to London every time something important has to be discussed. In other words we can manage demand rather than feed a growth in demand through an increase in capacity and/or subsidy. The National Theatre and Royal Opera House could also be in one or more of Manchester, Liverpool, Leeds and Newcastle and thereby be much more accessible to more people than those who live in London and those who can afford rail fares costing more than the entrance ticket to the performances hosted by these publicly funded national organisations.

Traffic reduction and demand management have a great deal to offer to the world of economic success, which is not the same as growth, but those who write key policy statements in Brussels and those in London who urge Brussels to set the tone of the growth paradigm, do not intend to stray very far from the world of "mobility for growth."

On aviation the document says that world air transport is growing by 4-5% pa and "we should therefore seize all opportunities associated with this growth." The aviation discussion then proceeds to emphasise the importance of reducing travel time for flying and increasing air capacity, both of which will contribute to the growth in demand for air travel and together with huge subsidies for aviation will produce the self-fulfilling prophecy of growth in this dimension of mobility.

I return to the question of subsidy in Chapter 5 but it is pertinent at this point to draw attention to the huge subsidies that aviation receives and the role this has to play in generating higher levels of demand for flying. The annual subsidy to European aviation is 30 billion Euros (Cramer, 2014).

On rail and road transport there is the same uncritical acceptance of growth in demand with a nod towards the need to make all modes of transport cleaner, greener and smarter and reduce noise and air pollution. Interestingly there is no discussion about the costs of all this growth in transport demand and who will fund the public expenditure share. Current levels of subsidy to transport already exceed some estimates of Greek national debt at 270-290 billion Euros pa (European Environment Agency, 2007) and the message from Brussels is keep on spending because the growth in mobility is good.

The document even manages a section on reducing congestion without mentioning the scope for reducing the number of cars and trucks on the roads. This is a remarkable achievement. It does, however, mention the importance of walking, cycling and public transport with the insertion of an important condition:

"Exploring how a favourable environment can be created for a significant growth in public transport at limited extra costs" (page 37).

There is no use of the phrase "at limited extra costs" when the discussion deals with the billions of Euros needed to fund high speed rail estimated to be £50 billion on the UK high speed rail project known as HS2 (House of Commons, 2015) or, indeed, additional airport capacity or new motorways.

The total research allocation funding in this European Commission document for "smart, green and integrated transport" and its unbridled support for growth in mobility is 579 million Euros in 2014 and 287 million Euros in 2015.

We are very clearly locked into a mobility growth paradigm with high level political and budgetary support and low level thinking about what it really means. What will the world look like if we all (and this includes the populations of Africa, India, China and South America) travel very far, very fast and very often for as many destinations and trip purposes as possible? This is the logical end point of a policy called "mobility for growth" but those advocating higher levels of mobility are most reluctant to flesh out the details of the world that will have been created.

Interestingly Schaefer (2005) has given us a clear picture of this end point. Schaefer makes a valuable contribution to the mobility debate by calculating the total per capita distance travelled at a future point in time based on a number of "givens." The starting point is the travel time constant for the amount of time human beings will travel each day (approx. 1.1 hours) discussed in detail by Zahavi (1979) and Marchetti (1994). This is then linked to a generalized estimate of increases in speed of travel over a long time period. Schaefer then calculates that the logical end point for every person on the planet is that he or she will be travelling 262,800 kilometres per year. This is based on the equation:

600kph x 1.2 hours per day x 365 days per annum= 262,800 kilometres.

This calculation is shown graphically in Figure 1.1.

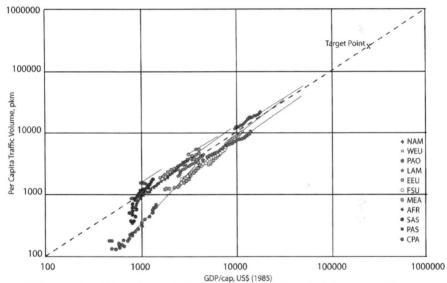

Fig. 1.1: Scenario for mobility and income for 11 regions, 1991-2050. A hypothetical "target point", to which all trajectories converge, is shown. For comparison, historical data (1960-1990) are shown with symbols.
Source: A. Schafer, D.G. Victor / Transportation Research Part A 34 (2000)

Schaefer's calculation is logically watertight and is supported by the rhetoric in "Mobility for Growth." Those that support higher levels of mobility have a responsibility to be very clear about how far this growth can or should continue and the extent to which it is fuelled by subsidy and sloppy spatial planning. They are silent on all these points.

How did we get here?

Transport history and economic history provides a detailed analysis of growth in transport demand in the last 300 years. Dyos and Aldcroft (1969) provide an excellent signposting service tracking this growth and its links with industriali-sation, technological change and urbanisation. The journey from London to Edinburgh by passenger coach took 10 days in 1754 and two days by 1836. London and Manchester were 3 days apart in 1750 and 18 hours in 1836. York was 4 days out of London in the 1750s and in the 1830s could be done in 20 hours. Movement between the major towns was 4 or 5 times as fast around 1830 as it had been in 1750.

The period of passenger coach dominance, approximately 1750-1850 saw an increase in the numbers carried (Dyos and Aldcroft, 1969). This is a clear example of an increase in mobility linked to technological and organisational changes and dramatic improvements in road maintenance. This increase in mobility was closely associated with improvements in disposable income and economic growth that have cemented the whole mobility discourse into a solid "feel good" narrative. Mobility is a good thing and why would anyone want to suggest otherwise?

The passenger coach era came to an end with the growth of rail travel and once again mobility increased and came to be seen as a central part of human progress and political agendas.

The railway building era in Britain transformed the possibilities for travel and long distance movement and gradually replaced horse drawn coaches. The Liverpool and Manchester railway opened in 1834 connecting two of the largest cities in Britain and unlike previous railway schemes emphasised passenger traffic. It covered the 30 miles separating these two cities in 1.5 hours, halving the time taken by the coach and at a cost of five shillings a ticket.

	Track length (miles)	Total number of passen-gers (millions)
1870	15537	336.5
1880	17933	603.9
1890	20073	817.1
1900	21855	1142.3
1912	23441	1294.3
1924		1746.9
1933		1575
1937		1819

Table 1.1: Railway growth in Britain
Source: Dyos and Aldcroft (1969), page 156 and 325

Railway use in Britain grew rapidly in the 19th and early 20th centuries (Table 1.1). The growth in numbers was also accompanied by longer distance trips and by a social revolution so that travel over longer distances was no longer the preserve of the wealthy as was the case with horse drawn coaches.

In a very early example of what we would now call social engineering or reducing social exclusion, an Act of Parliament in 1844 made provision for one train daily along every new passenger line stopping at every station and carrying third class passengers at 1d (one old, pre-decimalisation, penny) per mile. The process of

widening train travel to include "workmen" and other low income groups accelerated through the 19th century after third class ticket prices were reduced to 1d per
mile in 1883 on most trains and the average fares declined even further to 0.5d (a
halfpenny) by the early twentieth century.

Marchetti (1994), making extensive use of the findings of Zahavi (1979) has
quantified the rate of growth of mobility over time from 1800-2000 in France and
calculated that the average annual increase in distance travelled is 3%. In Figure 1.2
he tracks the development of each mode and transport technology over this long time
period and concludes:

"The share of the fastest mode of transport in the budget of the traveller keeps
increasing, with the costs decreasing and his disposable income increasing."

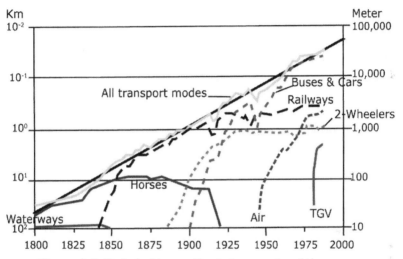

Figure 1.2: Technical innovation in transport and the
increase in mobility for France.
Originally Figure 16 in Marchetti (1994)

Figure 1.2 charts the distance travelled per day by vehicles and does not include
walking and cycling. It provides us with a clear benchmark. Mobility has been
increasing at 3% pa over the last 200 years and whilst this result is specific to
France we can assume from what we know about railway, cars and aviation
trends over time that the result will be similar in other western European
countries. Ausubel and Marchetti (2001) produce comparable data for the USA
(Figure 1.3).

The average annual increase in passenger distance in Figure 1.3 is 2.8% which is
very similar to the French data referred to above.

The authors conclude: "Let us review our picture of mobility. Speed matters.
Humans search for speed because travel time being fixed, speed gives us
territory, that is, access to resources…as a rule the choice is to consume both

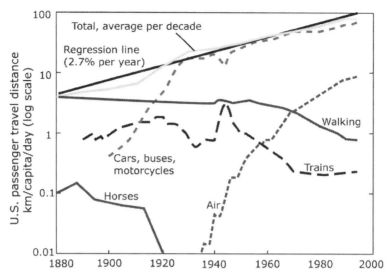

Figure 1.3: Passenger travel distance per capita per day in the USA
Source: Ausubel and Marchetti (2001), originally figure 2

the travel time budget hour and the disposable money budget maximising the distance, that is, the speed."

Interestingly Marchetti confirms that over this long period of time and across different regions and cultures we still have a stable propensity to spend one hour per day travelling. If we walk that means we cover a distance of 5km (2.5kms on both outward and return journeys) which Marchetti says is a radius of 2.5kms and therefore covers an area of 20 sq kms. If we go by car we cover a distance that is 6 or 7 times greater than the linear walk distance and if this linear distance is translated into an area we can cover an area by car that is 50 times greater than on foot (assuming an average speed of 35kph producing an area covered of 1000 sq kms).

Marchetti's (1994) view of this one hour "invariant" is very clear:

"It shows the quintessential unity of travelling instincts around the world above culture, race and religion, so to speak, which gives unity to the considerations relative to the history and future of travelling, and provides a robust basis for forecasts in time and geography."

Ausubel, Marchetti and Meyer (2005) expand the discussion of invariants to include the finding that "on average people make 3-4 trips per day, rich or poor."

They also expand on the USA case study showing an average annual growth in mobility of 2.7% and offer a rare view of where this will take us:

"Staying within present laws, a 2.7% per year growth means a doubling of mobility in 25 years and a 16-fold increase in a century."

It remains one of the most remarkable blind spots in transport policy and the totality of public policy and budgeting that this doubling or 16-folding remains on target and is not discussed.

The historical development of transport and mobility, as discussed above for passenger coach and rail travel in the 18th and 19th centuries, goes some way towards explaining the contemporary fascination with mobility as a policy driver, a readily available pre-packaged source of promises for politicians seeking votes and something that filters out any suggestion that lower levels of mobility might produce much better outcomes for everyone. In western Europe we have lived through 300 years of impressive continuous development of transport technology, time savings and the widening of opportunity fields, with no attempt to evaluate the costs and benefits of alternative scenarios compared to the "business as usual" scenario, and this has hard-wired a mobility fetish into human development that is resistant to debate.

The growth of mobility itself is a powerful source of positive feedback. As average annual distances travelled increase and the media recycles exciting stories about exciting things that flow from travel so the idea that mobility is on an endless growth trajectory becomes more deeply embedded. If it goes up every year it must be good. The positive feedback in the case of mobility is multi-layered and synergistic. Every year spatial planning (or the lack of it) increases the distances between "things", subsidies encourage the perception that car travel or aviation is cheaper than it really is and the constant flow of media stories around the growth of mobility supports and sustains more mobility. All of these factors then multiply the effects of the other factors and it becomes very difficult indeed to discuss the possibility that reductions in mobility might actually bring multiple benefits.

Mobility: the Faustian bargain

Marchetti in his many publications has made it very clear that mobility is a powerful human imperative linked to territory and resources. We have an absolute need to cover more ground so we can access more resources so anything that increases our range e.g. a higher speed is a "good thing." His comparison of 20 sq. kms of territory based on walking and 1000 sq kms based on the car (a 50-fold increase in territory and resources) is a powerful image.

This powerful image and its attractive simplicity cannot be relied upon to explain current trends in mobility or signpost the future. In this important respect Marchetti is wrong. For most of the 20th century human beings have not needed to wander around and dominate a large territory in order to survive and prosper and the idea has no relevance to the 21st century. It is accepted that the idea of territory and resources may still lie buried in the perceptions and motivations of those who take important decisions on transport infrastructure, spending and mobility and it is certainly the case that more mobility is attractive to politicians of all colours, except the European green parties who Marchetti (1993) criticises in his article "On Mobility." If it does sit in those minds like some kind of aberrant virus intent on replicating itself in every cell so that all decision taking is pro mobility then we have an explanation for the scale of current problems. This must not, however, be conflated with some kind of predictive capability or justification for ill-judged decisions or smugness about our ability to predict the future.

	1995	2005
Graz	8824	8102
Copenhagen	10877	11234
Helsinki	8255	8628
Dusseldorf	9384	9731
Oslo	10133	12155
Hong Kong	5003	6344
Madrid	6721	8251
Stockholm	11333	10221
Berne	12145	13707
Geneva	8484	10206
London	8021	8978
Vienna	7072	8196
Manchester	6262	7053
Stuttgart	9055	10324
Brussels	5383	5862
Prague	9239	12533
Brisbane	13712	14429
Melbourne	13330	12957
Perth	14568	14711
Sydney	12341	13301
Calgary	12210	12519
Montreal	8764	7780
Ottawa	9410	9772
Toronto	7945	7514
Vancouver	10359	11204
Berlin	6732	8222
Frankfurt	8686	10858
Hamburg	10305	10792
Munich	9411	11864
Singapore	6200	6472
Zurich	11172	11997
Atlanta	25209	24639
Chicago	16708	17887
Denver	18203	22348
Houston	25624	21304
Los Angeles	17875	17653
New York	13998	14888
Phoenix	15364	16009
San Diego	19039	19877
San Francisco	18337	19108
Washington DC	18236	21663
Overall Average	11706	12482

Table 1.2: Total mobility in 41 world cities in 2005. Total kms travelled per person in 1995 and 2005 by car, motorbike, public transport, walking and cycling
Source: Kenworthy (2014)

It is also the case that we now know a great deal about mobility and accessibility and transport and quality of life in cities and how to produce very attractive urban lifestyles which by definition are low mobility lifestyles. This level of understanding has been advanced by, amongst others Jacobs (1961), Gehl (2010), ITDP (2012) and Holzapfel (2014). All of these authors and sources demonstrate that there are many benefits associated with compact cities, high density cities, high quality walking, cycling and public transport use, low levels of car use (which means lower levels of mobility) , a high concentration of destinations within easy reach of everyone without having to own a car, rich social interaction possibilities, low levels of noise, low level of pollution and an overall total environment that is welcoming, friendly and valuable for those groups normally ignored by pro-mobility advocates i.e. the old, children, and women with child care duties.

Kenworthy (2014) has shown that mobility levels in 41 world cities vary from a low of 5682 kms travelled per person in Brussels to a high of 24639 in Atlanta (USA) (Table 1.2).

The large range of annual kms travelled per person in Table 1.2 (see previous page) reveals a completely different dimension to the mobility debate to that described by Marchetti. Mobility varies enormously and it varies directly as a result of spatial form, urban density and the number of destinations available to residents within a given geographical area. The latter component of mobility can more accurately be described as accessibility. Accessibility is essentially a performance measure of how an urban system or locality works. How many destinations e.g. shops, school, church, doctor, post office can a resident access on foot in (say) 30 minutes or by bike in (say) 15 minutes. The time threshold can be varied but it is the concept itself that is important. A city with a high accessibility score will facilitate a large number of potential origin-destination pairs within a small time budget and at a small (or zero) monetary budget. A low accessibility city, region or locality will require a car trip to support trips to destinations that few and far between.

To illustrate this point let's look at Atlanta (24639 kms per person in 2005) and Brussels (5862 kms per person in 2005). First in Marchetti and anthropological terms it is clearly possible for Brussels residents to live a full life, access resources and support a reasonable quality of life at a much smaller expenditure of energy and cash than his or her Atlanta comparator. In human evolutionary terms the Brussels resident is very successful because the expenditure of cash and energy is smaller than Atlanta and this will leave more of both commodities for other things and these other things can enrich quality of life. For now we will note that there is no time benefit for the Brussels residents compared to the Atlanta resident. Both will still travel for about 1 hour each day.

We could possibly argue that the Atlanta resident is approximately 5 times better off or 5 times happier than the Brussels case but this would need some very robust evidence and would also fly in the face of a large literature on the miseries of a long distance commute and time stuck in traffic jams.

The logical conclusion is that the Brussels resident has got a really good deal in terms of everyday living, budgets and stress levels compared to the Atlanta case.

It is also the case that Atlanta has carried a significant amount of budgetary stress in building, repairing and expanding freeways and highways, bridges and tunnels. It is more expensive to support 24639 person kms pa than it is to support 5862 kms per person pa (Vivier, 2006).

The high mobility of the Atlanta resident simply means that he or she has to travel further at a bigger cost than a Brussels person and this is unequivocally a "bad deal" and a failure of public policy.

The failure of public policy is multiple. The Atlanta system burdens city and regional administrations with unaffordable costs and a widening gap between revenue and expenditure. It also causes enormous problems for ordinary families. The impact on ordinary families of similar situations in Australian cities has been very well documented by Dodson and Sipe (2008). The consequences of misguided policies in Australian cities to encourage urban sprawl, longer distances for most journey purposes and high levels of dependency on private cars has been to give ordinary families huge problems of managing budgets, coping with rising petrol prices and in extremis being unable to get to work and joining the ranks of the urban poor. Urban poverty in this case is directly linked to all those policies that have combined to produce sprawl, car dependency, and lack of destinations that are easily accessible and grossly inadequate public transport. This is the case in Parramatta in the western suburbs of Sydney and there could not be a clearer demonstration of the failures, perversity and uselessness of a public policy based on mobility and policies that ignore high quality accessibility scenarios.

Two German families

In the Introduction I quoted Holzapfel and his account of two German families, the Kebberich family in Tübingen and the Branger family in Kleinalmerode near Kassel.

It is a central argument of this book that the Kebberich family in Tübingen is better off than the Branger family. It should be the purpose of public policy and transport policy to make it possible for all those wishing to pursue a high accessibility, low cost, high quality of life style to do so. Current transport and public policy encourages mobility which is a very different objective and is high cost for individuals and city-regional governments and adds to the carbon burden generated by the transport sector to the detriment of climate change policy.

These questions accurately describe the full multi-dimensionality of the mobility and accessibility interplay and point to bigger societal questions around choice and resilience. If we have more mobility in total across society does this extinguish the options that have been selected by the Kebberich family? Is it the case that a lifestyle choice for more mobility for some actually takes away the option of a lower mobility life style for others? Maybe mobility is a bit like passive smoking in that it (allegedly) gives a great deal of pleasure to the primary user but has many deleterious side effects for those who choose not to smoke. Passive smoking carries the potential to damage the health of those who have chosen not to smoke and those choosing high mobility lifestyles most certainly erode the quality of life of those pursuing low mobility options. The erosion mechanisms are well known. Higher level of traffic (high mobility) erodes the potential for walking and cycling as traffic danger increases. Low mobility becomes even more difficult as destinations disappear. Health care, education and shopping all show signs of a reduction in number, an increase in size and a lengthening of trips between origins and destinations. Trip lengthening rapidly exterminates walking and cycling choices.

This is the reality described eloquently by Illich (1974) when he concludes that no one can save time without forcing another to lose it (page 42) and "motorised vehicles create remoteness which they alone can shrink. They create distances for all and shrink them for only a few" (page 42).

Resilience can be defined as our ability to absorb and adapt to shocks in ways that are that are manageable because we have built into our planning and organisational systems a robustness and resilience that minimises the impact of those shocks and in advance. The National Health Service in the UK would be far more resilient if it maintained a network of hospitals closer to where staff and patients lived and if it embraced a logistics concept based on "near" rather than "far." A system based on long distance travel by staff and long distance sourcing of drugs and surgical supplies is much more likely to break down, at a time when it is really needed, than a more localised system. It is not resilient. If we have more mobility are we more susceptible and vulnerable (less resilient) to the kind of stresses identified by Dodson and Sipe (2008) or the consequences of climate change or permanent gridlock interrupting the increasingly long supply lines now the norm in the National Health Service and food logistics?

A growth in mobility will always produce a decline in resilience.

In the next chapter I elaborate further some of the more serious consequences that flow from the mobility growth paradigm.

Chapter 2
Consequences

H igh levels of mobility widen opportunities, increase the number of jobs available within acceptable travel times, allow car owners and those with access to cars to visit distant shopping centres, get to national parks and their walking, climbing and caving opportunities and visit friends and relatives in rural areas with no buses on a Sunday. All of these things are difficult without a car and it is not surprising that 92% of all trips to the English Lake District are by car. Car based mobility allows those who benefit to range widely over a large area in search of work and promotion and increasingly is part of the consumerist approach to schools and hospitals. It is now routine in the UK to inspect schools and hospitals and produce rankings and performance measures with the result that we "shop" for a good school or a good hospital that may be further away than more local facilities. The idea that all schools and hospitals should be of high quality and serve a local area with no need for residents to travel beyond the nearest facility has not been recognized as something worthy of adoption.

Mobility is not just about physical access to a given destination. It can also have important social benefits and consequences. A visit to an elderly relative or friend who lives (say) 30kms away reduces social isolation and contributes to positive health outcomes for both parties. Such visits matter and if they are possible only by car then the car is the correct choice. What is not acceptable from a public policy perspective is the assumption that the car is the default option in all circumstances. It is perfectly possible to have a high quality public transport system, a high quality community transport system run by local volunteers and an accessible car-share club and with some intelligent joined up thinking all these options can be used interchangeably to facilitate social interaction. The current situation in most parts of rural England falls far short of this joined up thinking. If I want to visit a relative or friend on the main Shrewsbury-Ludlow corridor which is served by the 435 bus I can't do this on a Sunday because the bus does not run on a Sunday (or on a bank holiday). The non-car owner is prevented from making a simple trip. Much of the UK bus network outside of large cities closes down on a Sunday or public holiday.

These benefits and consequences are real and they are important and it is not part of my plan to ignore them or downgrade their significance. The problem with mobility discussions in general is twofold. First there is no generally accepted policy imperative or will to re-engineer the land use planning, facility location and transport systems to make more of these trips currently possible only with a car, more easily accomplished without a car. There is no accessibility policy. Secondly there is no attempt to learn from 5 decades of cost-benefit analysis in transport and employ rigour and data in an assessment of the costs and benefits of higher levels of mobility. Even if increases in mobility in the 1950s and 60s brought benefits that exceeded costs by a large margin there is no logical or theoretical basis for assuming that the curve or growth trajectory is a straight line (as mobility goes up so the benefits go up by the same percentage points). The curve may be asymptotic and have a clear discontinuity demonstrating that as mobility rises beyond a given number of kms per person per annum there are no detectable increases in benefits. There may even be an explosion in negative externalities and a decline in quality of life. The point is we do not know and we do not ask and we should ask.

This chapter is the start of a discussion that opens up the way to this rigorous assessment of costs and benefits but in a way that puts human beings and not monetary values at the centre. I will not attempt a full cost-benefit analysis (CBA) because I do not think that the conversion of important human, ethical, social justice and community issues into monetary values actually helps. How could we put a monetary value on the enormous grief, distress and pain that spreads across a whole network of friends, relatives and neighbours when a child is killed crossing a road and we know that we could have prevented this death. It is offensive to reduce human tragedy to monetary values.

In the late 18th and early 19th century there was a vigorous debate in England about slavery and the abolition of the slave trade (Hague, 2008). Powerful arguments were deployed on both sides of the debate and there was a strong case for slavery when looked at through the eyes of those involved in the slave trade and those worried about the economic fortunes of Bristol, Liverpool and Lancaster. William Wilberforce and others took the view that slavery was wrong and that it should be abolished. It would not be very convincing to equate mobility with slavery and that is not my intention but there is a shared dimension that is worth exploring.

Slavery was an accepted part of late 18th century national life. It was seen as "normal", it was good for the economy and there was a strong element of logic in the proposition that if Britain did not "do it" then this would simply hand over the trade to the Dutch or French. They would "do it", there would be no change to the lives of slaves and the British economy would be damaged. Very similar arguments are currently deployed in the world of climate change policy (the French and Dutch are replaced by the Chinese) but the relevance to mobility lies with the strength of economic arguments which "trump" all the other arguments. The slave trade was wrong and had to go and it took time for the ethical and other arguments around slavery to outperform the economic case for slavery. Mobility is inextricably linked to economic growth and economic performance and any arguments that we would gain from having more accessibility and less mobility are very quickly trumped by the economic arguments. The language of economic growth, better connections, regeneration and assisting lagging regions delivers a rich diet of untested but powerful images around progress, jobs and growth being linked to transport infrastructure improvements and more mobility. It is currently unthinkable that a policy of reduced mobility would be promoted by politicians seeking to be elected for another term of office. The economic has trumped all the other arguments around health, quality of life, climate change and local economic resilience and continues to do so just as the economic arguments trumped any arguments that were deployed to support the case for the abolition of the slave trade.

The abolition of the slave trade, it was claimed, would destroy our economy and damage Britain's global ambitions militarily and economically. The abandonment of high mobility growth trajectories will be seen as damaging our economic performance in an increasingly competitive globalised economy and we would lose jobs. This is identical to the pro-slavery arguments deployed in Liverpool in the closing years of the 18th century. The correspondence is even more remarkable when looked at through the competitiveness lens. It is now a routine part of political discourse to bemoan our poor quality infrastructure (not enough roads, motorways, airports or high speed rail lines) and argue for more of these things so that we can maintain international competitiveness and sustained economic growth. Economic considerations and international competitiveness were key planks in pro slavery arguments in late 18th century Britain and are still with us in the early 21st century discussion around transport infrastructure and mobility.

In this chapter I want to shift the centre of gravity in transport and mobility discussions away from the ideological dominance of economics and towards a wider concept of quality of life and local economic resilience. I want to assert the primacy of a strong, citizen-based, democratic imperative that recognizes the importance of exploring and defining a desirable future and then working out how to get there. This has nothing to do with the cost benefit analysis world based on negotiable methodologies about the value of time, the value of green belt land or the value of peace, quiet and tranquillity. These attributes of the world we live in are shaped by mobility and by decisions about whether or not to build a new road, a new high speed rail line or a new runway and that is unacceptable. They should be and must be shaped by a clear sense of what we want in the desirable future and this cannot be left to the vagaries of arbitrary methodologies claiming a spurious scientific identity but serving to deny the importance of human scale thinking about the world around us.

Let me give an example of a situation where the language and ideology of mobility has created a serious road safety problem for children on the way to and from school and the way in which the discourse prioritises "traffic" i.e. cars, and does not take into account the safety of children and the fears of parents. This debate is about a strongly expressed teacher, parent, school governor and local elected councillor worry about traffic danger and the refusal (so far) of the public body responsible for both schools and highways to provide a school crossing patrol person who would supervise children crossing this road. The road is Keswick Rd in Lancaster (UK) and the children are on the way to and from Ridge Community Primary School.

In response to a request for school crossing person the person responsible has said:

"The national criterion for establishing a School Crossing Patrol Point is a PV2 of 4 million with 15 unaccompanied children. The PV2 is determined by counting the number of vehicles and unaccompanied children and multiplying them as 'pedestrians x vehicles x vehicles'.

In Lancashire the criterion has been reduced to a PV2 of 2 million with 10 unaccompanied children, which as you will see is rather more generous than the national one. I have attached a copy of the criteria used for your information.

The crossing patrol point in question was used to cross children over Kentmere Road and Keswick Road, consequently this junction has been counted which showed that there were twelve children in the morning and ten in the afternoon, but when multiplied with the vehicles the PV2 amounted to 1.4 million in the morning and 0.77 million in the afternoon, and therefore does not meet the required criteria."

Source: e-mail from Mr Ken Speak, Lancashire County Council School Patrol officer, 23rd October 2013.

This refusal to agree to a request that would reduce the probability of a child death or serious injury whilst crossing this road provides a clear insight into ideology of mobility. It rejects any consideration of the human elements e.g. the fears and concerns of parents, children and teachers. It promotes a totally arbitrary decision rule based on an arbitrary equation (P= number of pedestrians and V2 = number of vehicles squared) and an arbitrary threshold that must be crossed to justify the introduction of a road safety measure.

The rejection of the request has increased the probability of a child death as a result of being hit by a car in this location and has promoted the interests of car drivers (a reduction in the number of times a car would be stopped) above the interests of the child. The human element and the over-riding priority to eliminate all deaths and serious injuries on the roads (Whitelegg and Haq, 2014) has been air-brushed out of the picture.

The Lancashire school-crossing case study exposes the insidious nature of policies, programmes and decisions that are rooted in the prioritisation of mobility, especially car-based mobility, above every other consideration. Professionals and politicians work within this dominant mobility ideology and cannot see that they are working to reward the mobile car users regardless of the consequences for the vulnerable road user. Higher levels of mobility do confer benefits but it can never be acceptable to promote the interest of the mobile above all other interests regardless of the consequences.

A second case study illustrates the same point. Congestion in London is a major headache for businesses, motorists and the Mayor of London who quite understandably wants to be associated with alleviating such a serious problem. The London congestion charge has made a difference and reduced vehicle numbers and congestion but congestion is creeping up again and giving the Mayor severe reputational problems. His response has been to reduce crossing times for pedestrians at over 500 traffic light controlled pedestrian crossings:

"Green Man time has been reduced at 568 crossings across London since 2010. Reduced crossing times encourage pedestrians to take greater risks. For other groups, particularly older and disabled people, it can affect their confidence when crossing the road. The Committee is concerned to note that there has been little analysis of the effect of reducing Green Man time on crossing behaviour." (London Assembly, 2014, page 24).

The mayor of London has taken a clear decision to prioritise motorists over pedestrians. This is the reality of a mobility ideology. The ideology operates to exclude any other considerations so decisions are made that increase risk of death and injury to pedestrians and discriminate against children, older people and those who cannot move very fast for a variety of health related reasons other than age.

The significance of the Lancashire and London case studies lies in the clarity that they reveal about priorities and the ease with which other considerations do not even register on the radar screen of decision takers. Those involved with promoting mobility and its flawed economic growth support system have successfully exterminated from consideration the system wide negative impacts of that mobility fetish.

There are at least 8 negative consequences that flow from higher levels of mobility. All these consequences cast a shadow over ordinary everyday life and present a series of problems for many of society's vulnerable groups e.g. children and the elderly. They detract from quality of life and they soak up resources that are desperately needed in other areas of collective life. They are:

1. Air pollution

2. Death and injury on the roads

3. Energy consumption

4. Climate Change

5. Obesity and related health impacts

6. Community disruption

7. Equality and social justice

8. Fiscal burdens

Each of these will be dealt with in turn in the following chapters.

Chapter 3
Death and injury

One of the most obvious, pervasive and unacceptable consequences of motorised mobility is death and injury in the road traffic environment. It is over 60 years since John Dean addressed the problem in his book "Murder most foul" (Dean, 1947):

"It is common ground that the motor slaughter ought to be stopped; it is also common ground that it can be stopped, or at least greatly reduced..it is realised that the killing or maiming every year of about a quarter of a million persons ..are not items that any country can afford to ignore..it is also realised, if less clearly, that the motor slaughter leaves behind it an ever widening trail of private misery-bereavement, poverty resulting from the death of the breadwinner, crippledom and the rest and that this, too, ought to be stopped. Finally, it is realised, if again it is less clearly, that the motor slaughter is bad in itself: that it is bad that human beings should kill and maim other human beings in this cold blooded way: worst of all that as happens in a very large proportion of the cases, vigorous adults should kill or maim children and elderly and infirm persons and then criminally and meanly put the blame on their victims: that in short, it is not only the lives and well-being of about a quarter of a million persons and the material loss every year that are at stake, but to a high degree, the standards of decency and the moral health of the nation. Never before in the history of civilisation has it been so easy to kill and maim without incurring punishment or even censure. Never before in all history has it been common custom to kill and maim people because they get in your way when you are in a hurry, or even when you are not in a hurry but merely wish to feel you are. It is a fantastic and unprecedented situation; a fit prelude to race extermination and Belsen. Murder indeed most foul, strange and unnatural." Dean (1947, page 5).

These words will sound harsh and maybe unreasonable to those used to a more sedate and unchallenging discussion of road safety but no matter how harsh and unreasonable they may sound to modern ears accustomed to anodyne words and an inability to face up to serious moral responsibilities they are as nothing compared to the harshness and total unacceptability of death and injury on an industrial scale that is inextricably linked to the mobility paradigm. The overwhelming and unbearable suffering and misery associated with the global total of 3,400 deaths every day is "murder most foul" and a stunning condemnation of the amoral and unethical environment in which the growth of mobility thrives. Indeed, the growth of mobility absolutely depends on this amoral, unethical and inhuman approach to road safety. For the growth of mobility to take deep root in all our thinking, planning and funding it is necessary to delete the horror, misery and tragedy of road traffic deaths and injuries from our consciousness.

For the avoidance of doubt let me be very clear. The growth of motorised mobility exposes an ever increasing proportion of the world's population to road traffic danger. The number of vehicles on the street, their weight, mass, kinetic energy and speed all produce a direct effect on the numbers killed and the severity of the injuries. The pursuit of growth in motorised mobility is the pursuit of higher levels of death and injury to vulnerable road users especially the poor, the old, those who cannot run very fast and those who for a few critical moments might misjudge the space-time trajectory of a tonne of metal driven by someone using a mobile phone, lighting a cigarette or simply enjoying the "high" of fast driving.

The death of a 10 year old girl walking home from school crossing a road in the circumstances described by Roberts (2010, page 34) where it is known that the time available to cross the road is 4 seconds is a tragedy of enormous proportions. The tragedy is a direct result of the pursuit of the mobility paradigm, a paradigm that cannot envisage reducing the speed and volume of traffic to assist a child in these circumstances. The tragedy is then magnified and compounded by blaming the child. The coroner's verdict on this death was "I find that [name] died at [place] accidentally, sustained when she ran out into the path of an approaching vehicle without checking that the road was clear of traffic." Mayer Hillman (Hillman et al, 1990) found that children are blamed for 90% of child pedestrian deaths.

To pursue the growth of motorised mobility in the absence of an absolute, deliverable, overriding commitment to reduce death and injury in the road traffic environment to zero is fundamentally flawed, fundamentally wrong and fundamentally unethical.

The World Health Organisation has estimated that approximately 3400 people die every day as a result of being hit by a motorised vehicle or being an occupant of a motorised vehicle involved in crash. This is 1.24 million deaths pa. Between 20 and 50 million suffer non-fatal injuries and 59% of all deaths are amongst young adults (15-44 years old). I will not refer to these events as "accidents." The word "accident" carries a message of unpredictability and a suggestion of inevitability. The opposite is the case. Deaths and injuries are predictable and preventable (WHO, 2013).

The WHO (2004) is very clear about how we should deal with deaths and injury in the road traffic environment:

"Every day thousands of people are killed and injured on our roads. Men, women or children walking, biking or riding to school or work, playing in the streets or setting out on long trips will never return home, leaving behind shattered families and communities. Millions of people each year will spend long weeks in hospital after severe crashes and many will never be able to live, work or play as they used to. Current efforts to address road safety are minimal in comparison to growing human suffering."

"The time to act is now. Road safety is no accident. It requires strong political will and concerted, sustained efforts across a range of sectors. Acting now will save lives. We urge governments as well as other sectors of society to embrace and implement the key recommendations of this report" WHO (2004).

Clearly a body count cannot convey the enormity of the impact of death, injury and distress on parents, families and friends. A more discursive, ethnographic and narrative assessment is needed to capture the full extent of impacts on people and relationships. We need to find a way to give a much stronger voice to the victims in shaping road safety policy if we are to build a way out of the accepted parameters of the road safety debate and chart a course towards a "Vision Zero." Vision Zero is the name given to the Swedish road safety policy adopted by Parliament in 1997 which established a target of zero deaths and zero serious injuries in the road traffic environment (Haq and Whitelegg, 2014).

Notwithstanding the strong caveat on the inability of numbers to convey the enormity of the impact of death and injury and the fact that the numbers are almost certainly underestimates the World Health Organisation (WHO, 2004) uses them to good effect:

- Worldwide an estimated 1.2 million people are killed in road crashes every year and approximately 50 million are injured.
- This annual total approximates to 3000 deaths every day.
- These figures will increase by 65% over the next 20 years unless there is "a new commitment to prevention."
- Road traffic deaths will increase in the period 1990-2020 from 0.99 million to 2.34 million.
- Low income and middle income countries account for 85% of the deaths and 90% of the annual disability-adjusted life years (DALYs) lost because of road traffic injury.
- Without appropriate action by 2020, road traffic injuries are predicted to be the third leading contributor to the global burden of disease and injury.
- A large proportion of the road crash victims in low and middle income countries are vulnerable road users such as pedestrians and cyclists.
- In the period 1975-1998 road traffic fatality rates rose by 44% in Malaysia and by 243% in China.

The WHO (2013) report updates the 2004 report and gives a detailed account of the global variation in road traffic deaths and deaths by users group (Figure 3.1).

The report identifies the main characteristics of the road deaths epidemic:

- 1.24 million deaths in 2010.
- 87 countries saw an increase in the number of fatalities in the period 2007-2010.

- Africa has the highest road traffic fatality rate.

- 23% of all deaths are amongst motorcyclists, 22% are pedestrians (but this rises to 38% in Africa), 5% are cyclists, 31% are car occupants and 19% are unspecified.

- Almost 60% of road traffic deaths are aged between 15 and 44.

- For every fatality there are 20 non-fatal injuries.

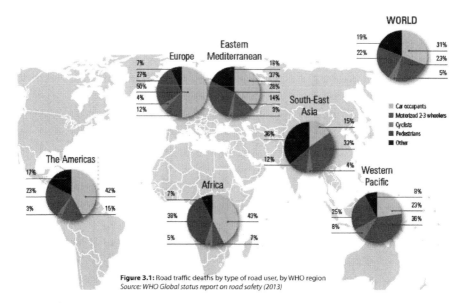

Figure 3.1: Road traffic deaths by type of road user, by WHO region
Source: WHO Global status report on road safety (2013)

The road death epidemic is very severe indeed in Africa, China and India and I return to a more detailed discussion of the relationships between the mobility paradigm and its strongly negative consequences in Chapter 13. India and China illustrate the pervasiveness of the mobility paradigm and the way it shapes the totality of public policy to worsen the road deaths outcomes and exclude those policies that reduce and eliminate road traffic danger.

The mobility paradigm is deeply embedded in China and India but started its life in Europe and North America. The degree to which it is hard-wired into the world view and thinking of politicians, businesses, decision-takers and journalists is difficult to convey but is assisted by a series of linguistic and conceptual distortions that have been exposed by Roberts (2010). These include:

- The use of the word "accident."

- The flawed interpretation of statistics to promote the idea that deaths and injuries are declining as a result of road safety interventions.

- The avoidance of social justice and ethics as a legitimate framework for looking at deaths.

Accidents

Road traffic "accidents" are predictable and preventable. The main determinants of injury risks are the volume and speed of traffic (Roberts, 2010, page 35). Children living in the busiest streets were fifteen times more likely to be injured than children living in the quietest streets. Roberts is very clear about cause and effect:

"Traffic and not erratic jaywalking children is the cause of child pedestrian injury. Children get hit by cars because the cars are there. There is one street and it is either a place for children or a place for cars. Mixing the two at least at average urban speeds does not work without bloodshed. A vehicle driving down a residential street at 40 mph packs more destructive energy than a bullet."

Roberts provides evidence that in circumstances where traffic volumes fell e.g. in the Middle East oil crises of 1974 and 1979 child pedestrian deaths fell. In New Zealand between 1975 and 1980 child pedestrian deaths fell by 46% in response to car free days and a weekend ban on petrol sales "but when the oil started flowing and traffic volume resumed its upward trajectory, the number of children killed and injured on the roads increased along with it…when petrol prices rise fewer children die; when they fall, more children die."

The World Health Organisation (WHO, 2004, page 7) recommends against the use of the word "accident." Road deaths and injuries are predictable and preventable:

"While the risk of a crash is relatively low for most individual journeys, people travel many times each day, every week and every year. The sum of these small risks is considerable. The term "accident", which is widely used, can give the impression, probably unintended, of inevitability and unpredictability - an event that cannot be managed. This document prefers to use the term "crash" instead, to denote something that is an event, or series of events, amenable to rational analysis and remedial action."

Deaths and injuries are declining

The road safety literature is often self-congratulatory. Apparently we are reducing death and injury and can take comfort from the fact that in the 1930s road traffic deaths in the UK were running at 6-7,000pa (Dean, 1947) and in 2012 this has been reduced to 1,754. This is a very convenient story that is used to promote the mobility paradigm and to make sure that inconvenient truths are excluded from the discussion.

Hillman et al (1990) produce hard evidence to show that over the period 1970-1990 there has been a progressive withdrawal of children from the street environment. In statistical terms the denominator has shrunk and the number of people exposed to the risk of death and injury has declined. This produces a decline in the numbers of deaths and injuries but the reason is the abandonment of streets and public space and it is not a road safety gain. Roberts is characteristically blunt:

"As the volume of road traffic increased and the streets became rivers of lethal kinetic energy, the pedestrians got out of the way. Parents kept their children indoors and those who could afford a car started driving rather than walking, even for short distances. The body counters at the ministries of transport of course claimed that death rates were falling because the traffic planners and police were doing a great job...no one bothered to count how many live people there were on the streets."

The decline in road traffic deaths and injuries does not represent a decline in road traffic danger and simply reflects the abandonment of streets and public space by people.

Social class variability

It is a general assumption that in an advanced, sophisticated, rational, democracy like the UK there should be an assumption of fairness across all aspects of public policy, spending and health outcomes. I show in chapter 5 that this is not true in transport spending. The UK spends disproportionately more of its increasingly scarce budget on things that benefit richer people. It is certainly not the case in road safety where the risk of death for a child in the lowest social group was five times that of a child in the highest social class (Roberts, 2010, page 39). This is another dimension of the denominator problem referred to above. Poor people will spend more time on the street, walking, not in car and not in a well equipped garden. This means they are exposed to more risk and so will exhibit a higher death and injury rate.

The social class variability and its significance for public policy has been summarised by IPPR (Grayling, 2002):

"We are able to show that the higher injury rate in deprived areas does not appear to be simply because the environment is inherently more dangerous, for example because deprived areas tend to be dense urban areas with more roads and traffic. Environmental factors are important but there appears to be a deprivation effect over and above the effect of the built environment. We estimate that the likelihood of a child pedestrian injury is four times higher in the most deprived ward in England compared to the least deprived ward, independent of factors such as population and employment density and the characteristics of the road network. A reasonable explanation is that the higher rates of child pedestrian casualties in more deprived areas are the consequence of more dangerous environments combined with higher exposure rates. Children in more deprived areas are likely to make more journeys on foot because their parents are less likely to have a car and more likely to play on the street unsupervised because they are less likely to have access to gardens and other safe play areas."

The data are clear (Figure 3.2 and 3.3).

The IPPR report provides an excellent evidence base for highlighting the impact of death and injury on so-called "lower socio-economic" groups and adds weight to the need to end this strongly discriminatory impact. It is unacceptable that children from poorer backgrounds should experience a higher probability of death and injury than those from "higher" socio-economic groups (SEGs) and the existence of the discriminatory effect tells us far more about road traffic danger and road safety measures than statistical tabulations showing a decline in numbers of those killed and seriously injured (known as KSI in the road safety literature).

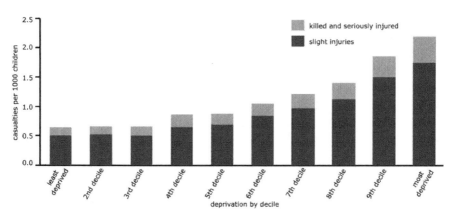

Figure 3.2: Inequality in child (0-15) pedestrian deaths in England and Wales
Source: Grayling (2000)

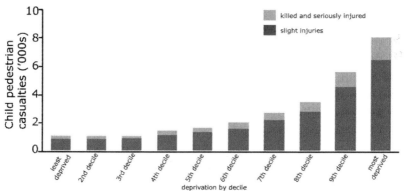

Figure 3.3: Number of child pedestrian casualties in deciles of English wards in 1999 and 2000
Source: Grayling (2000)

Sadly the IPPR report misses the main point that needs to be made. The main point that is missed is that traffic volume and traffic speed kills and injures children. Traffic volumes are on an upward trajectory, fuelled by the mobility paradigm and by the thousands of daily planning and funding decisions that pander to this increase. This increase in volume may well be associated with a reduction in KSIs as more human beings abandon the unequal competitive struggle for the right to use street and footpaths and retreat to the car, or just stay indoors and tweet. The car is perceived as inherently safer than the world outside of the car, and more fun. It has serious entertainment systems, airbags, ABS, computer control technology, reinforced impact resistance, and the prospect of GPS assisted automated driving and parking. As the new world of no involvement in human interaction on the street takes hold so the number exposed to risk goes down (children are not crossing roads) and the KSI number goes down and roads safety professional can congratulate each other on the success of their professional efforts.

A genuinely human-centred, community rich, ethical road safety policy would delete the mobility paradigm, reduce vehicle numbers drastically, reduce vkms drastically, ban cars from the majority of residential streets and have an absolute, non-diluted commitment to zero deaths and zero injuries in the road traffic environment. Zero KSIs will eliminate the social class bias and give everyone an equal chance of not being squashed by a tonne of metal as they struggle to cross a road with only 4 second gaps between vehicles available for that crossing.

Vision Zero

The responsibility for road safety has traditionally been placed on the individual road user rather than on the designers of the system. Road safety has tended to focus on encouraging good behaviour by road users via licensing, testing, education, training and publicity. Sweden is among those countries with the lowest number of traffic fatalities in relation to its population. However, in spite of this excellent record, in 1997 the Swedish Parliament introduced a new approach to road safety called "Vision Zero" (Whitelegg and Haq, 2006).

Vision Zero is based on a refusal to accept human deaths or lifelong suffering as a result of road traffic accidents (Elvik, 1999 and Elvik and Amundsen, 2000). It requires moving the emphasis away from reducing the number of deaths to eliminating the risk of chronic health impairment caused by crashes. Vision Zero in Sweden requires fatalities and serious injuries to be reduced to zero by 2020.

Vision Zero has had a mixed reception in the academic and professional literature and is by no means immune from criticism (Elvik, 1999 and Elvik, 2008, Elvebakk and Steiro, 2009). The policy has stimulated fundamental thinking around the nature of policy itself including whether or not it is "rational" (Rosencrantz, Edvardsson, and Hansson, 2007) and including explicit discussions of the role of ethics in road safety policy (Hokstad and Vatn, 2008) and including a useful discussion of "backward and forward responsibility" in Fahlquist (2006).

The 1990 Swedish National Traffic Safety Programme set a target of less than 600 fatalities by 2000. In 1993, the Road Safety Office merged and became the Swedish National Road Administration (SNRA). In 1994 the SNRA, now responsible for national traffic safety work, presented a National Traffic Safety Programme for the period 1995–2000. A new target of 400 fatalities for the year 2000 was adopted. This original target was achieved in 1994. The intentions of the National Traffic Safety Programme, with ten sub-targets for traffic behaviour, were not reached but abandoned with the discussion of the Vision Zero concept. An interim target of reducing the number of road accident fatalities from 600 in 2000 to 270 in 2007 was adopted as a move towards the Vision Zero target. The annual number of fatalities has been constant during the period 1994 to 2001. In 2000, there were 591 deaths and 4,103 serious injuries in traffic in Sweden (Koornstra et al., 2002). The number of fatalities in 2013 was 260 (European Commission, 2015).

Swedish fatalities in 2013 were 27 per million inhabitants, the lowest in the EU (European Commission, 2015). The EU-28 average is 51 fatalities per million inhabitants. The decline in fatalities in Sweden, 55.4% in the period 2001-2013 was higher than the two countries normally regarded as good performers in road safety (Netherlands and the UK).

Vision Zero requires a paradigm shift in addressing the issue of road safety (Rechnitzer and Grzebieta, 1999). It requires abandoning the traditional economic model where road safety is provided at reasonable cost and the traditional transport model in which safety must be balanced against mobility. At the core of the Vision Zero is the biomechanical tolerance of human beings. Vision Zero promotes a road system where crash energy cannot exceed human tolerance. While it is accepted that crashes in the transport system occur due to human error, Vision Zero requires no crash should be more severe than the tolerance of humans. The blame for fatalities in the road system is assigned to the failure of the road system rather that the road user (Wadhwa, 2001).

Vision Zero is based on the ethical imperative that (Tingvall and Haworth, 1999):

"It can never be ethically acceptable that people are killed or seriously injured when moving within the road system."

Crashes have to be prevented from leading to fatalities and serious injuries by designing roads, vehicles and transport services in a way that someone can tolerate the violence of a crash without being killed or seriously injured. Common long-term disabling injuries and non-injury accidents are outside the scope of the Vision. Vision Zero is estimated to achieve a possible reduction in the number of fatalities by a quarter to one third over a ten-year period (SNRA, 2003).

Vision Zero strategic principles are:

- The traffic system has to adapt to take better account of the needs, mistakes and vulnerabilities of road users.

- The level of violence that the human body can tolerate without being killed or seriously injured forms the basic parameter in the design of the road transport system.

- Vehicle speed is the most important regulating factor for safe road traffic. It should be determined by the technical standard of both roads and vehicle so as not to exceed the level of violence that the human body can tolerate.

The approach is:

- To create a road environment that minimises the risk of road users making mistakes and that prevents serious human injury when designing, operating and maintaining the state road network.

- To analyse crashes that have resulted in death or serious injury in traffic and, where feasible, initiate suitable measures so as to avoid the repetition of such crashes.

- To stimulate all players within the road transport system to work resolutely towards achieving mutually targeted objectives conduct the work on road safety in close co-operation with all players within the road transport system.

- To take advantage of and further develop the commitment of the general public to safer traffic.

Vision Zero emphasizes what the optimum state of the road should be rather than possible ways of reducing current problems. The main change instigated by Vision Zero is a new way of dividing responsibilities for road safety. Rather than emphasising the responsibility of the road user alone, Vision Zero explicitly states that responsibility is shared both by the system designers and the road user:

1. The designers of the system are always ultimately responsible for the design, operation and use of the road transport system and thereby responsible for the level of safety within the entire system.

2. Road users are responsible for following the rules for using the road transport system set by the system designers.

3. If road users fail to obey these rules due to lack of knowledge, acceptance or ability, or if injuries occur, the system designers are required to take necessary further steps to counteract people being killed or seriously injured.

In 1999, a short-term action plan was launched by the Swedish government, containing 11 points aimed at strengthening and stimulating traffic safety work in accordance with Vision Zero principles:

1. A focus on the most dangerous roads (e.g. priority for installing centre-guardrails for eliminating head-on collisions, removing obstacles next to roads, etc.).

2. Safer traffic in built-up areas (e.g. a safety analysis of street networks in 102 municipalities led to reconstruction of streets; the efforts are continuing).

3. Emphasis on the responsibilities of road users (e.g. creating more respect for traffic rules in particular with regard to speed limits, seat belt use, and intoxicated driving).

4. Safe bicycle traffic (e.g. campaign for using bicycle helmets, a voluntary bicycle safety standard).

5. Quality assurance in transport work (e.g. public agencies with large transportation needs will receive traffic safety (and environmental impact) instructions on how to assure the quality of their own transportation services and those procured from outside firms).

6. Winter tyre requirement (e.g. a new law mandating specific tyres under winter road conditions).

7. Making better use of Swedish technology (e.g. promoting the introduction of technology - available or to be developed - that relatively soon can be applied, such

as seat belt reminders, in-car speed adaptation systems (ISA), alcohol ignition interlocks for preventing drinking and driving, and electronic driver licences).

8. Responsibilities of road transport system designers (e.g. establishment of an independent organisation for road traffic inspection is proposed by a commission of inquiry on the responsibilities of the public sector and the business community for safe road traffic).

9. Public responses to traffic violations (e.g. a commission of inquiry is reviewing existing traffic violation rules in the light of the Vision Zero principles and of ensuring due process of law).

10. The role of voluntary organisations (e.g. the government is evaluating the road safety work of the 'Nationalföreningen för trafiksäkerhetens främjande' (National Society for Road Safety (NTF)) and its use of state funds).

11. Alternative forms of financing new roads (e.g. possibilities are studied for other forms of supplementing public financing of major road projects).

Implications of Vision Zero for road fatalities

Proponents of Vision Zero see human life as a basic human right to be protected from fatal injuries. While humans are fallible and make mistakes in using the road system, these mistakes should not carry the death penalty (Elvik, 1999). The ethical principle on which Vision Zero is based is that death is unacceptable means that there is a moral obligation to design cars, roads and the rules of the road to protect road users from being killed in traffic. Vision Zero explicitly rejects the trade of human life against other objectives. It also rejects the use of cost-benefit analysis (CBA) to guide priority setting in road safety policy. Tingvall (1997:56) states:

"If a new road, new car design, new rule etc. is judged as having the potential to save human life, then the opportunity must always be taken, provided that no other more cost-effective action would produce the same benefit."

Although Sweden has a comparatively good road safety record, Swedish policies are still considered to be ineffective in improving road safety. Elvik and Amundsen (2000) indicate that current policy priorities are inefficient in Sweden and concluded that road safety could be substantially improved if policy priorities were based more on CBA then they are today. They argue that cost-effective road safety measures can prevent more than 50 per cent of road fatalities in Sweden. However, current policies prevent approximately 10–15 per cent of the current number of road fatalities over the next 10 years. Many cost effective measures are not being implemented. By rejecting the use of CBA to set priorities, Elvik (2003) argues that advocates of Vision Zero are in effect rejecting a road safety policy that would give far better results than current road safety policies.

The main sources of inefficiency in current road safety in Sweden are (Elvik, 2003):

- Lack of power to introduce new vehicle safety standards – this power now resides with the European Union.

- The existence of social dilemmas that is situations in which measures that are cost-effective from a societal point of view are loss making from the point of view of individual road users.

- Priority given to other policy objectives, which cannot be adequately assessed by CBA, primarily objectives related to regional development.

Elivk (2003) concludes that the amount of resources that are currently spent on road safety policy in Sweden are sufficient to cover all cost-effective road safety measures, provided the use of inefficient measures ceases.

Elvik (1999, 2003) is rather sceptical about Vision Zero and presents an economic argument against the concept. Other authors e.g. Rosencrantz, Edvardsson and Hansson (2007) conclude that the policy has strengthened Sweden's efforts to eliminate death and serious injuries in road crashes, a view supported by Nihlen Fahlquist (2006) who argues that adopting Vision Zero as a national transport policy goal has signified an important shift of responsibility from individual road users to system designers.

Conclusions

Deaths and injuries in the road traffic environment very clearly point to serious problems associated with the mobility paradigm and the assumption that mobility growth is unavoidable, desirable and a key component of progress, economic development and quality of life. It cannot be acceptable that 3,400 people die every day in road crashes and it is not right that streets are colonised by vehicles and replace people. The language and rhetoric of road safety plays a significant part in promoting motorised mobility. It downplays the progressive withdrawal of people from public space and it airbrushes out of the picture the social class discrimination that produces disproportionately larger numbers of deaths amongst the poor and disadvantaged. It is an important agent of legitimation and collaboration with a policing, judicial and urban planning system that blames victims and shapes the built environment in favour of the car and to the detriment of the pedestrian, cyclist and public transport user.

The Swedish Vision Zero policy is not without faults but it sets out a clear ambition that is so much better than the lack of a clear vision. Reducing deaths and serious injuries to zero is possible and leads inexorably to a fundamental re-engineering of the mobility paradigm. The key components of a Vision Zero strategy are the same as the key components of a new approach to traffic, transport, mobility and road safety that would bring about the much needed paradigm shift and the abandonment of the mobility paradigm. It would be identifiable by promoting the following policies, targets and interventions:

- A total, system-wide, default speed limit of 20mph/30kph on every street in every urban area and through every village on every road going through a settlement. This would be vigorously enforced.

- An accessibility policy to produce the city of short distances (Holzapfel, 2014) and to maximise access by all groups in society to all daily destinations (education, health care, work, local shops, recreational facilities). Such a policy would impose a duty on providers of education and health care to deliver those services in accessible locations so well within walking, cycling and public transport range and to deliver a uniformly high quality of service. An accessibility paradigm rejects the notion that if we travel longer distances to a school or clinic or hospital we can find a "better" one.

- A steady decommissioning of car parking spaces to produce a reduction in the number of spaces available in cities by 50%.

- Highway space reallocation so that subject to local circumstances streets would be re-engineered laterally so that one third of the available width (from building line to building line) would be allocated equally (one third each) to pedestrians, cyclists and vehicles.

- Traditional approaches to planning would be abandoned in favour of mixed uses, car-free housing, zero tolerance for large traffic generators e.g. out of town shopping centres would be decommissioned.

- Budgets currently spent on new roads, car parks and high speed rail would be reallocated to walking, cycling, trams, buses and local facilities.

All these policies, spending plans and interventions would be designed and tracked so that they produce zero deaths and injuries in the road traffic environment, zero air pollution from traffic, zero carbon transport, zero social discrimination and maximum human use of public space and streets.

All this is possible, desirable, fundable, ethical and a logical development as a necessary next step in a long line of "impossible" paradigm shift going back to the Magna Carta, the end of feudalism, the abolition of the slave trade, the end of child labour in factories and mines, clean drinking water and sanitation in our mid-19th century cities, votes for all and votes for women and the end of colonialism. Of course there will be massive resistance just as there was to each of the previous paradigm shifts but those who front the resistance will be reminded of one thing: the current system is dirty, expensive, kills people and deprives hundreds of millions of people of basic human rights. We can carry on with the dirty, nasty system but we should not.

Chapter 4
Air Quality

A RECENT report from the Massachusetts Institute of Technology (Agren, 2013) estimated that the total combustion emissions in the USA accounted for about 200,000 premature deaths pa due to changes in particulate matter (PM2.5) concentrations and about 10,000 deaths due to changes in ozone concentrations. The sources of these emissions were industrial, vehicles, shipping and rail operations. The greatest number of emissions related premature deaths comes from road transport with 53,000 early deaths pa attributed to exhaust emissions from cars and lorries. Electricity generation came in at 52,000pa. In a state by state analysis California accounted for 21,000 early deaths "mostly attributed to road transportation, and to commercial and residential emissions from heating and cooking."

A report on air quality in Europe (European Environment Agency, 2015) estimated a total of 491,000 premature deaths in 28 European countries of which 52, 430 were in the UK. Air pollution is very clearly a major public health hazard in Europe and the USA.

In June 2012 the International Agency for Research on Cancer (IARC) classified diesel engine exhaust as "carcinogenic to humans":

"The IARC today (12th June 2012) classified diesel engine exhaust as carcinogenic to humans (Group 1), based on sufficient evidence that exposure is associated with an increased risk for lung cancer" (IARC, 2012).

Air pollution is a major public health problem globally, regionally and locally and in the UK is characterised by massive indifference to the scale of the problem and a seriously inadequate governmental (central and local) response.

London is typical in this respect and its air pollution problem has been analysed in great detail by the Clean Air London Campaign (2013):

What are the health impacts of air pollution in London?

- Air pollution comprises particles and gases. The particles are categorised by their maximum diameter in microns e.g. PM2.5 and PM10. In practice, nitrogen dioxide (NO2), a toxic gas, is the only molecule within the gas category with relevant WHO guidelines and legal limits.

- Poor air quality has a significant impact on the health of London residents. The Mayor published a study in 2010 estimating 4,267 premature deaths in London in 2008 attributable to long term exposure to fine particles (PM2.5). These occur mostly as heart attacks and strokes. The Department of Health estimates

6.3% to 9.0% of all deaths in London in 2010 were attributable to long-term exposure to man-made PM2.5 alone.

- Children, the elderly and people with existing respiratory illness suffer disproportionately from the effects of air pollution. Over 1,100 schools in London are within 150 metres of the city's busiest and most polluted roads (i.e. those that carry over 10,000 vehicles a day). Traffic pollution from such roads may be responsible for 15-30% of all new cases of asthma in children and chronic obstructive pulmonary disease in adults of 65 years of age and older.

The response of the London administration and the Mayor of London to the premature deaths of over 4000 London residents pa has been very weak indeed and the Clean Air London (CAL) campaign has repeatedly called for measures that would produce improvements in air quality e.g. the complete abolition of diesel fuelled buses and taxis in London.

The European Commission declared 2013 as the "Year of Air" (Potočnik, 2012). Commissioner Potočnik highlighted the seriousness of the EU air quality problem:

- 81% of citizens live in areas where air quality does not meet WHO standards set to protect public health.
- 3.6 million years of life are lost each year in the EU due to the emission of particles.
- The annual cost of this health damage is estimated to be in the (rather wide) range 189 billion -609 billion Euros in 2020.
- 200,000 premature deaths pa due to particle emissions alone are expected by 2020.

EEA (2013) has quantified the proportionate responsibility of transport emissions in the totality of air pollution:

"The contribution of transport to air quality ..was responsible for 58% of all NOx emissions…and 27% of PM 2.5 emissions..and the contribution of urban and local traffic to PM10 concentration is 35%, while it is up to 64% in the case of NO2 concentrations."

Air quality policy and practice in the UK is a clear case of policy failure and decisions at all levels not to do anything to improve air quality (Whitelegg, 2013). Local authorities in the UK have a legal duty under the 1995 Environment Act to monitor air quality, declare Air Quality Management Areas (AQMAs) if air quality fails to meet the EU standard and put in place an Air Quality Action Plan (AQAP) to improve air quality. There are approximately 405 AQMAs in the UK and there is no documented case in the UK of the removal of the AQMA designation because the AQAP has improved air quality and solved the problem.

There is a stark contrast between the accumulated knowledge on the severe effects of poor air quality on human health (52,430 deaths in 2012 in the UK) and the gross inadequacy of the policy response.

The Lancaster City Council Air Quality Strategy (Lancaster City Council 2013) does not contain a single action or intervention that the local authority will initiate or implement that is likely to produce an improvement in air quality. This is a serious public policy and public health failure. The statutory responsibility for improving air quality has been in place for 20 years and there is still no action plan that contains actions and this is in spite of the clear evidence in the strategy that air pollution deaths occupy the 3rd rank after smoking (1) and obesity (2). This is shown in Figure 4.1.

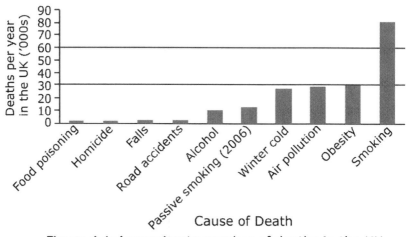

Figure 4.1:Approximate number of deaths in the UK from various causes
Source: Lancaster City Council (2013) page 16

The paucity of measures and interventions to improve air quality is very difficult to understand when set against the large number of measures that can be implemented to improve air quality but very easy to understand when set against the powerful life support system devoted to mobility growth and support of motorised transport. As in the case of grossly inadequate action to eliminate death and serious injury in the road traffic environment, the failure to do anything meaningful to improve air quality is an integral part of the overriding importance given to mobility. The support of mobility and the growth of motorised transport absolutely require that we do not intervene to eliminate poor air quality or to eradicate deaths in the road traffic environment. We will not solve our road safety and air quality problems until we recognise this stark internal conflict and decide to abandon the mobility fetish and replace it with a clear public policy duty to improve accessibility and reduce car use.

What can be done to reduce air pollution from traffic sources?

- Adopt policies that will deliver the Freiburg modal split. A city with 28% of all trips by car and 28% by bike (Freiburg) will have cleaner air than a city with 58% of trips by car and 2% by bike (Manchester). The Freiburg modal split details are discussed in Whitelegg (2013a).

- Replace all diesel buses and taxis with alternatively fuelled vehicles. Nantes in France has replaced 80% of its bus fleet with CNG fuelled buses (Civitas, 2009). Graz in Austria has a 100% bio-diesel bus fleet "fed" by waste oil from catering establishments (Civitas, 2008). Civitas (2010) contains more information on similar work undertaken in Bremen.

- Create low emission zones (LEZ) that will only allow the cleanest cars into the city and eventually will only allow zero-pollution cars into the city. The London LEZ is expected to reduce particulate emission by 6.6% by 2012 (Transport for London, TfL, 2008). Adopt LEZs in all urban areas above a population of 100,000. 47 cities in Germany have implemented the LEZ approach with the specific intention of improving air quality. There are none in the UK outside of London.

- Suspend traffic when there is a danger of EU limit values being exceeded. The city of Milan was totally car free for 10 hours on 9th October, 2011) because pollution had exceeded permitted levels for 12 consecutive days (Transport and Environment, 2011). This policy suggestion originated with the European Commission in 1999 but has not been actioned in the UK: "An important option offered to city authorities by the framework directive is the right to 'suspend activities, including motor-vehicle traffic when there is a risk of limit values being exceeded" (European Commission, 1999).

- Implement urban logistics projects to intercept trucks on the edge of cities and tranship the freight onto smaller and less polluting vehicles for final delivery. Urban logistics already exists in a number of German cities and is implemented in the Broadmeads shopping centre in Bristol and at Heathrow Airport. Urban Logistic solutions are defined and evaluated in Bestufs (2007). In the Tenjin Joint Distribution System in Fukuoka in Japan there was a decrease of 65% in the number of lorries entering the area served and a decrease of 28% in total distance travelled. This has a direct effect on improving air quality.

- Implement large scale car-share/car club schemes (Glotz-Richter, 2010). The detailed monitoring of car share schemes in Bremen show that one car share car can replace 9.5 individually owned vehicles (Civitas (2010). Based on the proportion of the Swiss population that car shares (100,000 out of 8 million) the potential car-sharer population of the EU27 is 6 million (Momo, 2010). Car-sharers have much reduced car ownership levels, a car share car emits 15-25% less CO_2 per kilometre driven and car share club members make much heavier use of bus, train, bike and foot contributing to reductions in greenhouse gas emissions and air pollution.

- Implement large scale new residential developments to cope with any growth in housing demand on the model of Vauban and Rieselfeld in Freiburg. These new residential areas have very low car ownership and use rates (Stadt Freiburg, 2010).

- Implement congestion charging/road pricing schemes along the lines of the London and Stockholm schemes (Victoria Transport Policy Institute, VTPI, 2011) and scale up the geographical extent of the charging area so that in the case of London (but generalisable to all metropolitan regions in the EU27) the charging area would extend to the whole of the administrative area of London with a population of 7 million (Whitelegg, 2011).

- Allocate a high political importance to improving air quality and put this into practice in all land use, spatial planning, housing, economic development and regeneration strategies and policies. Developments must pass the air pollution test. If they add to air pollution then they cannot go ahead. If they are designed in line with a de-coupling agenda (OECD, 2006) and with best practice on traffic reduction, demand management and the absolute prioritisation of walking, cycling and public transport, they can go ahead.

- Introduce new planning legislation along the lines suggested by the Campaign for Clean Air in London (House of Commons, 2011): "The campaign for Clean Air in London (CAL) urges the Environmental Audit Committee to recommend a requirement under UK planning law to protect sensitive populations (e.g. children and the elderly) from air pollution. This should build upon standards applied to school siting in California."

- Decommission parking spaces in all urban areas in step with detailed planning to increase the share of walking, cycling and public transport. If we are to increase the use of these sustainable modes we do not need the same amount of car parking and generous car parking provision is a stimulus to higher levels of car use.

- Develop and implement clear accessibility strategies so that we can create the city of short distances. Policies that increase distances e.g. closure of post offices, schools, local shops, health clinics, GP surgeries and swimming pools will be terminated.

- Design for the community as a whole with mixed uses the norm. The UK planning system is not fit for purpose as long as it maintains the 1940s notions of carving up a city or part of a city/town/locality so that areas look like monoculture agriculture (one area for housing, another area for retailing and another area for employment). These can and should all be mixed up together.

- Bring the UK planning system into line with air quality reduction objectives. This means rejecting planning applications that will add to air pollution through extra traffic generation in or close to an AQMA. It also means working with developers to design their proposals to minimise car use. A site like R89 (a greenfield housing development) in Grange-over-Sands in Cumbria with 42 homes and over 100 car parking spaces is clearly designed to deliver its contribution to the mobility agenda and to resist any suggestion that those residents buying a house on this site might be inclined to walk, cycle and use public transport (Whitelegg, 2013b). If these sustainable modes of transport were designed as an integral part of the proposal from the start and implemented in full before occupation, we could expect a much reduced level of car trips generation and its associated congestion and air pollution. The R89 site has over 100 car parking spaces and zero provision for bike parking and has made no effort whatsoever to assist with improving public transport and making the homes attractive to those who can be persuaded to use bus, bike or feet for local trips. R89 is a small site but is first in the queue for this small town and another 600 new homes are in the same high mobility/non-sustainability pipeline and will generate approximately 4000 additional car trips per day when built.

Conclusion

The strength of the mobility paradigm and its ability to air-brush alternative approaches out of any serious consideration leads directly to 52,430 deaths every year in the UK and 491,000 premature deaths each year in the EU (EEA, 2015).

The public policy failure associated with the scale of the air quality problem and the extremely limited nature of what is done to improve air quality can be explained by the degree of entrenchment of the mobility paradigm. The scale of the commitment to supporting and promoting traffic growth is large and manifests itself in 5 ways:

1. The allocation of eye-wateringly large amounts of money for infrastructure projects that are designed to stimulate higher levels of traffic flow (usually described as improving connections) e.g. the 26.3 billion Euros for Trans-European network funding announced on 19 November 2013 as a tripling of EU finances.

2. The acceptance of an annual subsidy bill for transport in the EU-27 of 270-290 billion Euros.

3. The lack of progress in implementing the full internalisation of external costs (making sure all transport modes pay the full costs they impose on society as a whole) despite over 20 years of lip services to this principle.

4. The prevalence of the Nelsonian approach to knowledge e.g. new roads generate new traffic and do not solve congestion and new roads may or may not create jobs, may move them around and may result in jobs draining away and all this is unpredictable.

5. The prevalence of an empirically flawed belief system that moving around a lot is a good thing and that doing it faster is better.

Under these circumstances any public policy intervention that has a chance of deviating from the mobility growth mantra will not even get on the agenda of measures proposed for adoption to improve air quality. The measures listed above all include elements of traffic reduction, lorry bans, road closures, car-free life styles and higher costs for car drivers and lorry operators. These would not be well received. They contradict the mobility paradigm and they deliver significant improvements in air quality and human health.

This is why the problem of poor air quality is persistent or as the European Environment Agency puts it (EEA, 2013, page 71):

"Air quality remains a key concern. Limit values for NO2 and PM10 continue to be exceeded in a large number of locations. Worryingly, the most recent data on transport emissions of air pollutants indicate that the long term trend of decline is no longer taking place in 2011."

The World Health Organisation (WHO, 2014a) estimates that approximately 3.7 million people globally die each year as a result of poor outdoor air quality:

"Only 12% of the people living in cities reporting on air quality reside in cities where this complies with WHO air quality guideline levels. About half of the urban population being monitored is exposed to air pollution that is at least 2.5 times higher than the levels WHO recommends - putting those people at additional risk of serious, long-term health problems."

The public policy response to poor air quality is grossly inadequate and that is because key decisions takers and opinion formers are deeply embedded in and committed to a world of high and growing mobility. They cannot contemplate measures and interventions that would eliminate traffic related outdoor air pollution. From an historical perspective this is the direct equivalent of early 19th century assumptions and perspectives about sewage. Just as it was acceptable at that time to dump raw human sewage in streets or rivers it is now acceptable to dump carcinogenic air pollutants into the air we breathe in cities. Just as we cannot understand why it was thought acceptable to dump raw sewage, so in the future will it be thought ridiculous, unintelligent and uncivilised that we accepted polluted cities and 3.7 million dead human beings.

Chapter 5
Fiscal Impacts

The newly approved and now under construction Heysham M6 Link Road in the north of England (also known as the Northern Bypass) is intended to provide a link between the M6 motorway, the main road to Morecambe and the port of Heysham (Gate, 2014 and James, 2014). It is 4.8kms long, is costed at £129 million (158 million Euros or 217 million US dollars) and has been justified by Lancashire County Council, the promoting transport authority, on its congestion busting credentials even though the same Lancashire County Council admitted in a public inquiry that it would not produce a solution to congestion and other measures will be needed. The road will cost 32,916 Euros per metre.

Mobility is a very expensive commodity and it is being promoted in the UK, and more generally, with no attempt to impose the austerity measures or public expenditure cuts being imposed on other public projects and services. It would make a very interesting thought experiment to put those who make cuts in education, welfare and the National Health Service in charge of transport and vice versa. We could then have unlimited growth in high quality health care, new schools, class sizes equal to the private schools (which are called public schools in England) so that instead of 30 children in a classroom there would be 8-10 in a class and we would have a dense network of mental health, dementia and alcohol/drug rehabilitation centres in every locality. In this imaginary world, transport spending would be cut, mobility would decline (but not accessibility) and there would be no more new roads built at 32,916 Euros per metre when the evidence presented to public inquiries shows that the new road will not reduce congestion and will not create new jobs.

Back in the real world (the UK in 2016) we have the well-established business as usual arrangement with £56 billion allocated to high speed rail projects and £15-£27 billion (estimates vary) to London's cross-rail project and large numbers of bypasses and motorway widening schemes to promote and encourage the growth of mobility. In addition we have huge cuts in local authority budgets which feed directly into cuts in the support given to bus services. The result is much more mobility by expensive and faster modes of transport and much reduced accessibility for those dependent on buses who are largely made up of lower income groups, children, women and older people.

It is obvious to any reasonably awake observer of transport spending that personal passenger transport is very expensive indeed. The high cost of infrastructure, maintaining that infrastructure, dealing with death and injury in the road traffic environment, policing, the courts system, 52,000 deaths in the UK per annum from poor air quality, obesity and much more is very high indeed.

In addition to public costs there are personal costs to be met from after- tax disposable income including rail and bus fares, petrol and diesel, car purchases, parking charges and fines, vehicle maintenance and the replacement and renewal of tyres, exhaust systems and other vehicle components.

A UK study, now rather dated (Maddison et al, 1996), calculated that all the costs generated by cars and trucks totalled £45-£52.9 billion and all forms of road taxes totalled £16.4 billion which as a percentage of all "external costs" is 31%-36%. Every time a car driver makes a journey of any length and complains about the high cost of the taxation element in fuel and vehicle purchases she is in fact paying less than 50% of these external costs.

External costs are costs that are generated by the activity (e.g. the car trips or lorry journeys) are "externalised" in the sense that the costs are passed onto society at large or government agencies. The main examples of these external costs are greenhouse gases and climate change, congestion, road damage, deaths and injury on the roads and health damage caused by exhaust emissions. A subsidy (EEA, 2007) is an actual cash transfer or taxation that is specifically foregone. Trains and buses are subsidized, roads built and kerosene (aviation fuel) is not taxed leading to a loss of over £10 billion pa to the UK treasury (Sewill, 2003).

The European Environment Agency (EEA, 2007) has calculated the annual transport subsidy in EU member states and put the figure at 269-293 billion Euros. The subsidies were allocated across modes as shown in Table 5.1.

	Billion Euros
Road	125
Air	27-35
Rail	73
Water	14-30
Multiple modes	30
Total	269-293

Table 5.1: EU transport subsidy, 2005
Note: The data on infrastructure subsidy is taken from 15 member states but all other components of subsidy are taken from 25 member states.
Source: EEA (2007)

The subsidies in Table 5.1 reflect actual financial transfers from the state to each mode of transport either through infrastructure support or tax relief. The data do not reflect externalities. These external costs total 650 billion Euros pa (EEA, 2007, page 8).

The transport sector of the economy is very heavily subsidised which contributes to the growth in demand. If the cost of a km of vehicle travel or a tonne of freight carried by a lorry is much less than it would be without the subsidy or without "fair and efficient pricing" (to include externalities) then more vehicle kilometres of car travel and tonne kilometres of road freight will be consumed. This can properly be regarded as a market failure. There is a failure to send the right price signals to the person driving a car or the truck operator.

The very large size of the externalities at 650 billion pa is another layer of cost insulation. European and most national governments including the UK support the principle known as "the polluter pays principle." The car driver should pick up the "tab" for all the costs she imposes on others and by extension she should not expect all these costs to be picked up by the state.

Fiscal rules over many decades have promoted the growth in mobility.

The high cost of the annual EU subsidy in Table 5.1 to all transport modes at around 270-290 billion Euros pa is very similar to the Greek bailout, the repayment of which has caused so much anguish and political crisis in Greece and the Eurozone in the first 7 months of 2015. This is not the place to discuss the woes of the Greek economy but it is relevant that across the EU as a whole we make no fuss at all about throwing such a large amount of money at a subsidy every year and the profligacy and indebtedness of states like Greece is almost daily news. This is not the same thing as suggesting that the annual transport subsidy be switched to bailing out struggling national economies but once again it raises the fundamental ideological issue around mobility. High levels of subsidy and high levels of uncovered external costs are accepted as part of normal life and are not subjected to the same austerity and stringency processes that have been imposed on Greece and are part of public expenditure cuts in the UK.

At the level of the ordinary citizen and daily trip making experiences it is obvious that there are economies to be made and better ways on offer when it comes to sorting out urban transport. It is clearly very silly indeed to endorse a situation where every journey that every person makes every day for any distance should be by car and this car must have a parking place at every destination. This is so silly that I assume there is no need to explain why it is silly. It is at the same time approximately the situation we have in the USA with vast amounts of space allocated to highways and parking lots and little attention (with some honourable exceptions) given to walking, cycling and public transport. Donald Shoup at Berkeley has described this as "the high cost of free parking" and has pointed out that the spending on highway and parking capacity is cumulatively greater than the US defense budget (Shoup, 2005):

"All this free parking is charity for cars. In 2002, the total subsidy for off-street parking was somewhere between $127 billion and $374 billion a year. If we also count the subsidy for free and underpriced curb parking, the total subsidy for parking would be far higher. In the same year the federal government spent only $231 billion for Medicare and $349 billion for national defense. Do we really want to spend as much to subsidize parking as spend for Medicare or national defense..spending so much to subsidize parking dramatically alters the transportation system, land use patterns, the economy, and the environment- all in the wrong direction." (Shoup, 2005, page 591).

The "wrong direction" referred to in this quotation is the rapid progress towards maximum car-based mobility and road shipment of freight. The growth of mobility is fuelled by eye-wateringly large sums of money devoted to a growth in traffic, generating new trips and ensuring that land use systems require a car for origins to be connected to destinations. This is the reality of a sophisticated life support system for higher levels of mobility.

Referencing the USA is not a sign that Britain is doing things better. On the contrary the British planning system is doing an excellent job leading us in the same direction, though heavily disguised by waves of rhetoric proclaiming the importance of sustainability and the relevance of walking and cycling to the sustainability agenda. Once again the details reveal all. A recent planning application from a house builder in the small tourist town of Grange-over-Sands (Cumbria, UK) has been approved by the local planning authority. This was an application to South Lakeland District Council to build 42 new homes on a greenfield site on the edge of the town with no cycling facilities in place or requested by the planners and very narrow, discontinuous footpaths to connect the site to any destination (shops, schools, health care) and poor public transport. The application was for 42 new homes and 112 parking places and zero bike parking. This is contrary to many years of thinking around sustainable transport (Whitelegg, 2013b) but it was accepted by the planners who recommended approval to the councillors who then gave approval. We are on our way to the American destination.

The local planning authority could have taken the view that 42 new homes should be defined as a total package taking into account how the new occupants would travel under various assumptions about what could be done to improve walking, cycling and public transport. The professional planners and the politicians acting on their advice opted for maximum growth in car-based mobility. Each household will generate 6 extra car trips per day or 253 car trips per day for the site as a whole. This application is for 42 new homes only but 673 new homes are planned and they will follow in rapid succession and at the same trip generation rate will generate an additional 4000 car trips per day. This is happening in every local authority area in England so the planning system is working at full speed to deliver higher levels of car-based mobility which in turn will impose higher costs on the community, public budgets and individuals.

	Modal share of public transport (%)		Cost of transport to the community (%GDP)	
	1995	2001	1995	2001
Geneva	18.8	21.7	10.2	9.4
London	23.9	26.8	8.5	7.5
Madrid	27.2	30.2	12	10.4
Paris	27.1	27.5	6.8	6.7
Vienna	43.2	46.6	6.9	6.6

Table 5.2: Relationship between public transport modal share and community costs
Source: Vivier (2006)

A report from a global organisation representing public transport operators has used a global data base on mobility to shed light on the costs of mobility at the level of a city and the way this varies with modal split (Vivier, 2006). Unsurprisingly and in line with citizen expectations and common sense the costs of mobility are much less in a city with a high level of use of walking, cycling and public transport (Table 5.2).

Table 5.2 shows a number of results of importance to all of us concerned with the costs of running cities and the availability of public expenditure for health, education and social welfare. It is not just a matter of technical or academic interest if public budgets are being consumed by a growth in mobility and this leaves much less for other areas; it is a hugely important quality of life and democratic matter. Have we really decided to spend "as if there is no tomorrow" so we can all go faster and further rather than on important budgets that directly affect the quality of life of all citizens and the quality of urban areas as places we would choose to live?

Table 5.2 shows that as the modal split for public transport goes up so the cost of transport as a % of GDP goes down. Cities that managed an increase in the modal share of public transport saw a decrease in the cost of transport. Elsewhere in the report Vivier says "the cost of transport for the community in cities with a high share of public transport is up to half the cost in cities where the private car is dominant. The difference represents a saving of 2000 Euros per inhabitant per annum."

Vivier goes on to emphasise that "Cities characterised by the lowest cost of transport to the community are often those where expenditure on public transport is the highest."

% modal share of walking, cycling and public transport	community cost as % of city GDP
>55	6.3
40-55	8.8
25-40	10.2
<25	12.5

Table 5.3: The cost to the community of transport as it varies by modal split
Source: Vivier (2006)

He then quantifies the cost of transport (% of GDP) as it varies by the percentage of all trips by walking, cycling and public transport (Table 5.3).

Figure 5.1 (next page) shows the full data set referred to in Table 5.3 graphed and a very clear relationship can be seen.

The relationship between the two variables in Figure 5.1 and Table 5.3 sends a very clear signal to urban planners, economists and all those responsible for fiscal matters in any city in the world. It is essential to raise the % modal share of walking, cycling and public transport if city finances are to be well managed and a high quality of life achieved at a low cost. To go for high mobility as implied by EU policy documents and the UK planning system is a recipe for fiscal melt-down and the decline of cities. It is unaffordable, unfair, unnecessary and unwelcome.

A future organized around much reduced consumption of distance and speed and much improved accessibility based on higher levels of walking, cycling and public transport is a fiscally prudent and affordable future. It also brings a much increased probability of enjoying the multiple benefits of living in well-run, well-funded cities, no longer living on the edge of drastic budget cuts and bankruptcy. It also brings with it the potential to have world best education, health care, clean air and public spaces because we are no longer squandering billions on the futile quest for more mobility.

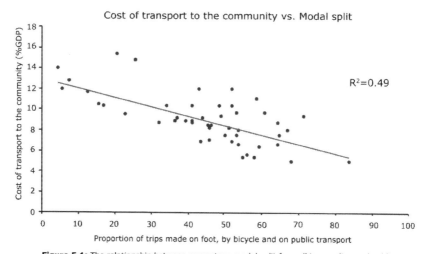

Figure 5.1: The relationship between percentage modal split for walking, cycling and public transport and the total cost of transport to the community as a percentage of GDP
Source: Vivier (2006)

Chapter 6
Energy

Transport is responsible for 22% of total global energy consumption (United Nations, 2013). The breakdown of energy use by mode is shown in Table 6.1.

Mode of Transport	Share of total energy use (2001) (%)[a]		Share of CO_2 emissions (2000) (%)[b]	
	Passenger transport	Goods transport	Passenger transport	Goods transport
Road transport	77.3		74.7	
Cars	44.5	-	42.5	-
Buses	6.2	-	6.3	-
Other (2- and 3- wheeler etc.)	1.6	-	2.4	-
Heavy trucks	-	16.2	-	23.5
Medium trucks	-	8.8		
Rail transport	1.5		2.3	
Air transport*	11.6	-	12.4	-
Sea transport*	-	9.5	-	10.6

Table 6.1: World Transport Energy Use and CO2 emissions by mode
Note: * Air and sea transport has been allocated to passenger and goods transport respectively for simplicity
Sources: [a] Kahn Ribeiro, 2007, p328 (citing Fulton and Eads, 2004); [b] OECD/ITF, 2011b, p17

The combination of global population increase (a 40% increase is predicted in the period 2010-2030), rapid economic development and car ownership growth in China, India and South American countries and a decline in oil availability (the peak oil problem) all conspire to create serious difficulties for traditional forms of oil-based mobility. A growth in mobility will increase the demand for energy and it is European Union policy to reduce the demand for energy whilst at the same time promoting growth (European Commission 2013a and 2013b). This is a fundamental policy conflict that remains unaddressed.

The European Commission energy policy R&D document (European Commission, 2013b) states that EU energy policy has the objective of holding 2020 energy consumption down to no more than 1474 Mtoe of primary energy consumption and 1078 of final energy consumption. The forecast for 2020 is 1680 Mtoe of primary energy consumption.

EU policy on energy is highly interventionist and focuses on ways in which buildings can be made more energy efficient, consumer behaviour can change in the direction of smarter energy choices and products can be designed to minimise energy use in manufacturing and energy use during the lifetime of the product. The emphasis on design, behavioural change, energy efficiency and renewable energy has a direct relevance to energy demand in transport. The conceptual equivalent of wind, wave and solar energy if transferred from energy to transport policy would be walking and cycling. In both domains the energy being used does not need fossil fuels or complex supply chains (e.g. the nuclear fuel cycle) to function, is widely available, does not consume finite resources and is renewed every day.

There is no renewable transport policy to run alongside the EU renewable energy policy.

We can design cities so they have higher population densities and more destinations within shorter distances. This is the direct equivalent of designing buildings so that they will use less energy. We can build cities so that they use less energy, a concept increasingly referred to as the "city of short distances" (Holzapfel, 2014). We can improve energy efficiency by transferring as many short trips as possible (say under 5kms in length) from the car to walking, cycling and public transport. This is the direct equivalent of designing products so they use less energy and we can influence consumer behaviour so that those making transport choices are much more aware and much better equipped to reduce car use and switch to alternatives. In one UK study of behavioural change interventions, the York intelligent travel project (Whitelegg and Haq, 2004) a reduction of car use of 16% was achieved from within a target population of confirmed car users.

Transport policy in the main is a "no go" area for the kind of interventions that are now routine in energy policy. This is surprising given the fundamental importance of the transport-energy interdependence.

Most national governments and European level policy making are enthusiastic about alternative fuels in transport e.g. biofuel and shifting the energy demands of cars from petrol and diesel to electricity with the possibility that this electricity can be generated from renewable sources (European Commission, 2013b, page 58 et seq). There are serious flaws in a policy that assumes a technological fix. Switching from petrol and diesel to electricity whilst growing mobility is a deeply flawed policy (Whitelegg et al 2010; Kenworthy 2013) but one that will consume billions of Euros in the next 20 years to provide the R&D support to vehicle manufacturers and networks of charging stations. Expensive changes will also be needed in the grid distribution infrastructure and balancing of demands in space and time to cope with the possibility that several hundred million vehicles will be plugged in and charging at the same time. All these considerations and costs are much more problematic and expensive if they are based on a maximum mobility scenario. If there is a major paradigm shift to reduce and eliminate the mobility bias in transport policy so that (for example) we reduce vehicle kilometres of motorised transport by 50% by 2025 on a 1990 base then e-mobility becomes a much realistic possibility and much more affordable.

E-mobility is currently promoted as part of the maximum mobility objective and to provide a green smokescreen to reinforce the mobility paradigm by suggesting that mobility can be zero carbon/lower carbon and non-polluting. If e-mobility can be delivered to the extent that it can replace the vast majority of petrol/diesel car trips in Europe (and this has not yet been demonstrated) the result will be hugely expensive and many more roads with all their damaging effects will be funded and built. Urban sprawl will continue to consume valuable land that could be used for food production and land also provides valuable landscape, ecological and biodiversity services that are destroyed when new roads occupy that space. Distances travelled will increase and as distances increase so walking and cycling decline. With the decline in "active travel" (walking and cycling) obesity prevalence will increase (Roberts 2010) and citizens will be living in increasingly remote suburban communities with all the problems identified by Dodson and Sipe (2008) and paying for their mobility with larger percentages of their disposable income.

This is an undesirable future.

E-mobility offers some relief from damaging exhaust emissions and their health impacts but sits very uneasily in the wider context of polices and measures that could increase accessibility reduce congestion and reduce deaths and injuries in the road traffic environment. It cannot deliver on these wider societal objectives and should be more correctly seen as a device to maintain the growth of mobility and in particular the growth of private motorised transport and urban sprawl. It is not located within a coherent sustainable transport policy context characterised by the demotion of mobility as a societal objective. This demotion is now recognised as an overdue policy change by a United Nations report (United Nations, 2013) and this same report recommends its replacement by comprehensive accessibility objectives:

"Achieving transport affordability objectives require actions that support non-motorised transport; reduce the financial costs of transport services; and increase transportation affordability through improved land-use accessibility."

"Urban planning has a major role to play in organizing spatial activities in cities so that they are in close proximity to their users. Two important factors are at work here. First, if travel distances are reduced then accessibility is improved as activities can be undertaken with less travel. Second, if travel distances are short, then it becomes more attractive to walk and cycle- particularly if space is allocated for exclusive rights of way- and to use public transport, and this in turn reduces the energy use and the environmental impacts of transport."

"Accessibility as a priority rather than transport."

"Recasting the sector's primary objective as one of enhancing accessibility invariably lead to a different set of policies and strategies, like transit-oriented development and the provision of highly interconnected bikeway networks. These strategies not only conserve, land, energy and financial resources, but also help the poor and those without privatized motorised vehicles to access goods and services within the city. In short, accessible cities are inclusive, resourceful and pro-poor."

Accessible cities are also much more resilient. They can deal with shocks that might disrupt transport systems (strikes, civil unrest, and severe weather) and also with fuel price hikes that might result from peak oil and global shortages of oil as India,

China and Brazil accelerate their "progress" towards Californian or Swedish levels of car ownership and use. It will be a mistake of some considerable historical significance not to build resilient cities.

Holger and Dalkmann (2007) have provided a coherent structure that locates e-mobility in the sustainable transport conceptual framework. They call this the "Avoid, Shift, Improve" strategy or for short ASI.

A= Avoid so that through land use planning and accessibility planning destinations are co-located with residential areas and distances are kept short. This leads to a lower level of car use and a higher level of use of non-motorised transport. Curitiba in Brazil and Singapore have developed spatial strategies and land use patterns that lead to lower CO_2 emissions from transport than cities that pursue low density developments or extensive suburbanisation. Petersen (2002) presents a detailed checklist for policy makers on how to manage land use and urban structures to reduce the prevalence of car use, increase the use of non-motorised transport and reduce CO_2 emissions.

S= Shift so that wherever possible transport demand can be shifted from cars to public transport, walking and cycling and freight can be shifted from truck to rail and water. The objective is to transfer demand to less carbon intensive modes.

I= Improve so that vehicles that use fossil fuel can be designed to be more fuel efficient.

Electric vehicles properly belong to the "I" category. They perform much better than fossil fuelled vehicles but they still need to nest in a Russian Doll fashion within the two outer layers of sustainable transport policy (the A and the S).

The study of energy futures in the UK by UKERC (2009) explicitly recognises this structured approach by constructing a scenario that reduces annual distances travelled by car by 74% by 2050. This approach is more consistent with ecological efficiency and sustainability than exchanging one kind of car for another kind of car. This is associated in the same study with a steady growth of the "multi-modal" approach so that by 2050 there is both a reduction in car use and an increase in the use of the alternatives to the car. Cycling for example grows from 1% of all distance travelled in 2009 to 13% in 2050.

This structured approach was also adopted by the Stockholm Environment Institute study of zero carbon transport in the UK (Whitelegg et al, 2010). In this study spatial planning and accessibility planning measures produced a 60% reduction in CO_2 emissions from the road transport sector and fiscal measures produced a 25% reduction. The remaining amount of car use was then assumed to be EV powered by electricity that was 100% decarbonised. This combination of spatial, fiscal and technological measures together with some behavioural changes produced a 100% decarbonisation of the road transport sector in the UK and a decarbonisation that was assisted by electric vehicles but was delivered through highly integrated layers of policies that first of all reduced demand for car transport and then applied the EV technology to the residual demand.

Any consideration of mobility and accessibility must fully embrace the spatial dimension and the degree to which mobility measured in vehicle kilometres goes up in cities and metropolitan areas operating at low densities. This, in essence, is the core of US transportation, energy and climate change policy difficulties and has been extremely well documented by Newman and Kenworthy (1999) and their detailed work on world cities, density and the relative importance of cars, walking, cycling and public transport. This is captured in Table 1.2 where I listed 41 cities from recent work by Kenworthy (2014). Density or the lack of density (urban sprawl) is the most important factor explaining the differences between Atlanta (USA) and its annual per capita vehicle kilometres of 24639 and Brussels (5862) or Berlin (8222).

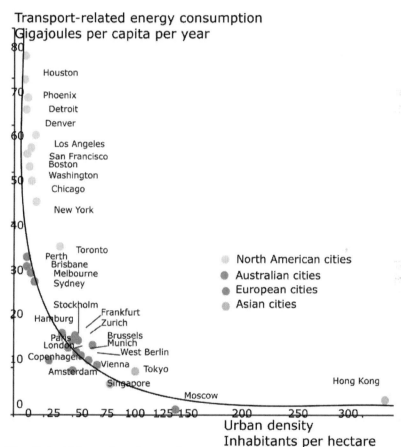

Fig 6.1: Urban density and transport-related energy consumption

Source: Newman and Kenworthy, 1989; Atlas Environment du Monde Diplomatique

There is a very clear relationship between urban density and transport related energy consumption per capita in world cities (Newman and Kenworthy, 1999). Energy consumption is a useful surrogate measure for tracking CO_2 emissions. This is presented in graphical form in Figure 6.1.

Vivier (2006) has shown how sustainable urban transport policy achieved through policies that prioritise walking, cycling and public transport (WCPT) over cars can produce significant reductions in energy consumption. This is the same point as already made about urban density. WCPT modes cannot thrive in an urban system that is characterised by sprawl and longer/lengthening distances. Distance can only be shortened by a clear diminution of policies that promote mobility and their replacement by policies that promote accessibility.

The discussion in Chapter 1 about invariants and the long term, cross-cultural allocation of just over one hour per day of travel time has a powerful influence on societal development, energy use and greenhouse gas emissions. Given that we have an internal thermostat (Chronostat) that fixes travel time at about one hour per day the result of technological change to speed up transport modes and switch choices from walking and cycling to cars has the effect of increasing distances. If we can reduce travel time we don't. We compensate for a reduced travel time opportunity by increasing the distances so that the reduced travel time is consumed as extra distance and we maintain the 1.1 hour time budget. The "Chronostat" has kicked in and the result is sprawl.

Vivier produces evidence to show that energy consumption per person per annum is lower in dense cities with a higher modal share for WCPT modes (Table 6.2).

Modal share of WCPT (%)	Energy consumption MJ/person/year
>55	11900
40-55	14600
25-40	19100
<25	55500

Table 6.2: Variation in per capita energy consumption by % modal split for WCPT modes
Source: Vivier (2006)

Is there something important missing in energy policy? It is rather obvious that an energy policy should embrace a sector of energy consumption (transport) that is responsible for 22% of total energy use and that the opportunities offered by spatial planning and accessibility planning to reduce energy consumption as shown in the above table should be fully developed and implemented.

This possibility is referred to in the European Commission (2013b, page 80) document:

"The key challenges for Smart Cities and Communities are to significantly increase the overall energy efficiency of cities, to exploit better the local resource both in terms of energy supply as well as through the demand side measures."

Sadly, the enormous potential for transport policy, spatial planning and modal shift to increase energy efficiency of cities is absent in the energy policy R&D document.

It is remarkable that energy policy does not embrace transport issues in this way and does not embrace urban density and accessibility measures. It is even more remarkable as I have shown in the case of Grange over Sands in Cumbria that UK planning policy and the planning system actively encourages lower levels of WCPT, higher levels of urban sprawl and higher levels of energy consumption.

Vivier puts the point even more succinctly: "Energy savings between cities with a high WCPT mode share and cities relying mainly on the private car represent around 500-600 litres of petrol per inhabitant pa."

The relationship between modal share (proportion of trips made on foot, by bicycle and on public transport) and annual energy consumption is shown graphically in Figure 6.2.

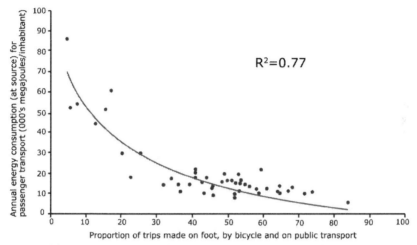

Figure 6.2: Energy consumption for passenger transport versus modal split
Source: Vivier, 2006

There is also a very important dynamic element. It is not too late to shift an urban system into a low energy/low carbon state. Cities which managed to increase the modal share of WCPT saw a decrease in the consumption of energy per person (Table 6.3).

	Modal share of WCPT modes %		Average consumption of energy for transport per person/pa MJ	
	1995	2001	1995	2001
Athens	34.1	40.9	12900	12600
Geneva	44.8	48.8	23600	19200
Rome	43.2	43.8	18200	17100
Vienna	62	64	10700	9050

Table 6.3: Change over time in energy consumption per person and modal share of WCPT modes
Source: Vivier, J (2006) Mobility in Cities Database. Better mobility for people worldwide. Analysis and Recommendations, UITP (Union Internationale Transports Publique), Brussels

Conclusion

The links between energy policy and transport policy are poorly developed and at the EU level there is a clear policy conflict. The undiluted commitment to the growth in mobility is a direct contradiction to the ambitious policies to reduce energy use. The potential for both sets of policies to work synergistically and harmoniously is enormous and would embrace spatial planning and urban density at its core.

Heaps et al (2009) have shown a clear way forward that embraces energy use, transport, climate change and detailed mitigation scenarios. Their analysis is a scenario-based consideration of all the economic sectors contributing to energy use and greenhouse gas emissions and includes transport. The preferred mitigation scenario works towards 40% reduction in CO2 by 2020 and a 90% reduction, on a 1990 base, by 2050. These reductions are achieved through 3 main sets of policies:

- Radical improvements in energy efficiency.
- Accelerated retirement of fossil fuels.
- Dramatic shift to renewable for electricity generation.

Very large changes are envisaged in buildings and transport sectors.

For homes they envisage that 90% of all homes will be retro-fitted to German "passiv haus" standards at a rate of 5% of the stock pa. There would also be reductions in house size (sq metres of living space) to 2005 levels and increases in urban density along the lines I have discussed above.

On urban density the authors say that a change in transportation planning and thinking will be needed to support:

"Compact, transit-friendly, walkable communities instead of developments that expand and sprawl into the countryside."

Heaps et al (2009) demonstrate that it is possible to build mitigation scenarios that are realistic, feasible and costed and "ready to go" and can achieve multiple policy objectives. This same approach was also adopted by Whitelegg et al (2010) demonstrating that it is possible to decarbonise transport systems, replace mobility fetishism with an accessibility objectives and improve quality of life for all citizens.

It is a source of deep regret that within the EU both national governments and EU-wide policies have fundamentally failed to understand these issues and have set us on a trajectory that will, as a result of an illogical commitment to mobility, multiply a large number of negative consequences including severe climate change.

Chapter 7
Climate Change

"Reducing global transport greenhouse gas (GHG) emissions will be challenging since the continuing growth in passenger and freight activity could outweigh all mitigation measures unless transport emissions can be strongly decoupled from GDP growth (high confidence)." (IPCC,2013)

"Reducing [climate change] emissions from the on-road transportation sector is particularly attractive because this action yields both rapid and longer term climate benefits." (Unger, 2010, page 3)

The transport sector in the 27 member states of the European Union (EU27) is responsible for 25.5% of total CO_2 emissions and these are expected to rise by 120% in the period 2000-2050 (UITP, 2009). Transport is the fastest growing source of greenhouse gas emissions and its emissions are effectively cancelling out the gains made in reducing CO_2 emissions in other sectors of the economy.

The very strong commitment to the growth in mobility at both national and EU-wide levels is the root cause of this policy failure and is very likely to be the main factor in the explanation for the failure of climate change policies overall and the likelihood that many or all of the predicted severe consequences of climate change will happen.

On the 19th November 2013 the European Commission announced a tripling of the budget available to encourage higher levels of passenger and freight transport and to make sure these opportunities were "smoother and quicker" (European Commission 2013c). The announcement says "mobility is the key to quality of life and vital for EU competitiveness." On both counts the authors are wrong. Higher mobility is not associated with these outcomes. There is no evidence that quality of life goes up as we travel more or move goods over longer distances. Similarly "competiveness" cannot be reduced to the ease with which we can move around. We do know that higher levels of mobility add to congestion and this imposes large costs on individuals and businesses and will add to the greenhouse gas inventory. Higher costs are unlikely to improve competitiveness.

The growth in mobility and its ideological support network carries the extremely serious burden of bringing about the failure of climate change policies.

A detailed scientific assessment of the climate change debate and the importance of reducing greenhouse gases if we are to avoid the worst consequences of climate change can be found in Rockstrom et al (2009) and Heaps et al (2009) and is not repeated here. The accepted scientific view, and one shared by this author, can be summarised as follows:

- Climate change is real, accelerating and anthropogenic in origin.
- It is mainly caused by the emission of so-called greenhouse gases (GHG) largely generated by the burning of fossil fuels.
- The evidence on impacts is persuasive and points to an increase in the frequency and severity of severe weather events.
- The impact on human populations especially the poorer groups in global society is severe and will lead to substantial loss of life.
- The damage to ecosystems is severe e.g. coral reefs.
- There is an urgent need to mitigate GHG emissions i.e. reduce.
- There is a strong argument for across the board reductions which include transport.
- Mitigation must proceed with a great deal of care for social justice and equity and to protect the poorest people on the planet.
- The costs of GHG reduction and climate change strategies are less than the costs of ignoring the problem.
- There are a large number of co-benefits associated with GHG reduction.

The links between mobility, lifestyle and climate change

The scientific debate around climate change is important but it can obscure lifestyle issues and the ways in which a decarbonised world (i.e. at least a 90% cut in CO_2 by 2050 on a 1990 base) would be different to the world we now know. This is possibly even more important in a mobility discussion where we are exploring a scenario characterised by less mobility measured in vehicle kilometres of motorised transport but much more accessibility and many more of our journeys than now would be made on foot, by bike and by public transport. In addition it is not "just" a transport issue. Our cities, in a decarbonised world, would be different. They would be more compact, denser, more walkable, cleaner, less congested and with health damaging air pollution largely eliminated. This delivers significant improvements in quality of life (Whitelegg, 2013).

To capture the real significance of mitigation in transport we need to paint a picture of what the world (well at least Europe for now) would look like in a 100% decarbonised transport future or as close to that future as we can get. This is what it would look like:

The Vision

A zero carbon transport future will provide better access for more people to more things than is currently the case. Traffic congestion and time wasted stuck in jams will be a thing of the past and time currently wasted on commuter trips will be spent on rewarding and enriching activities. By 2050 all urban and rural areas will have significantly enhanced public transport and cycling facilities bringing high quality and low-cost transport choices within everyone's reach. Those who opt not to use a car will save thousands of pounds a year by avoiding the fixed and variable costs of car ownership and use, and will also avoid the uncertainties and potential disruption of oil price shocks as the world adjusts to shortages of supply and increased demand from developing countries and the rapidly growing economies of China and India. Individuals and families will have much improved air quality, reduced noise and stress from traffic and much improved community life stimulated by reduced levels of motorised traffic and reduced traffic on streets and through villages.

The shift to bike, foot and public transport will increase the spending of people in their local areas. This will result in a local renaissance with shops and newly created jobs in local communities serving the increased level of local spending that previously leaked out to global oil and car-making sectors of the economy. Those that have given up individual car ownership will benefit by an average of £4,000 per annum which will be available to spend on local goods and services giving a further boost to local economies.

The passenger car will still exist and be used by those who have limited transport alternatives but fuel prices will rise to cover the full costs of supporting motorisation (the polluter pays principle) and parking will be recognised as a valuable asset that must be charged for at market rates. Speeds will be limited to a maximum of 20mph/30kph in all residential areas and through villages to support the rapid take up of walking and cycling and to create high quality living environments. Speeds on motorways and dual carriageways will be limited to 60mph to reduce CO_2 emissions and to encourage the take-up of eco-driving techniques. Cars will be either plug-in electric vehicles (PEVs) or powered by hydrogen fuel cells. The electricity required, both for re-charging the PEVs and for producing the hydrogen, will come from a decarbonised electricity supply system largely based on renewable energy and micro-generation in all businesses, homes, schools and health care facilities.

Businesses of all kinds will find ways to introduce flexible working, videoconferencing, more family and child friendly working practices and will actively promote the end of the long commute. Links between businesses, businesses and customers and workers at home or in local "area offices" will be facilitated by a large number of electronic methods. Deliveries of raw materials and goods to manufacturing sites will exploit the advantages of canals, inland waterways, estuaries and the UK's excellent network of 300 ports as well as making better use of the rail network e.g. as in the German "Rollende Landstrasse" system where whole lorries go on trains for sections of their journeys. Lorries will operate in ways that avoid cities, avoid long trunk-haul routes on motorways and are powered by alternatives to diesel that significantly reduce CO_2 emissions.

Tourism in 2050 will still be important but a combination of higher fares and air traffic delays will reduce the demand for flying and increase the number of holidays taken in the UK. There is evidence that holidays involving personal development, child-centred activities, outdoor activities and artistic activities are already on the increase and this process will accelerate putting more emphasis on what is done rather than on where it is done. Holidays in the EU will still be popular and will be accessible by much improved train services, including overnight trains, which provide a journey experience that is also part of the holiday and will steadily supplant air travel.

The aviation industry will still be important but no larger than in 2005 and airlines and companies owning airports will be far more profitable and successful as they diversify into all kinds of communication and mobility activities and services. There will be significant job gains across all sectors of the aviation, rail and bus industries.

The health of all citizens will improve in a low carbon transport future. There will be more lively local economies making jobs available in the community. There will be more social interaction giving everyone the health generating social context of living in a supportive community. There will be less noise and air pollution with attendant health benefits and much more physical activity contributing to a reduction in rates of obesity and heart disease.

The demands on public finance and spending will be reduced. There will be no need for new roads, bypasses and motorway widening at current prices approaching £25 million per mile. A healthier and more supportive population and community will reduce National Health Service (NHS) costs e.g. the predicted £50 billion per annum costs of obesity by 2050.

Local communities will be far more resilient in the sense that a larger proportion of jobs, food and other items of consumption will be sourced locally. This will reduce the risks of disruption that are likely to be associated with long distance sourcing in the future such as oil price hikes, interruption in supply as transport infrastructure succumbs to damage from extreme weather events and shortfalls in fuel availability.

Cities will change so that there is far more green space and woodland and a higher number of homes and employment opportunities than is currently the case in low density developments. Land for eco-efficient, car-free housing can be released from car parks that will now be surplus to requirements and the projected need for new homes therefore, can be met without taking away valuable rural land that will be needed for increased food production.

Cities will be far more friendly and supportive of children and the elderly with calmer environments, reduced traffic and increased feelings of confidence and security. The shift away from the car will increase the amount of walking and cycling and the degree of mutual, friendly "surveillance" making everyone feel safer. Children will rediscover the delights of independent mobility, the joys of getting to and from school and visiting friends and local swimming pools under their own steam. The elderly will find it much easier to cross roads, hold conversations on the street and engage with neighbours in ways that ends social isolation and its related health damaging consequences.

Urban and rural residents alike will be happier in this zero carbon future. Layard (2005) has shown that happiness can be measured and that the objective of public policy is to increase the amount of happiness and/or the number of people reporting that they are happy. He shows that in many societies happiness has declined as indices of material welfare have gone up raising the intriguing possibility that a society or culture moving at a slightly slower pace with more opportunities for social, interaction and less noise and pollution might be warmly welcomed. A low carbon future delivers such a society.

A much improved local environmental quality linked to higher levels of integration with local food production, heightened involvement with neighbours and community activities and a greater feeling of security and comfort from a more resilient society will all contribute to increased happiness and to higher levels of social cohesion.

The transformation of society from having a rather one-dimensional emphasis on economic growth to one based on community growth, increased happiness, reduced pollution, improved health and the creation of jobs that are far more evenly distributed and resilient to potential shocks, will bring enormous benefits to all. Examples of community growth would include more social interaction as people meet each other in a much more pleasant public realm as they walk and cycle. A decline in traffic levels is associated with more friends and acquaintances at the level of an individual street (Appleyard, 1981) and more friends and acquaintances are associated with higher self-reported happiness.

This transformed society, combined with increases in transport choice and improvement in safety and security, all point to the absence of "losers" in the zero carbon world. Society will be much fairer with much improved access for everyone, much fewer demands on those with constrained budgets through the elimination of the need to own a car as a default option and the availability of many more transport choices.

Achieving the Vision

Achieving a maximum decarbonised future by the year 2050 is desirable and achievable on quality of life, fiscal and climate change grounds. It will involve more action than those applied to the transport sector including a decarbonised electricity generation system and a new grid distribution system to support a very different pattern of domestic and transport production and consumption of energy. Nevertheless transport holds the key to decarbonisation simply on the grounds that it is a fast growing source of greenhouse gases and, so far, shows very little sign of following successful reductions in GHG emissions in industry, offices and homes.

Achieving the maximum level of decarbonisation in the transport sector is not a technical or a fiscal problem. We know how to do it and we have the cash to pay for it and recent spending decisions in the UK e.g. £56 billion on high speed rail (with a lot more than this to come as costs escalate) and £15-27 billion on London's cross-rail project indicate that there are funds available. More importantly we know there are a large number of co-benefits flowing from carbon reduction and mobility reduction and these co-benefits produce savings in other budgets. This is often referred to as "spend to save" so for example a large expenditure on combined heat and power (CHP) and a wind turbine at Lancaster University reduces carbon emissions and energy bills.

This "double-win" also operates in transport. York University has a 25% modal share for bikes compared with approximately 8% for Lancaster University. This means that staff and students at York University save money on personal transport expenditure and York needs fewer car parking places and has a lower bill for construction, supervision and maintenance of parking. It also means that York University has a lower carbon inventory than Lancaster.

A significant improvement in modal share for walking, cycling and public transport can produce much larger reductions in congestion than is claimed for new road construction. This is the case in most of the UK's planned new road schemes including the Westbury bypass (Kinnersley, 2014), Heysham M6 Link Rd (Gate, 2014) and the Aberdeen Western Peripheral Route (Walton, 2014). It is also the case in Melbourne where a hugely expensive new road, the East-West link, is consuming far more resources than are available for urban rail projects (Morton, 2014). A switch to a decarbonised paradigm will cut billions off the budget for new roads, deliver improvements in quality of life and bring transport policy in line with climate change policies.

Road building and increasing capacity on existing roads is especially problematic for the climate change discussion. New roads generate new traffic (SACTRA, 1994) and stimulate the progression to higher levels of mobility with higher levels of CO_2 emissions e.g. the HM6L road in Lancaster was estimated by the highway authority promoting the road to generate an additional 20,000 tonnes of CO_2 pa (not counting any emissions generated by construction, concrete, tarmac etc). Adding to CO_2 emissions when there is an urgent need to reduce them (Rockstrom et al 2009) is a significant policy failure.

The measures that are available to policy makers to deliver a decarbonised transport system are well known and in many cases already in place in the better run cities and regions of Europe. One of the best examples is the region around Freiburg-im-Breisgau in the southern German state of Baden-Württemberg. Much of the detail can be found in Whitelegg (2013) and the physical reality of what has been achieved in one city-region sends a powerful message to global policy makers that it works, it can be done and it is especially good for the economy. Sadly it is a message that is widely ignored.

Freiburg has invested heavily in renewable energy, mainly wind turbines and solar, and is regarded as a European best practice "solar city." Its transport system is highly integrated with excellent bus, tram, local train, walk and bicycle facilities delivering a 28% modal share for bikes and very low levels of car use. Its planning systems are organised around compact city principles and investment in high quality public transport offers such as trams and the recently electrified branch railway line from Bad Krozingen to Munstertal. The electrification of this small branch line with new rolling stock shows what can be done. The population of the valley served by this line is approximately 10,000. This can be compared with dreadful, dirty, diesel operated services in the UK using vehicles that are 40 years old e.g. the Lancaster-Morecambe branch line serving a population of approximately 100,000. There is no prospect of new investment on this line.

Freiburg is well known for its highly acclaimed car-free residential areas of Vauban and Rieselfeld (Folleta and Field, 2011). Vauban is not 100% car free but has very low levels of car ownership (160 cars per 1000 residents) and low levels of car use, 16% of all trips are by car. Residents must sign a legal agreement not to own a car or pay for a parking space in a shared public garage at a cost of 18,500-22,500 Euros (Foletta and Field, 2011). Parking on the residential streets is not allowed.

Vauban is not an isolated example of best practice. In Germany there are other excellent examples of highly intelligent, integrated spatial planning and transport planning producing high quality of life outcomes and justifiable on carbon reduction alone but bringing with them a large number of co-benefits. Tübingen referred to in Holzapfel (2012) is another best practice example and Foletta and Field (2011) describe 7 other locations under the title "Europe's vibrant new low car(bon) communities."

Spatial planning is an under-used policy instrument for reducing GHG and at the same time increasing accessibility. Figure 7.1 shows a very clear relationship between energy use and density (energy use tracks GHG emission very accurately).

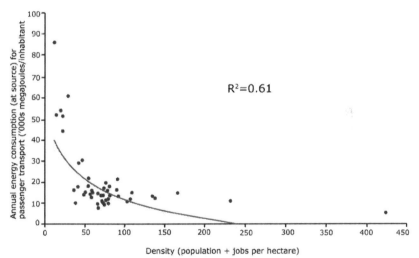

Figure 7.1: Energy consumption for passenger transport versus density
Source: Vivier, 2006

Increasing density in our large urban areas brings significant reductions in energy use and GHG emissions.

UITP (2009) has provided a very strong evidence base for the relationship between the percentage of all trips made by walking, cycling and public transport (WCPT) and per capita annual CO_2 emissions.

Cities with a modal share for WCPT above 55% produce on average about 2.4 tonnes less CO_2 from passenger transport than cities below that level of performance (UITP, 2009). This is good news. We know how to reduce CO_2 emissions in our urban areas in Europe. We know how to do it but with the exception of some remarkable cities like Freiburg we do not do it.

Evidence on successful transport policies that are reducing carbon emissions

One of the many paradoxes surrounding transport, CO_2 reduction and climate change policy is the huge disparity between the large number of authoritative studies on how to go about reducing CO_2 emissions from this sector and the low level of serious implementation of these suggestions.

As early as 1992 the European Commission funded a detailed study of policy measures to reduce CO_2 in the transport sector (TNO, 1992). This study evaluated 94 separate measures that had the potential to reduce CO_2 emissions. The study concluded that the "target scenario" of a 12% reduction in CO_2 emissions on a 1990 base by the year 2000 was feasible. Interestingly the study concluded (TNO, 1992 page xxii):

"Tackling each issue separately will not yield the required results. This means that any policy would have to be formulated to address the need for all the following:

- Better technology and alternative fuels.

- Reduction of traffic volume (fewer vehicle kilometres).

- More energy conscious driving behaviour.

- Enhanced traffic circulation (by infrastructure changes and electronic methods)."

The same conclusion was reached in a European Conference of Ministers of Transport study published in 1995 (OECD, 1995). This study listed 29 measures grouped under 4 headings:

- Land use management.

- Road traffic management.

- Environmental protection.

- Pricing mechanisms.

As in the TNO (1992) study the authors argued:

"All the policy instruments listed are potentially helpful but no single one of them has the power to achieve the objectives of sustainable development: to do this governments need to introduce packages of policies that are mutually reinforcing."

In 2004 the UK Department for Transport funded a study on how to reduce CO_2 emissions in transport by 60% (Hickman and Banister, 2005).

The authors identified 11 policy packages, clusterings of packages and policy pathways and 123 policy measures to reduce CO_2 emissions in the UK transport sector. A detailed description of the policy measures and packages can be found in DfT (2006).

The Yorkshire and Humber regional study already discussed above (Yorkshire and Humber Regional Assembly, 2008) also identified specific measures that would reduce CO2 emissions in the transport sector. These measures are listed in Figure 7.2 together with an assessment by transport professionals of their acceptability in the policy making process.

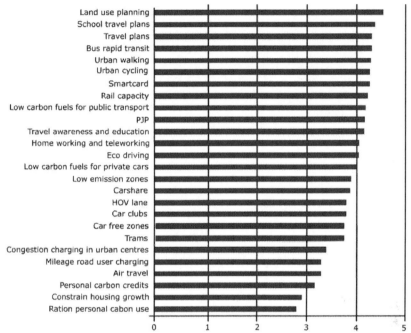

Figure 7.2: Policy measures and interventions used in the Yorkshire and Humber study of a regional low carbon transport system
Source: Yorkshire and Humber Regional Assembly (2008)

Note: Respondents were asked to assess the acceptability of the proposed measures on a 1-5 scale where 1 = very unacceptable and 5 = very acceptable

The studies quoted above of regional, national and European level packages of measure to reduce CO2 emissions from the transport sector are supported by specific examples of individual measures or packages where detailed monitoring and evaluation have taken place. Table 7.1 (next page) summarises this evidence.

The European Environment Agency (EEA, 2008c) has produced a review of six policy interventions and shown the CO2 reduction in each of the policy areas. The review covers:

- Eco-driving in the Netherlands (97,000-220,000 tonnes reduction in CO2).
- Speed control measures in Rotterdam (Netherlands) producing a 15% reduction in CO2 in the pilot area.

- Congestion charging in London producing a 16.4% reduction in CO2.

- Environmental zone in Prague (Czech Republic) producing a reduction of 1650 tonnes pa in CO2.

- Freight consolidation centre in London producing a 75% reduction in CO2 emissions.

- Teleconferencing in the UK producing a reduction of 100,000 tonnes of CO2.

Policy measure	Reduction	Reference
London congestion charge	13%	http://cchargelondon.com/effect.html
Stockholm Congestion charge	14%	http://www.c40cities.org/bestpractices/transport/stockholm_congestion.jsp
Cycling in Copenhagen	90,000 tonnes of CO2 per year	http://www.c40cities.org/bestpractices/transport/copenhagen_bicycles.jsp
Freiburg, Germany (car-free, 20mph zones, integrated public transport	5%	http://www.c40cities.org/bestpractices/transport/freiburg_ecocity.jsp
Portland, Oregon (Optimisation of signals)	15460 tonnes of CO2 per year	http://www.c40cities.org/bestpractices/transport/portland_traffic.jsp
Stockholm (clean vehicles)	200,000 tonnes of CO2 per year	http://www.c40cities.org/bestpractices/transport/stockholm_vehicles.jsp
York (UK) Intelligent travel project	16%	http://www.sei-international.org/mediamanager/documents/Publications/Future/intelligent_travel_york.pdf
UK wide travel smart project	0.9 million tonnes pa	https://www.gov.uk/government/policies/improving-local-transport/supporting-pages/working-with-businesses-and-people-to-reduce-the-need-to-travel
City of Bremen, Germany (public transport, car share and cycling	17,500 tonnes of CO2 per year	Freie Hansestadt Bremen (2008)
"Typical Latin American cities" (BRT, pedestrian and cycle up-grades)	25.1%	http://www.internationaltransportforum.org/Topics/Workshops/WS4Sundar.pdf
TransJakarta BRT and CNG buses	32,302 tonnes of CO2 pa	Yunita (2008)
Milan, Italy "Ecopass" access charge	12%	ITDP (2008)

Table 7.1: The CO2 reduction performance attributable to specific policy interventions
Note:
BRT = Bus Rapid Transit where the bus service has a dedicated track and buses cannot be delayed by general traffic congestion
CNG = Compressed Natural Gas used as an alternative fuel to diesel

A recent paper by Vallack et al (2014) shows how it is possible to totally decarbonise all road and rail transport in the UK by 2050 and reduce aviation emissions of CO2 by 56% and shipping by 48%. The overall impact of all measures is a 76% reduction in transport's CO2 emissions when the 2050 "maximum impact" scenario is compared with the business as usual scenario. The reductions are achieved by a carefully constructed and mutually supportive package of fiscal, behavioural, spatial planning and technological interventions.

It is possible for the transport sector to play its full proportionate role in achieving ambitious GHG reductions and avoiding the worst consequences of climate change.

The failure to grasp this opportunity is another manifestation of the power of the mobility paradigm and its life support systems. Just as we are unable to embrace zero deaths and injuries in the road traffic environment and zero air pollution from traffic sources we are incapable of zero (or near zero) carbon emissions in transport.

Climate Justice

Dealing with climate change requires significant reductions in GHG emissions of at least 80% on a 1990 base by 2050. Even this level of reduction may not be enough to prevent some of the worst consequences of climate change becoming reality and impacting very hard indeed on the poor of the world. This reduction requirement has caused a great deal of difficulty in obtaining global agreement on the scale of reduction needed. Politicians in the UK frequently argue there is no point in reducing emissions here because any reduction would be quickly swamped by the annual average increase in China and India. In both China and India there is a strongly held view that the severity of climate change problems is the result of long periods of fossil-fuelled economic growth in the USA and the EU and it is unacceptable to deny the same opportunity for economic growth and poverty alleviation in those countries through the imposition of cuts. More importantly this long history of adding carbon to the atmosphere and triggering climate change means that the USA and the EU are responsible for the bulk of the these impacts and this greater historical proportionate responsibility must be recognised and translated into a financial transfer mechanism to assist China and India with development and decarbonisation. The implication of this viewpoint is that China and India and similar countries should be excluded from the reduction regime and given the opportunity to develop and eradicate poverty. This is referred to as "climate justice" or "climate debt" (Klein, 2014) or "Greenhouse Development Rights" (Baer et al, 2008).

Pape (2014) has put some numbers on this that reveal the scale of climate injustice:

"Cumulative global emissions have been around 1200 GtCO2 between the years 1850-2008. Of this figure Annex 1 countries (the developed world) accounted for 864 GtCO2 which is 72% of the total. Since their share of population was nearly 25%, their fair CO2 emission share would have been 300 GtCO2 and their overuse or carbon debt was therefore about 564 GtCO2. Non Annex 1 countries accounted for 336 GtCO2 which is 28% of the total CO2 emissions. Their fair share would have been 900 GtCO2 and thus they had an underuse of 564 GtCO2 of emissions."

Pape goes on to quote IPCC calculations that set out the case for restricting cumulative CO2 emissions to 900 GtCO2 in the period 2011-2050 and that on a population basis Annex 1 countries should emit only 122 GtCO2, since they represent only 13.5% of the global population. Developing counties with 86.5% of global population should be limited to 778 GtCO2.

This is then translated into an equity-based financial compensation mechanism (Pape, 2014):

"On top of this, in order to be able to claim this carbon budget of 122 GtCO2 emissions, the developed countries would have to repay the 564 GtCO2 of climate debt that they accumulated in the previous period, 1850–2010. This payment could be made by re-allocating the fair shares for the period 2011–2050. Thus, Annex I countries would have responsibility for negative emissions of 441 GtCO2 (122 GtCO2 minus 564 GtCO2), while non-Annex 1 countries would have responsibility within a budget of 1,372 GtCO2 (778 GtCO2 plus 564 GtCO2). If it is not possible for Annex I countries to implement their responsibility fully, keeping in mind the difficulty of achieving such a high level of negative emissions by 2050, these countries could arrange for non-Annex I countries to take on some of the responsibility through a scheme that involves payment of financial resources to implement mitigation or avoidance of emissions."

The implications of the logic, methodology and calculations described by Pape are that the developing world should receive financial compensation from the developed world as payment towards the investments, technology and policy changes that will deliver development to these poorer countries but at a lower level of carbon emissions than if they had followed the same model as the USA and Europe over the last 100-150 years.

This is of particular relevance to the mobility paradigm because transport is responsible for a significant share of the increase in GHG emissions in these two countries and redefining this paradigm so that it does not pursue the same path as that followed in the USA and European will require assistance with funding and technology which could be provided by a climate debt compensation mechanism.

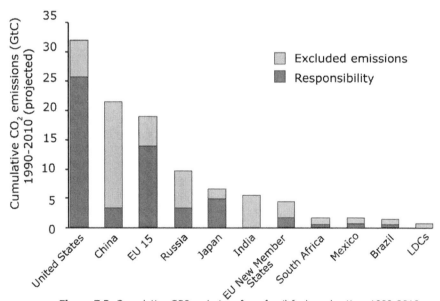

Figure 7.3: Cumulative CO2 emissions from fossil-fuel combustion, 1990-2010. Each bar is divided between a green section that shows "responsibility" and a yellow section that corresponds to emissions associated with consumption below the development threshold.
Source: Baer et al (2008)

Baer et al (2008) have suggested a way of quantifying the degree to which countries are responsible for climate change and which countries should be given "space" to continue their development trajectories unhindered by reduction requirements. This is shown in diagrammatic form in Figure 7.3.

Sunita Narain, Director of the Centre for Science and the Environment in Delhi (quoted in Klein, 2014, page 414) said:

"The solution is not for the wealthy world to contract its economies while allowing the developing world to pollute its way to prosperity (even if this were possible). It is for developing countries to develop differently. We do not want to first pollute and then clean up. So we need money, we need technology, to be able to do things differently. And that means the wealthy world must pay its climate debts."

Another group of climate change researchers have calculated the actual monetary amounts that must be transferred from Annex 1 countries to named Annex 2 countries (Table 7.2).

	Receives (billion US dollars)	Provides (billion US dollars)
China	497	
India	151	
France		51
Germany		72
UK		49
USA		634

Table 7.2: Financial transfers associated with climate debt calculations
Source: http://www.climatefairshares.org/tables

The financial transfers would pay for the paradigm shift in full. China and India could confidently build a high quality pedestrian and cycling infrastructure for all urban and rural residents as well as a high quality public transport system designed to meet the needs for all income groups and all social groups to reach the destinations they choose to use. The mobility paradigm would be transformed into an accessibility paradigm with a budget in place to deliver the infrastructure, including the provision of high quality pedestrian pavements alongside every road in every urban and rural area in both countries. Additionally the two countries would dramatically reduce their spending on roads, high speed rail and aviation that traditionally forms part of the high spend, highly damaging, high carbon option that has been employed in the developed world. All of China and India's citizen would benefit, climate change mitigation would be delivered and a socially just future assured.

Chapter 8
Obesity

A recent World Health Organisation report (WHO, 2014b) has identified the key components of the global obesity "epidemic":

- Worldwide obesity has nearly doubled since 1980.
- In 2008 more than 1.4 billion adults, 20 and older, were overweight. Of these over 200 million men and 300 million women were obese.
- 35% of adults aged 20 and over were overweight in 2008 and 11% were obese.
- More than 40 million children under the age of 5 were overweight or obese in 2012.
- Obesity is preventable.
- Around 3.4 million adults die each year as a result of being overweight or obese.
- 44% of the diabetes burden is attributable to overweight and obesity.

Obesity is not directly caused by motorisation, poor quality urban planning or deficient infrastructure for walking and cycling but there is a strong connection between transport policy, the promotion of motorised mobility and obesity outcomes. The WHO (2014b) document expresses this connection as follows:

"The fundamental cause of obesity and overweight is an energy imbalance between calories consumed and calories expended. Globally, there has been:

- An increased intake of energy-dense foods that are high in fat; and
- An increase in physical inactivity due to the increasingly sedentary nature of many forms of work, changing modes of transportation, and increasing urbanization.

Changes in dietary and physical activity patterns are often the result of environmental and societal changes associated with development and lack of supportive policies in sectors such as health, agriculture, transport, urban planning, environment, food processing, distribution, marketing and education."

It is clear that changes in transport choices in recent decades leading to a decline of walking and cycling and a switch from those modes to cars is part of the explanation for increasingly high levels of obesity. It is also clear that changes in urban form and structure and the poor quality of walking and cycling infrastructure contribute to this decline and to an increase in physical inactivity. It is also clear that interventions are possible to reverse the decline in physical inactivity and deliver higher rates of walking and cycling. The problem is we are not doing this on a large scale and with conviction and just as in the case of death and injury on the roads and mortality from poor air quality, physical inactivity thrives in an environment that promotes mobility and its ideological life support systems.

There is a remarkable conceptual linkage between climate change and obesity. Obesity is generally accepted to be the result of a situation where calorific intake (often linked to high energy density foods/fast foods, sugar) is greater than energy expended with the result that physiological changes produce what we call obesity or at a lower level of seriousness, overweight. This is a physical imbalance where we are loading one system (the human) with an excessive input and this produces undesirable consequences.

There is a significant positive association between the density of traffic around children's homes and obesity, as measured by the Body Mass Index (Jerrett et al, 2010). A research project carried out in Atlanta (USA) found that each additional hour spent in a car per day is associated with a 6% increase in the risk of obesity (Frank et al, 2004). The relationship between declining levels of active transport (walking and cycling) and obesity has been explored in detail by Roberts and Edwards (2010) and very clearly summarised by Pucher (2010) and Bassett et al (2008) and this is reproduced as Figure 8.1.

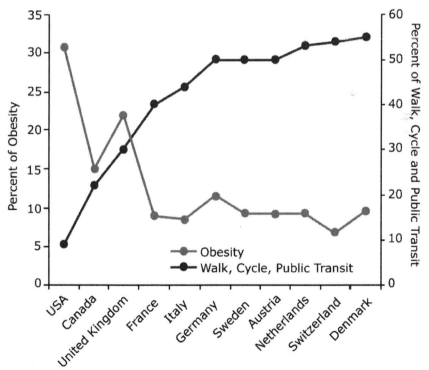

Figure 8.1: Relationship between active travel and obesity
Source: Pucher (2010)

Woodcock et al (2009) estimated the health effects of transport policies that would meet greenhouse gas emission reduction targets. They conclude that meeting emission targets in the transport sector will require substantial increases in walking and cycling, with correspondingly large reductions in car use. Based on scientific evidence linking physical activity and health, it was estimated that the increase in walking and cycling would dramatically cut rates of chronic disease, with 10-20% less heart disease and stroke, 12-18% less breast cancer and 8% less dementia (Woodcock et al, 2009).

There is a very clear and useful policy opportunity in the promotion and advancement of walking and cycling. Higher levels of so-called active transport will improve population health and will also reduce greenhouse gas emissions by substituting walk and cycle trips for car trips. Roberts and Edwards (2010) make explicit links between obesity and climate change:

"If you think that obesity and climate change are unrelated, you are wrong. The human race is getting fatter and the planet is getting hotter, and fossil fuels are the cause of both….obesity is a normal human response to a sick environment, the bodily consequences of living in a world flooded with cheap energy. As a result of petroleum powered transportation and the road danger it creates, we walk and cycle less than ever before in the history of the world and our personal energy output has plummeted…climate change and fatness are different facets of the same basic problem."

We are much more likely to be able to solve climate change and obesity problems and deal with peak oil vulnerability if we harness the synergy that exists between public health, quality of life and climate change concerns. They are all part of the same debate and all require a serious and dramatic upgrade of our built environment to reward the cyclist and the pedestrian. The current "Zeitgeist" is to reward the motorist and to increase climate change and obesity problems.

Climate change is a larger scale imbalance phenomenon where the inputs (greenhouse gases from fossil fuel burning) are too great for the bigger system(s) to absorb/handle with the result that there are also severe negative consequences. Both are clear examples of structural imbalances characterised by strong rooted behavioural patterns that actually make the situation worse. We eat more when we could/should eat and we are less active in how we work and how we travel. We could eat less and/or be more physically active. We pump more CO_2 into the atmosphere when we could very easily reduce these emissions.

At a more practical level Davis, Valsecchi and Fergusson (2007) have shown how car use fuels climate change and obesity. The linkages are strong but rarely factored into wider public health and climate change discussions and they carry a very positive message that two pressing and enormously costly problems can be solved with a bit of joined up thinking to reduce car-based mobility and increase the accessibility for everyone to all routine destinations.

Davis, Valsecchi and Fergusson (2007) conclude that the dominant factor in explaining the obesity epidemic is the dramatic decline in physical activity after

1945. With a strong evidence base they conclude that the decline in walking accounts for much or the entire rise in obesity levels:

- Main car drivers walk only half the distance and for half the time of adults in non-car owning households.

- This equates to a deficit of 56 minutes of walking every week.

- Over a decade we calculate that this could lead to a weight gain of more than 2 stones (12.7 kgs).

- Passenger cars account for 13% of total UK CO2 emissions.

- On the basis of new main drivers halving their walking distance and travelling instead by car the cumulative impact on CO2 emissions over the period 1975-2005 totalled 5.8 million tonnes of CO2 which is 22% of the overall increase in CO2 emissions for passenger cars in the last 30 years.

The conclusion that a decline in walking has had such a serious impact on the rise of CO2 emissions and obesity prevalence has significant policy implications. It immediately draws attention to the possibility that policy makers can adopt an integrated suite of policies that reduce obesity and make a substantial contribution to the reduction of greenhouse gases. This suite of policies would focus on urban design, the need to enrich accessibility, increasing residential density and increasing the safety, security and quality of the walking environment.

The authors provide quantitative guidance on the scale of results that could be expected from an integrated suite of policies:

- If today we reverted to the walking patterns of 1975 we would save 5.7% of current emissions from passenger cars, which equates to a saving of 4.1 million tonnes of CO2 out of 72 million tonnes.

- If today all main drivers (a total of 26 million people in the UK) reverted to walking patterns they had before owning a car, 11.1 Mt CO2 could be saved amounting to 15.4% if total emissions from passenger cars.

Britain has one of the world's fastest growing rates of obesity. 23.6% of men and 23.8% of women are obese and there are similar levels reported for children.

WHO (2010) reported that physical inactivity is now identified as the 4th leading risk factor for global mortality and 5% of global mortality is caused by obesity and being overweight.

Obesity levels are high in the UK, USA and Australia with clear links to the amount of active travel (walking and cycling) undertaken by the citizens of those countries (Figure 8.1).

In Chapter 13 I discuss mobility, motorisation and obesity in the special circumstances of India and China. Obesity whilst still an enormous problem in rich countries like the USA is now a major public health and fiscal issue in India and China. Obesity generates huge costs which can be added to the costs of mobility discussed in Chapter 5. A country with high levels of obesity has to carry a very large burden of costs associated with type 2 diabetes, coronary heart disease, osteoarthritis, many cancers, respiratory disease, social stigma, mental health problems, loss of productivity, days off work and medical treatment.

Davis (2010a) reported that the annual cost of obesity to the UK National Health Service (inactivity, ill-health and premature death) was £8.4 billion pa at 2004 prices.

Davis et al (2007) concluded that the decline in walking accounts for "much or all of obesity." It follows that this additional cost burden can be laid at the door of low levels of walking and cycling and the obsessive pursuit of motorised mobility. Even if we do not accept the main conclusion in Davis et al (2007) about the proportional responsibility of transport choices (more car and less walk) the enormous costs of obesity will still add a significant amount to the costs of mobility which, once again, are not factored into the policy changes made in support of mobility growth.

Interestingly the case for giving more prominence to the decline in walking in the explanation of rising levels of obesity is strengthened by the finding (page 18 of Davis et al, 2007) that there has been a 20% decline in energy intake in the period 1974-2004 coinciding with an increase in obesity prevalence.

Conclusion

There are two major sets of global problems with roots in a shared set of public policy failures and causes. There is a global epidemic of obesity that imposes a very large amount of personal suffering, premature mortality and health costs on all countries and on developing countries already under fiscal pressure to alleviate poverty, provide sanitation and clean drinking water and provide basic health care facilities that are accessible to those who need to use them. There is also a major and as yet unresolved climate change problem. The current transport ideology and mobility paradigm contributes to both sets of problems and at the same time offers a range of policy interventions that can improve matters in both dimensions of the same problem.

A substantial component of the costs associated with the obesity epidemic can be laid at the door of mobility and the prioritisation of motorised mobility by global decision takers and politicians. Abandoning the current mobility paradigm and replacing it with a serious and thorough population-based accessibility paradigm has the potential to eliminate the obesity problem.

Similarly for climate change. CO2 emissions from the transport sector are rising rapidly at a time when emission reductions are being achieved in other sectors. The rise of transport emissions has the potential to wreck the totality of climate change policies through its growth potential and the damage this is doing and will do to our attempts to limit emissions, reduce atmospheric concentrations of CO2 and keep temperature rises lower than 2 degrees Celsius.

Abandoning the mobility paradigm and replacing it with one that emphasises accessibility and quality of life outcomes has the potential to produce a radical and urgently needed breakthrough in both dimensions.

Central to the design and implementation of joined up policies to reduce obesity and CO2 emissions is the urgent need to re-engineer our cities so that they are walkable, rich in destinations, highly accessible and are associated with all the attributes that make walking, cycling and public transport more attractive. This will include higher residential densities, safe, segregated, traffic free routes for walking and cycling, a reduction in vehicle numbers, an absolute prohibition of any speed greater than 30kph in any urban area and a major shift in budgets to benefit the non-car modes and remove all subsides to motorised transport, high speed rail and aviation.

The UK based National Institute for Health and Care Excellence (NICE, 2008) has issued guidelines on the promotion of physical activity to improve health outcomes including the reduction of obesity. It recommends that pedestrians, cyclists and users of other modes of transport that involve physical activity are given the highest priority. It suggests 5 specific interventions that would deliver this prioritisation:

- Reallocate road space so that more space is given to pedestrians and cyclists.
- Restrict motor vehicle access and reduce highway capacity.
- Introduce road user charges e.g. the London and Stockholm congestion pricing schemes.
- Introduce traffic calming measures to reduce the speed and volume of vehicles.
- Promote and deliver safe routes to school.

These interventions are already well known though still not applied in the majority of urban areas in a systematic and synergistic way. UK transport planning is especially resistant to highway space reallocation and vehicular traffic reductions, so that, for example, streets under severe pressure from rat-running could be closed off to through traffic. The involvement of a national public health agency, a governmental body, in a traditional transport sphere is significant and opens the way for an increase in public health interventions in areas traditionally monopolised by transport planners. Transport is a health issue and the public health gains in reducing obesity and reducing deaths from air pollution are very large indeed.

Currently 72% of Europe's population lives in urban areas. With very few exceptions these areas are characterised by what has become known as an "obesogenic environment" (Townsend and Lake, 2009). The streets, the road crossings, the ugly areas of parking, the distances between origins and destinations, the speed of traffic, the anti-social behaviour of the vast majority of drivers, the noise and the smells and the road traffic danger define an obesogenic environment. It is an environment where all the signals and perceptions point to the inadvisability or impracticality of walking and cycling. This must be reversed and the central argument of this book is that to make this reversal truly possible and effective we have to abandon the rhetoric and ideology that feeds year on year growth in motorised mobility. The gains that flow from this reversal are enormous. We have the possibility of eliminating obesity, solving climate change, supporting much healthier populations, reducing huge and unaffordable public budgets currently spent on things that make matters worse and increasing the quality of life for everyone with a special emphasis on social justice. We can improve the quality of life of the poor and improve access to jobs, education and training so that those on welfare or workless can participate in paid work. We can improve the quality of life of women whose child care responsibilities, lack of access to a car and part time work status currently give them far more transport and travel difficulties than those experienced by men and in a way made worse by policies that promote mobility rather than accessibility (Spitzner, 2008).

The elimination of an obesogenic environment is especially helpful to women, those with mobility difficulties, children, the sick and the frail and older people and it frees up budgets under pressure and reduces greenhouse gas emissions. It is what is sometimes referred to as a "no brainer."

Chapter 9
Inequalities

The pursuit of higher levels of mobility generates and promotes inequality. Kenyon (2003) defines transport related social exclusion as a process that reduces access and participation:

"It is the process by which people are prevented from participating in the economic, political and social life of the community because of reduced accessibility to opportunities, services and social networks, due in whole or part to insufficient mobility in a society and environment built around the assumption of high mobility."

Lucas (2012) makes a direct cause and effect link between increasing levels of mobility and the "exclusion of less mobile sectors of the population" from those activities and destinations they need to access:

"This definition is particularly cogent in the transport context because it identifies the relational nature of the problem i.e. that it is the high and increasing levels of mobility within the population as a whole that is a key causal factor in the reduced accessibility and, ultimately, exclusion of less mobile sectors of the population."

Transport and mobility represent major dimensions of inequality in developed and developing countries. The mobility trajectory I have explored in earlier chapters has remodelled cities and regions in a way predicted by Ivan Illich in 1974. Increasing dependence on the car and increasing distances between "things" shifts urban and regional systems so that over time there is an increasing level of difficulty and disadvantageness for those who do not have access to a car. The car promotes a reduction in those things we need to access, expands distances for everyone and permits only the car owning classes to cope with those increased distances. Non car owning groups in society are increasingly disadvantaged. The relationship between owning a car and not owning a car in terms of access to health care, education, training, work, leisure and family is a fundamental dimension of inequality.

Fundamental inequalities and inequalities that increase over time are well known (Wilkinson and Pickett, 2009). We live in a very unequal world. Some of these inequalities are staggeringly high such as the gap between rich and poor and the numbers of people in India (for example) living on $1 per day or less compared to the relatively wealthy segment of India's population, estimated to be 200 million. Inequalities on this scale are a major global problem and the subject of high level policy commitments most recently expressed in the Millennium Development Goals (United Nations, 2012).

The Millenium Development Goals are ambitious and show signs of progress especially in reducing extreme poverty, achieving universal primary education, gender equality and reducing child mortality. All of these goals have a transport and accessibility dimension which is largely absent from international activity to achieve the 8 goals by 2015. It is abundantly clear in many of the poor regions of the world e.g. India and sub-Saharan Africa that poor quality access to health care hinders progress with reducing child mortality and poverty eradication is hindered by inadequate attention to the needs of the poorest for access to jobs, education and markets utilising low cost modes of transport. The preference of banks and global agencies for grandiose projects to build roads does nothing for the poorest and swallows a large amount of "aid", which is not aid in any real sense of the word. Roberts (2010) has described the foolishness and inadequacy of funding road projects in Africa as recommended by Tony Blair in 2005.

The MDGs deserve success but as in mobility itself there is a strong element of policy makers and international agencies saying one thing e.g. "we must pursue a low carbon strategy" whilst doing the opposite. The funding by international agencies of roads in Africa or flyovers in Kolkata are part of a bigger process of feeding the system that builds more infrastructure, drives up motorised mobility, rewards the wealthy and creates more greenhouse gases. The involvement of many agencies e.g. the World Bank in both supporting MDGs on the one hand and then advocating road building on the other is another example of the triumph of rhetoric over reality. Roberts (2010, page 70) summarises these conflicting messages in his usual characteristically robust fashion:

"The wealthy world needs Africa to build more roads so that Western car makers can remain profitable."

Poverty, access to clean drinking water and sanitation are clearly major global issues and can be seen as much more important than mobility. It is the case, however, that there are linkages. Spending on new roads and motorised mobility in India consumes a huge share of the budget and in cities like Kolkata benefits a small segment of the population (car drivers) leaving 90% of the 16 million residents deprived of funding for walking, cycling, public transport and safer streets. The Kolkata urban environment is a text book example of how a city can be shaped so that it accepts and promotes inequalities. The spending on flyovers and new roads of benefit only to a rich minority co-exists with the starving of funds for the tram system which survives on a grossly inadequate budget, is in very poor condition and provides a transport service of benefit to everyone. The grossly unequal spending also makes sure that the poorest will have to put up with the highest levels of air pollution and deaths and injuries in the road traffic environment. They will also have to put up with life threatening poor quality access to health care.

Surridge et al (2014) in a study of access to maternal health care in Zambia have shown that there is a very high maternal, neo-natal and new born mortality rate caused directly by the inadequate provision of rural health care, poor quality transport links and lack of access to suitable transportation vehicles to get the women to a facility. Quoting World Health Organisation statistics they demonstrate that this is part of a global problem. 350,000 women die each year due to pregnancy and childbirth related conditions of which 99% are in low income countries. 75% of these deaths could be prevented "through timely access to essential health care."

The detailed case study in rural Zambia reveals a serious and fundamental planning, funding and delivery deficit that is common to all low income countries. A mobility policy per se does not intentionally cause these problems but there is nevertheless a direct link between transport policies, higher levels of mobility, rising inequalities and a deterioration of the living conditions and health of the poorest groups. The link between the mobility paradigm and its strongly negative outcomes is complicated by ideology and an inability to think about fairness and social consequences. Because national elites, politicians and transport decision takers pursue the path laid out by European and North American decision takers over the last 5 decades, access is not regarded as an issue to be addressed and transport is regarded as a mobility and economic issue around road building and motorisation. This shifts budgets towards the rich and deprives the poor of the most basic conditions for a healthy life and it is socially unjust.

The rural Zambia situation is replicated in the same socially unjust way at the other end of the scale. The mega city of Kolkata is a socially unjust place. The mobility ideology and paradigm has occupied the territory that should be populated by a concern for accessibility, living conditions of the poor and a healthy environment for all. This concern cannot become a reality until the mobility paradigm is extinguished.

Zambia and Kolkata represent extremes of social injustice and governmental policies that deliver very serious inequalities. The problems we face in Europe are not as severe as those that can be found in Africa and India but they are still significant.

Europe, the USA and Australia are characterised by very significant inequalities and Wilkinson and Pickett (2009) have shown that more equal societies such as Sweden and Denmark have much improved social and economic outcomes than less equal countries like the UK. They have also shown that inequalities are widening or put more simply we are becoming more unequal over time.

In those countries with higher levels of inequality there is also a higher level of unwanted/undesirable social and economic outcomes that accurately track inequalities. The list includes:

- Life expectancy.
- Mathematical and literacy levels.
- Infant mortality.
- Homicides.
- Imprisonment.
- Teenage births.
- Trust.
- Obesity.

- Mental illness including drug and alcohol addiction.
- Social mobility.

Every one of these indicators behaves negatively as inequality levels rise.

This relationship is graphed in Figure 9.1.

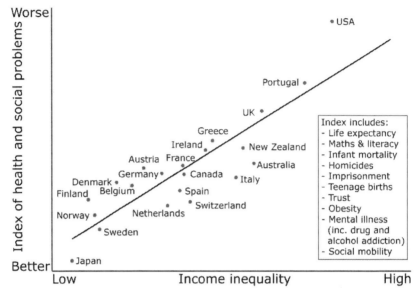

Figure 9.1: Health and social problems are worse in more unequal countries
Source: Equality Trust
http://www.equalitytrust.org.uk/sites/default/files/attachments/resources
/SpiritLevel-jpg_0.pdf

Transport policy and its dominant manifestation in policies that promote the growth of motorised mobility, aviation and high speed rail is not the cause of inequalities but is part of a deeply embedded set of preferences and prioritisations that support the status quo characterised by inequalities. Inequalities are propagated by thoughtless policies that have not been interrogated for their impact on inequalities.

As discussed in Chapter 5 on fiscal impacts, transport policies and spending disproportionately benefit the rich whilst costing a great deal of money funded from general taxation paid by all social groups and income levels. The poor are taxed to pay for the long distances and high speed preferences of the rich. Transport spending is regressive.

More importantly in democratic European societies transport priorities and transport spending have the effect of rewarding the overlapping space in a Venn diagram that embraces the rich, men, those who travel widely, fly a lot and are multiple car owners. The obverse is also true. Transport spending and priorities penalise the poor, women, those who by choice or force of circumstances do not travel widely and those who have to put up with degraded environments. They also penalise those with complex travel patterns (Spitzner, 2008). This group is dominated by women who take on the lion's share of dealing with work (often part-time, low paid or unpaid), care for relatives, children, schools, kindergarten, shopping and trips to doctors. This is a demanding task and needs an accessibility policy to make the task easier.

Children also suffer neglect. In a wide ranging study of children's independent mobility Hillman et al (1990) show how children's independent travel behaviour has been sacrificed over 2 decades in the pursuit of higher levels of car use and poorer quality walking environments.

Donaghy, Poppelreuter and Rudinger (2005) identified two groups that are largely ignored by transport policies and as a result experience serious difficulties in accomplishing everyday tasks involving gaining access to destinations with relative ease, safety and low costs. They are the socially excluded elderly and female transport users.

In this chapter I will review the evidence base for concluding that a focus on the growth in mobility actually disadvantages large segments of European society and promotes a vision of a transport future that is highly mobile, very expensive, discriminates against local trips and predominantly serves the interests of relatively affluent men. I will look at children, women and older people to explore these socially unjust dimensions of the mobility ideology.

The UK Social Exclusion Unit, a specialist unit within the office of the Deputy Prime Minister of the UK government (SEU, 2003) has carried out a thorough review of the main dimension of transport policy, trends and spending and the ways this discriminates in favour of wealthier groups in society. Amongst its findings are:

- Death and injury amongst children from crashes is 5 times greater in the lowest socio-economic groups (SEG) than it is in the highest group.

- The lowest SEGs experience the highest levels of air and noise pollution from road traffic and they have low levels of access to a car.

- Amongst the 20% of households in the lowest SEG, 63% do not have access to a car.

- Rail is used less by lower SEGs than it is by higher SEGs.

- Public transport fares in the UK are high. In an EU ranking the UK was the third highest after Denmark (1) and Sweden (2).

- Bus fares rose by 30% in real terms after privatisation in 1985.

- The Department of Transport in 2003 estimated that of the total transport expenditure anticipated in its 10 year plan, the bottom quintile of the population (low income) would get 12% and the highest quintile would get 38%.

The findings of the SEU report paint a very clear picture of a transport policy that is regressive, discriminatory, lacking in social justice and supportive of inequalities.

This remains largely unchallenged because it sits within the dominant ideology which promotes a growth in mobility.

Children

In Chapter 3 we discussed the steep social gradient associated with child death and injury on UK roads. This remains a major dimension of inequality and a major failure of public policy. It is unacceptable that children from low income backgrounds or so-called "low socio-economic" groups should experience a higher rate of death and injury than their more affluent neighbours.

Whitelegg (2013) described children as "the canary in the cage." In 19th century mines the canary was taken into the mine because it would be the first to register signs of deadly methane gas. It would fall of its perch giving the miners time to escape. In 21st century developed societies children are showing the signs of stress and distress; they are the latest incarnation of the canary in a mine.

In a major contribution to the study of children, transport, mobility and accessibility Hillman et al (1990) showed that in 1971 approximately 80% of children had made the journey to school on foot or by bike and without an accompanying adult. In 1990 this had shrunk to 9%. In much less than the space of one generation we had thrown away a hugely important part of child development, freedom and independence and at the same time added a great deal to traffic congestion and pollution.

The same study of children's independent mobility (CIM) compared Germany with the UK in a carefully matched comparison of localities, schools and age groups across both countries and found that 80% of German 10 year olds were allowed to travel to places, other than school in 1990 (unaccompanied by an adult), compared to 38% of 10 year olds in the UK.

The German-UK comparison is particularly compelling in an exploration of the mobility-accessibility relationship. Germany in 1990 had a higher level of car ownership than the UK but the widespread availability of better public transport, walking and cycling infrastructure coupled with higher densities and shorter distances produced a higher level of CIM in Germany. This can be interpreted as the effect of a largely non-obesogenic environment (qv Chapter 8).

Whizman and Pike (2007) quoting a term used by Mayer Hillman describe this loss of children's' independent mobility as a shift from free range children to battery reared children. Whizman and Pike also make very clear links between rising mobility, decline in CIM and obesity:

"In Australia this rapid decrease in CIM has been associated with a 5-fold increase in overweight and obesity amongst children along with a doubling or tripling of car traffic."

The 1990 study by Hillman et al has been brought up to date and incorporated new data from 2010 (Shaw et al, 2013). This offers a number of insights into mobility and accessibility as both sets of trends impact on children. Key findings include:

- Germany has become more like England with children being taken to school by car rising (1990-2010) to English levels.

- CIM for primary children in Germany was 83% in 1990 and 61% in 2010.

- 12% of trips to school were by car in Germany in 1990 and this rose to 30% in 2010.

- Overall 9% of primary children were accompanied by adults on the way to school in 1990 and this increased to 33% in 2010.

- German primary school children still had more freedom in 2010 than English children of the same age. German children allowed to travel home alone from school was 51 percentage points above the English level; for crossing roads alone it was 30 percentage points above the English level and for using buses alone it was 20% above the English level.

- English primary school children registered a decline of walking from 81% in 1971 to 63% in 2010, a decline in use of public transport in the same period from 9% of trips to 3% and an increase in car use from 9% of trips to 34%.

- The percentage of English secondary school pupils walking to school has increased in the period 1990-2010.

- The percentage of English primary school pupils accompanied on the school trip increased from 64% to 77% (1990-2010) and for secondary pupils the increase was from 9% to 17% in the same period.

The differences between England and Germany revealed by the 2010 survey of CIM reported in Shaw et al (2013) point to an international dimension in inequality. German children have more independence than English children (Figure 9.2).

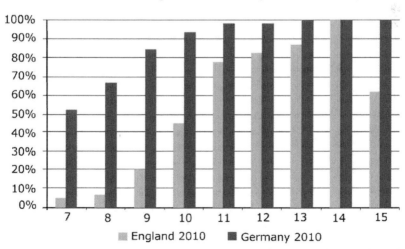

Figure 9.2: Percentage of parents reporting that their child is allowed to travel home from school alone, by age, England and Germany, 2010
Source: Shaw et al (2013)

German children also have more freedom to cycle than British counterparts (Figure 9.3).

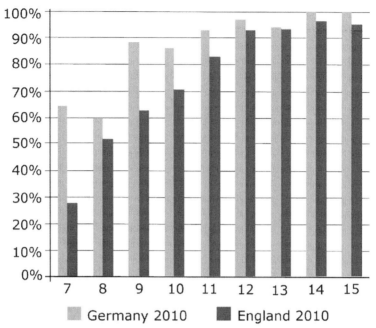

Figure 9.3: Percentage of children, by age, allowed to cycle on main roads alone in Germany and England
Source: Shaw et al (2013)

The differences revealed in figures 9.2 and 9.3 are the result of very different approaches in both countries to the design and funding of infrastructure and the quality of the public realm. The German approach to highly integrated public transport, cycling facilities and widespread "Tempo 30" (20mph) areas has promoted an environment that give children more choices and a higher level of actual and perceived security than that available to English children and parents who make the decisions about child welfare.

The two studies (Hillman et al, 1990 and Shaw et al 2013) represent an unusual and valuable 40 year perspective on mobility. The first survey data was collected in 1971 and the last in 2010. The 40 year period has seen a dramatic erosion of children's independent mobility. Children are now attached to adults far more than they were in 1971 and they are deprived of the freedoms that earlier generations took for granted. This also adds to road traffic volumes as parents take over a lot of the tasks formerly accomplished by children themselves and this adds to congestion and pollution at peak hours in school term time. Parents were questioned about the reasons for not allowing children to cross roads, cycle or travel unaccompanied by bus and the dominant factor was road traffic danger. Increased motorised mobility has created an environment that parents find fearful and are unwilling to go down the "free range" route. There was also a "stranger danger" fear around the possibility that a child would be abducted, assaulted or murdered but the authors of both studies conclude that the road traffic danger issue is the dominant factor.

The German-England comparison shows that Germany was able to "hold the line" for a lot longer than England and children were, and still are, to some degree more "free range" than their English equivalents. This is now changing in Germany but the differential is still there and the fact that Germany could resist the "battery-reared" route when England and Australia could not suggests that there are clues in German thinking, planning, funding and delivery that point the way towards a reversal of the theft of independent mobility from children.

Davis (2013) has shown how the mobility paradigm has taken deep root in policing, legal and judicial systems. In the very tragic circumstances where a child is killed by a vehicle whilst crossing the road the narrative quickly strays into victim blaming and takes no account of (a) what we know and can expect about child behaviour and (b) the very real difficulties associated with waiting to cross a road, finding a gap in the traffic and judging the acceptability of that gap when cars are arriving every 4 seconds. The extract below is lengthy but is one of the clearest expressions based on actual events that convey the powerful nature of the dominate mobility paradigm, the damage that this causes to children and their families and the way it diverts attention away from dealing with the unethical, unreasonable and unaccept-able presence of large volumes of speeding traffic in residential areas:

"Victim blaming in child pedestrian injuries is a strategy which serves to maintain the economic interests of the dominant groups in society at the expense and suffering of children, particularly those from low income families.

Roberts and Coggan (1994) analysed the processes involved in the aftermath of the death of a 10 year old girl walking home from school. This included the police officer's report from attendance at the crash scene. At this stage the officer coded his form as "Pedestrian: crossing road heedless of traffic, unattended child." A week later an engineer from the local highways department attends the site and notes the likely average speed of the motor traffic and the mean traffic flow per minute. From this Roberts and Coggan note that "there was a mean traffic flow at the injury site of 877 vehicles per hour, approximately 15 vehicles every minute. Thus the mean time available for crossing, assuming a steady flow, would have been only four seconds. It is quite likely therefore, that running was a necessary prerequisite for road crossing rather than an indication of impulsiveness.

In this case, a choice was made between the two main contenders for individual responsibility, the driver and child victim. Since the driver's claim of travelling at 40 kph (within the 50 kph speed limit) was accepted, no negligence was attributed to the driver. That responsibility was located with the victim. Although walking out into the road clearly did result in this child's death and might appropriately be considered a cause, it was nevertheless only one of a number of causes. Other causes of pedestrian injury which could equally have been chosen for consideration would include poverty, high traffic volumes and high vehicle speeds. However, a drawback of the multi-causal approach to causes is that it allows some causes to be singled out for attention above others. This is a choice motivated by ideology in which threats to road transport infrastructure must be resisted in order to protect vested interests which rest on economic expansion."

Conclusions on children

Children have taken a very large "hit" from the dominance of the mobility paradigm. The loss of freedoms and independent mobility (so-called "Children's Independent Mobility" or CIM for short) has created a fundamental inequality that crosses the boundary defining human rights. It is not at all an exaggeration to say that children have been deprived of their human rights. The deprivation is a natural consequence of the mobility paradigm. If national elites, decision takers and professionals focus on the growth of mobility (more road space, more car parking, more subsidies for road transport) the result is a huge increase in traffic, an increase in road traffic danger and the withdrawal of children from that dangerous environment.

The Swedish road safety expert Klaus Tingvall (quoted in Whitelegg and Haq, 2006) has said "a mistake in the road traffic environment should not carry the death penalty." For children and in most European countries it does carry the death penalty and then the child is blamed.

The mobility paradigm is blind to ethics and social justice. Killing children is not something that we should accept (Haq and Whitelegg, 2014) but the paradigm does not provide space for the consideration of ethics, social justice, human life or people of different ages and genders.

The need to reverse the decline in CIM is clear and policies that will produce this result are the same policies that will reduce the speed and volume of motorised traffic, reduce distances that separate "things" and increase the attractiveness of walking and cycling for all the journeys made by children and not just the school trip. Not to do this is to burden children with a significant part of the downstream problems caused by the growth of mobility. In addition to the probability of death and withdrawal of basic freedoms we add to obesity and remove the joy, discovery, learning and development opportunities that were once part of childhood.

Whizman and Pike (2007) put CIM right at the centre of the whole sustainable transport debate:

"Children's Independent Mobility is a vital pre-condition for the shift from car dependence to a more environmentally and socially sustainable society. The problem requires much more explicit attention from researchers and policy-makers than has previously been the case."

One could add by way of extra emphasis that reversing the 40 year trend and increasing CIM will also make a significant contribution to reduce greenhouse gases and reduce obesity levels.

The German experience points to the importance of a non-obesogenic environment, high quality, safe walking, cycling and public transport offers and an accessibility rich urban structure i.e. the city of short distances.

Women

It should not come as a surprise to find that the mobility paradigm discriminates in favour of men and against women. At a wider societal level there is a widespread recognition that women have more difficulty progressing to higher levels of salary and status than men (the "glass ceiling" problem), women earn less than men for doing similar work and the proportion of women in senior positions in local or central government is low or very low. Whitelegg (2013) analysed the proportion of women in municipal government (low) and linked this with the preferences of men and women for different outcomes to explain why, in the UK at least, there are poor quality outcomes from our local councils. Women with caring duties and responsibilities and with the lion's share of escorting children to school are acutely aware of concerns around accessibility and road traffic danger and are far more likely to bring this awareness to bear on major transport policy and budget decisions.

The links with CIM are important. The decline of CIM has imposed a serious burden on women who now have to arrange their daily schedules to deal with paid work (often part time and vulnerable in periods of economic downturn), child care, escort duties, trips to doctors and clinics and shopping. Hillman et al (1990) quantified this extra burden:

"During 1990, 1356 million hours per year were spent in Britain escorting children. The economic resource cost of this escorting using Department of Transport methods of valuation is estimated at between £10 billion and £20 billion annually."

Source: Hillman et al (1990, page 168).

The loss of child freedoms is serious public policy issue on many different levels including the importance of children benefitting in terms of cognition and spatial ability through searching and learning behaviour in their local environment. The discussion of escorting in Hillman's work raises wider economic issues around the value of time and the impact of unwanted and demanding escort duties on the lives of busy parents. Hillman accepts that some escort duties are desirable and welcome but the 4 fold increase in such duties in the period 1970-1990 suggests an element of growing parental concern about traffic and the necessity to protect their children. This has an economic cost in terms of time spent on such duties and a further economic cost in terms of the contribution of escorted trips to congestion.

Spitzner (2008) has elaborated the relationships between gender and mobility in some detail. She illustrates the complexity of gendered transport demand in a striking visual format (Figure 9.4).

The right hand part of this diagram illustrates the kind of trips, activities, origins and destinations that would be experienced by a person involved with the details of normal "whole working life." This person is usually female but the complexity would apply to any parent or grandparent of either gender taking on the primary responsibility for child care, schools, hospital appointments, shopping and cooking.

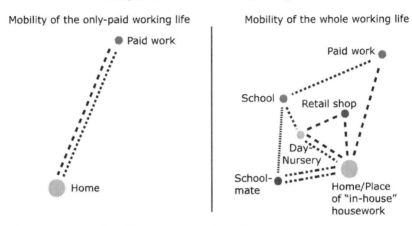

Figure 9.4: A gendered interpretation of mobility
Source: Spitzner (2008)

Put very simply women have to do a lot more than men and overcome far more difficult space-time scheduling problems than men. The journey to work is only a small component of total travel and is a relatively simple space-time problem and because it has traditionally been a male preserve (the man goes out to work, stays there all day and then comes home), it has occupied a disproportionately large amount of time and effort on the part of transport planners. The complex travel patterns of women have been largely ignored.

Spitzner has also illustrated a global pattern of gendered transport. She describes the modal split of men and women in Bonako (Mali), Pune (India), Dhaka (Bangladesh) Lima (Peru) and Ashgabat (Turkmenistan) to show that in aggregate women walk more than men, cycle less than men and use cars and motorbikes less than men. This is illustrative of a significant gender inequality and one that should not be accepted.

Tuong (2014) writing about Ho Chi Minh City in Vietnam has confirmed the pattern of gendered transport demand. In this city 93% of car drivers are men and the vast majority of bus users are women. Very few women cycle.

The lack of women cyclists tells us a great deal about the failure of urban design and safety considerations to deliver a high quality cycling environment (Pucher and Buehler, 2012). Women account for 30% of bike trips in London and 41% in Paris. (Pucher and Buehler, 2012, page 325). Clearly there will be many reasons why women do not take up cycling at the same rate as men but safety and security concerns are important and frequently articulated by women in cycling discussions.

Cycling rates have improved dramatically in many UK urban areas but large percentage increases from very low starting points don't convey the reality that cycling rates are still low. The general perception of road traffic danger discussed in detail in Hillman et al (1990) is a barrier to significant increases in cycling that is yet to be overcome. Road casualty data in London (Transport for London, 2011) reveals that in London in 2010 10 cyclists were killed, 457 seriously injured and 3540 slightly injured. This scale of death and injury is unacceptable given the WHO position that death and injury in the road traffic environment is predictable and preventable. The general awareness of road traffic danger also contributes to fear, caution and parental concern and this dampens walking and cycling rates.

In 2009 7 of the 8 cyclists killed by lorries in London were women (BBC, 2009). This attracted widespread publicity and adds to safety concerns. It is not appropriate and not my intention to develop an argument that female deaths are in some way more significant than male deaths but the debate in London about female cyclist deaths is intense and feeds into concerns about cycling as a whole. The BBC report refers to an internal "Transport for London" report that explains the severe gender bias in cycling deaths by reference to the behaviour of women at junctions. When they are waiting to turn left and stationary next to a lorry also waiting to turn left they obey the traffic lights and are then killed by the turning lorry. Men, on the other hand, jump red lights and/or have a much faster "getaway." Whatever the precise explanation it is clear that there are too many cycling deaths, there is a gender bias against women and there are solutions to the problem that are not being adopted. The problem continues. The Independent newspaper reported (13.11.13) that by that date in 2013 there had been 12 cyclist deaths in London.

Spitzner (2008) identifies the main dimension of failures in mobility policy from a gendered perspective:

- There is very little attempt in transport policy and spending to address the complexity of travel demand in space and time that women must deal with.
- Budgets are gender biased in that public funds are more likely to be spent on building roads and on the journey to work that mainly benefit men.

Women take on a very significant role in society in terms of caring for elderly relatives and child care and this is not factored into policy or economic analysis. The mobility paradigm does not serve the interests of women. It perpetuates the same kind of thinking and spending that has created a severe gender bias in transport outcomes which downgrades the significance of daily travel behaviour on the part of women and reinforces the importance of the much simpler, work-related, trip making behaviour of men. The replacement of the mobility paradigm by an accessibility paradigm would produce outcomes that are fundamentally rooted in the needs and aspirations of genders, all age groups and all income categories.

We need to add to this list of major problems created by the mobility paradigm, the deeply flawed methodologies for evaluating transport projects. Whether this is a traditional cost benefit analysis or a broader transport appraisal it still works in predictably perverse ways to produce the wrong answers. The complete method-ological baggage of valuing time (Whitelegg, 2012) should be abandoned. The constant travel time budget of c1.1 hours per day reveals time saving as a fundamentally flawed and misleading objective.

The relative valuations of working time and "non-working" time should be abandoned (this shows that men's time is more valuable than women's time).

Social justice and equity considerations require that we value whatever children and older people do when making their journeys and the valuation of travel time methodologies is blind to the importance of people and social groups.

The UK practice of downgrading the importance of walking, cycling and public transport by listing as a cost the fact that these modes would reduce fuel taxation revenue is perverse. If it is policy to get people out of cars and onto bikes we should not build into an appraisal methodology a sub-routine that disadvantages cycling by giving it a large negative number because it reduces fuel tax revenue.

Conclusion on women

Transport is an area of public policy and professional input that discriminates against women and in favour of men. Modal split statistics from many countries show that women are more likely to walk and use the bus than drive or cycle. Additionally wider societal trends that reduce accessibility and increase distances and confer child care and other caring tasks on women ensure that women have to do a great deal more than men in connecting disparate origins and destinations. Women have to reach many destinations within a limited amount of time and have much reduced access to the modes of transport used by men to allow them to do less.

Transport policy and spending perpetuates these inequalities and has not yet engaged with the gender issues that have been so clearly identified by Meike Spitzner (Spitzner, 2008).

Older people

Over 3000 post offices and 5,000 local shops were closed in England in the period 2001-2011. Post offices historically have played a large part in the lives of older people especially those who live alone (25% of people aged 65-74 and 44% of those over the age of 75 live alone in England). An older person would visit the post office to pick up the weekly pension and was not interested in direct bank transfers or bank accounts. He or she would make some other small purchases (a post office was often associated with a small shop) and most importantly he/she would have a conversation with the person behind the post office counter. The visit to the post office was a social occasion, an opportunity to catch up on local news, discuss the details of who was in hospital or recently sent home and who needed a visit or help with shopping. The post office was a social construct, an attractive destination, a place to linger for a little while and a way of avoiding the worst consequences of social isolation. For many hundreds of thousands of older people this all came to an end with the closure of the local post office.

Clifton (2011) reported on social isolation amongst older Londoners and quantified the numbers of older people who were socially isolated or felt lonely. He linked the problems of social isolation to the decline of facilities like shops, pubs and GP surgeries. He described the difficulties encountered by many of the older interviewees and quoted one interviewee on the subject of walking and social isolation:

"Before you had a lot more people walking, whereas [now] people leap in their car and pick their children up from school and things like that, driving here and there. I am not sure how we are ever going to change it round but [we need] more of a community spirit."

This reflects national surveys which have found that more than 1 million older people feel trapped in their own home and 20 per cent find accessing their local hospital difficult. A separate national survey found that just under half of those aged over 55 in Britain cannot walk to their nearest GP surgery, while 58 per cent cannot walk to their nearest bank. This is partly a result of the withdrawal of amenities such as banks, post offices, shops and pubs from local high streets, as they rationalise their operations or are forced out by competitors in "out of town" locations (Clifton, 2011, page 21).

Older people, unsurprisingly, make much more use of doctors' surgeries, clinics and hospitals than do younger age groups. Access to these facilities is very important and the centralisation tendencies of the UK National Health Service (NHS) are a source of worry for older people faced with long and difficult journeys to hospitals and clinics. This centralisation has been underway for at least three decades (Whitelegg, 1982) and it creates a great deal of difficulty and stress for older people.

The blindness of transport and mobility policy to the needs of women is repeated in the case of older people. The complete lack of an accessibility policy discriminates against older people who for reasons of lower income, social isolation and health problems have a much greater need for low cost, high quality access to the "things" they need. The closure of post offices and local shops and the centralisation of health care facilities disproportionately impacts on older people and reduces their quality of life.

Older people are especially vulnerable to two consequences that flow from the mobility paradigm:

- Social isolation linked to heavy traffic flows, difficulties crossing roads, poor quality street design and accessing local shops and post offices.
- Death and injury as a result of rising traffic volumes, inappropriate speeds and the anti-social behaviour of drivers.

Social isolation and heavy traffic flows

Steptoe et al (2013) in a study of social isolation and loneliness among older men and women conclude that social relationships are central to human well-being and are critically involved in the maintenance of health. Low scores on social isolation and loneliness are associated with raised mortality among older men and women and reducing social isolation and loneliness are important for both quality of life and wellbeing.

These findings should now be linked to the impact of traffic volumes on community interaction and the direct measurement of the number of friends and acquaintances that people have on streets with increasingly heavy traffic (Appleyard, 1981). As traffic volume goes up the number of friends and acquaintances goes down. Traffic volume has a direct effect on negatively affecting healthy outcomes and bringing about higher levels of mortality. Traffic volume is a public health hazard.

The general question of community disruption linked to traffic flows was originally explored by Appleyard (1981) and is discussed in more detail in Chapter 10. Older people have extra difficulties to overcome when leaving their homes and moving around in the urban environments.

These include:

- Large volumes of traffic that leave few gaps for the safe crossing of roads or junctions.

- Speeding traffic and judging the speed and timing of approach of vehicles.

- Using pedestrian actuated crossings (i.e. pressing a button to stop the traffic) and then cross. The timings on many UK crossings are set to minimise pedestrian crossing time so as to benefit the drivers (a very clear example of discrimination against older people).

London provides a very clear example of discrimination against older residents. A report from the London Assembly Transport Committee drew attention to the way in which pedestrians had been penalised by reducing crossing times:

"Green Man time has been reduced at 568 crossings across London since 2010. Reduced crossing times encourage pedestrians to take greater risks. For other groups, particularly older and disabled people, it can affect their confidence when crossing the road. The Committee is concerned to note that there has been little analysis of the effect of reducing Green Man time on crossing behaviour." (London Assembly, 2014).

Older people are not able to achieve fast crossing speeds necessitated by these reduced times and the re-adjustment of timings on crossings in this way shows a clear preference for the motorist and a willingness to make life more difficult for pedestrians in general and older pedestrians in particular. This takes the mobility paradigm into severely unethical territory.

Davis (2010b) summarises the severance and barrier effect of traffic:

"The traffic barrier is the sum of inhibiting effects upon pedestrian behaviour resulting from the impact of traffic conditions within a specific environment/street context. These effects can be either physical (observable) or psychological (unobservable) impediments to pedestrian movement."

Davis refers to a detailed study of pedestrian road crossing behaviour in Edinburgh based on video recording evidence of actual movements and concludes:

"The elderly are many times more disadvantaged than other adults – more than 10 fold on the basis of the crossing ratio indicator, and this on a street where shopping is the dominant trip purpose for both age groups and where crossing activity is closely linked to shopping as evidenced by variations in the ratios by time of day."

Severance as a result of traffic barriers is also linked to negative health outcomes (Davis, 2012a). Quoting Appleyard (1981) and linking this to epidemiological evidence he says:

"Various studies have demonstrated the severance effect of motorised transport on communities – that there is a dose response – the greater the traffic volume and speed the lower the level of pedestrian street activity and the less the street functions as place as opposed to space for the movement of vehicles. The study by Appleyard (1981) illustrated particularly clearly how numbers of friends and acquaintances reduced as traffic volumes and speed rose. Vulnerable groups, not least the elderly are likely to suffer disproportionately from traffic severance and any resulting reduction in social contact and social support which is dependent on independent mobility. Less attention has been given to connect the evidence of traffic severance with that of epidemiological evidence, which shows the importance of social contact and ties and friends and acquaintances to health and lifespan.

For every age group examined, and for both sexes, people with many social contacts had the lowest death rates and people with the fewest contacts had the highest rates. More recent studies have confirmed these findings and added evidence that social activities among older people – that may entail little or no physical activity – have a positive impact on lifespan. Meaningful social activities reduce the harmful effects of stress by enhancing the body's immune response function."

In both of the research summaries by Davis, older people are specifically identified as susceptible to traffic barriers and severance and in ways that damage health. Policies that lead to an increase in traffic damage older people. Policies that promote a growth in mobility lead to an increase in traffic and when these increases coincide with a decline in accessibility as in the case of deleting post offices and health care facilities, older people find themselves especially disadvantaged.

On a more positive note Davis (2012b) concludes that the UK free bus pass for people of pensionable age unsurprisingly increases bus use and this increased bus use is associated with more walking on the part of this age group and its associated health benefits. This, he concludes, reduces inequalities:

"Public funding enabling free bus travel for older persons may confer significant population health benefits through increased incidental physical activity. These potential benefits appear to be equitably distributed across socio-economic groups and this fact may make the intervention attractive in terms of public policy goals to reduce inequalities."

It is also the case, though currently not substantiated by empirical evidence that the free bus pass encourages more activity of all kinds out of the home and provides opportunities for combined activities with the same age group. A more active outgoing life style coupled with increased opportunities to meet people with similar interests is much more likely to be health promoting than one characterised by sitting at home alone in front of day time television.

The free bus is a very interesting example of a policy that helps older people and reduces inequalities. Like many other areas of public expenditure it is, however, under threat of cuts and also sits alongside real cuts in bus service subsidy and provision. The current scale of cuts in bus subsidy in rural England raises the very real possibility that older people will have a free bus pass and no bus.

Death and injury in the road traffic environment

Deaths and serious injuries amongst older people are a serious problem for older people. Living Streets (2009) has emphasised the issue:

"More pedestrians over 70 are killed on the roads than any other age group. Given that the proportion of the population aged 75+ is projected to increase from 7% to over 13% by 2018 to over 700,000 people…this has major implications for how we design and manage our streets."

It is also very important to recognise that there is a problem with official death and injury statistics. Statistics will often show that the number of deaths and injuries is low and road safety professionals including the police will conclude that a particular street, junction or location is "safe." This fails to recognise that there is another factor at work. If local residents perceive that there is road traffic danger they will try to avoid the danger. This is why older people will often stay at home and not go out if it involves crossing a busy road. The withdrawal of groups of vulnerable users from the street then lowers the number of deaths and injuries and leads to the false conclusion that a very dangerous location is "safe." The detailed analysis of CIM in Hillman et al (1990) demonstrate that the reduction in the size of the population exposed to risk (fewer children walking and cycling to school) results in lower absolute numbers of those killed and seriously injured (KSIs) and is not the product of so-called road safety interventions.

In the period June 2007-March 2008 the city of Portsmouth introduced system-wide 20mph speed limits on 94% of its road lengths and was the first city in the UK to do this. The new speed limit was a reduction from 30mph and was implemented with signage only and without the humps, bumps and chicanes normally associated with 20mph zones. In a detailed comparison of before and after road traffic casualties (DfT 2010) the report concluded:

"Comparing the 3 years before the system was implemented and the two years afterwards, the number of recorded road casualties has fallen by 22% from 183 per year to 142 per year. During that period casualty numbers fell nationally by around 14% inc comparable areas."

The DfT report did not contain a detailed analysis of statistical significance and this has subsequently been carried out by Campbell (2011). Campbell concludes that the headline finding of a 22% reduction in casualties is statistically significant at the p= 0.0005 level and "that the change in the observed rate is very unlikely to be due to chance year-to-year variation and that there is strong evidence that the introduction of the 20mph limits is associated with a fall in the total risk of road casualties."

A more detailed analysis of change over time in numbers killed or seriously injured (KSI) does not produce a statistically significant result. The change in KSI numbers is relatively small and falls within the year-to-year variation that can be expected in road safety statistics.

Garrard (2008) has identified road safety and speed issues as especially relevant to elderly groups. She presents evidence to show that older people are at greater risk of death and injury in the road traffic environment and discusses speed reduction programmes in Denmark and the impact of these projects on improving the quality of older people:

"Examples include an evaluation of speed reduction measures in Denmark which reported increased feelings of security and a reduced 'barrier effect', particularly for elderly pedestrians. Following the implementation of ten speed reduction schemes in Scotland, residents reported increased neighbourly interaction, improved perceptions of pedestrian safety, and improved neighbourhood appearance."

"Speed reduction interventions in three towns in Denmark led to similar improve-ments in safety perceptions. Intercept interviews with pedestrians and cyclists showed that feelings of security were improved considerably in the intervention towns. Perceptions of security improved for all age groups, but the greatest improvements were among older people. The authors concluded that the barrier effect (of high traffic speed) was reduced in the three pilot towns (Herrstedt 1992)."

Clearly older people need special consideration in the design of the built environ-ment and road traffic environment in which they live and access local shops and services including trips to the doctor, dentist, optician and other services used intensively by this age group. Current built environment priorities are not sensitive to older people. The Mayor of London has been reported as shortening the green phase on traffic light controlled pedestrian crossings (the time allowed for a pedestrian to cross) in order to smooth the traffic flow and reduce congestion (London Evening Standard, 2008). This is a policy that damages the quality of life of older people. The organisation and management of time in an urban environment is crucial to the quality of life of older people (Whitelegg, 1993a). Whitelegg characterises the way time is managed in an urban environment as "time theft." Transport planning and practice based on encouraging motorisation and car based trips achieves its success by stealing time from other groups especially the elderly who must now spend more time waiting to cross a road or be diverted through an unpleasant underpass, or having to negotiate ugly metal barriers that obstruct direct walking routes or find that local services they prefer to use have closed and they must now travel longer distances to shopping centres, hospitals or clinic because they have relocated to more inaccessible, pedestrian unfriendly locations. All these tendencies bring about substantial time penalties that must be endured by the very young, older people, women and those on low incomes.

Conclusion: older people

Appleyard and Lintell (1971) concluded that older people find it especially difficult to cope on heavily trafficked streets:

"On heavy street the older people, finding it too costly and too much effort to move, experienced severe discomforts."

An emphasis on mobility rather than accessibility discriminates against older people. The deletion of pubs, shops, post offices, banks and other services from High St and neighbourhoods reduces the quality of life of older people. In aggregate they do not have the resources (mental, physical and fiscal) to access facilities over longer distances. The dominance of traffic in local neighbourhoods and the decline of walking reduce the probabilities for social interactions and it is simply not possible for many old people to cross a road under the circumstances described above when the interval between cars can be less than 10 seconds.

The reality of road traffic danger and the fearfulness which is often associated with older people creates another set of difficulties leading to social isolation and difficulties in accessing destinations.

The association of social isolation and loneliness among older people with raised mortality is a serious public health problem that is unrecognised on the part of those responsible for deleting local facilities (e.g. post offices) and those responsible for policies that add to traffic volumes.

None of this is surprising. The mobility paradigm brings with it a host of ideological presumptions that are not open to public debate and democratic decision-taking. The timings on pedestrian crossings clearly identify the strength of this ideological bias. Even if there are pedestrian actuated crossings the crossing times have been selected to give preference to cars. Crossing times are designed to minimise delays to traffic (cars) and do not give enough time for older people to cross to the other side before the green pedestrian phase is over (pedestrians are not traffic). The loss of social interaction possibilities, the possibility that older people will be confined to their homes and the loss of destinations combine to provide a powerful cocktail that has been shaped in the interests of motorised mobility and has ignored the quality of life of older people.

Overall conclusions on children, women and older people

A transport policy shaped by strong commitments to the growth of mobility cannot grasp the importance of the needs for routine access to routine things required by children, women and the elderly. The mobility paradigm is not sensitive to people and is locked into a very old fashioned and discredited ideology that says moving around a lot by car and prioritisng expensive infrastructure is a good thing. This obsession with mobility produces a clear bias in transport spending. The vast majority of the spending is allocated to projects that benefit men, the relatively affluent, those who travel long distances and those who have a preference for speed. This discriminates against the three groups discussed above.

Holzapfel (2014) has discussed in some detail the long term historical bias in transport policy and spending in favour of long distance trips when the reality of most everyday trips by most citizens is that they are relatively local. Emphasizing long distance trips (e.g. the £56 billion high speed rail project in Britain) discriminates against the old, the young, women and the poor and exacerbates inequalities.

Transport infrastructure projects are very expensive and yet they emerge and are funded at precisely the same time as budget cuts are made in bus services, the public realm (e.g. street maintenance) and local facilities like libraries, post offices and social care for the elderly. There is a totally unacceptable fiscal bias towards projects that reduce accessibility for those groups discussed here and increase mobility for the relatively affluent (who are already very mobile).

Transport and mobility policies are immensely undemocratic, discriminatory, unethical, promote inequality, damage health and reduce the quality of life for many millions of UK citizens.

Chapter 10
Community Disruption

Transport is a well-developed professional area of expertise with many justifiable claims to scientific validity, rigorous analysis, logic and verifiable evidence-based theories and methodologies. It is also a defective area of professionalism. It is characterised by several important findings and debates that are not permitted to influence outcomes and are not factored into advice on policy, spending and infrastructure. At the top layer of those things that shall not be mentioned is the questioning of mobility itself and the possibility that the pursuit of growth in mobility is a mistake of historic proportions. This top layer could not exist without a clear list of other things that must not be allowed to infect transport professionalism. Prominent in this supporting cast of blind-spots is community disruption.

It is glaringly obvious that large amounts of traffic clogging up residential streets, rushing past schools and filling trench-like one way systems in our cities is an environmental and social problem. It is unpleasant. It separates friends and families, it creates barriers, it feeds the fear of road traffic danger, it stops our children moving around independently and freely and it creates neighborhoods that are inimical to frequent neighbour interaction.

Traffic planners, urban planners and traffic engineers know that traffic creates an unpleasant urban environment creates social isolation and robs communities of the many unplanned social interactions between neighbours that provide the glue that holds our communities together. They know this information but it is not factored into the deliberations about community and environmental quality on those occasions when the evidence is most relevant.

Just two examples will illustrate the severity of this professional and political rejection of the importance of community vitality and sustainability. In the small town of Grange over Sands in Cumbria the local authority (South Lakeland District Council) has signalled its determination to approve 673 new homes to be built largely on Greenfield sites and associated with an additional car-trip generation of 6 new car trips per day for each house built. If all the housing sites proceed in the agreed way there will be an additional 4000 cars per day on the narrow roads of Grange and through its delightful main shopping street, already marred by heavy traffic flows. Grange has a large proportion of elderly residents and still has local shops, local banks and health care facilities. With a little imagination and sense of priority and purpose Grange could easily become a European best practice example of very low car use, very high levels of active transport and a physical environment that celebrates high accessibility to local facilities and delightful car-free walking and cycling routes. None of this will happen. Planners and politicians are deeply embedded in mobility world and have approved the first site (Whitelegg, 2013).

The other sites will follow. The addition of 4000 extra cars per day will severely damage the walking environment and make crossing roads very difficult. It will damage community interaction, produce a decline in quality of life for older people and transform a pleasant small town into a noisy, traffic-soaked, polluted mess. These points have been made by local residents and rejected by traditional town planners, highway engineers and politicians. The mobility paradigm is dominant.

In Lancaster, a compact historic city of about 50,000 people with a lack lustre retail centre, there is a plan to build a large new edge of town shopping centre. Locally this is known as the "Centros" development. Centros is the name of the private company that submitted a planning application to Lancaster City Council for this development. This is predicted to add approximately 21,000 vehicles per week on local roads, on a congested one way system and on residential roads already used by rat running (Whitelegg and Pye, 2009). Planners and highway engineers have consistently rejected the argument that this additional traffic is on such a scale that the development should be refused planning permission.

In both Grange and Lancaster and in the vast majority of all local authorities in the UK the subject of traffic impacts on community life is dismissed and developments that add to traffic are routinely approved.

Donald Appleyard (Appleyard, 1981) captured the importance of the traffic environment in determining patterns of walking and social interaction.

His famous diagram is reproduced as Figure 10.1 (see next page).

Appleyard's diagram shows that at low levels of traffic there is a great deal of street life, walking and social interaction. Residents on the low traffic street have the highest number of friends and acquaintances. As traffic levels increase through medium to heavy so the amount of use of street space on the part of residents goes down, social interaction declines, conviviality evaporates and residents have fewer friends and acquaintances than they have on the lightly trafficked street.

This pioneering work has been replicated in Bristol in the UK (Hart and Parkhurst, 2010) with the same results. There is a clear dose-response relationship between traffic levels and people crossing the road and using street space. The higher the traffic volume the lower is the use of that space:

"The study methodology replicates the work of Donald Appleyard, who demonstrated that people living on a street with relatively heavy traffic had only one third as many social connections as people living on a relatively light-traffic street. Subsequent studies investigated street design, traffic, and neighbourhood quality of life; work that culminated with the publication of the seminal work Liveable Streets (Appleyard, 1981). Livable Streets revealed the social impacts of motor traffic in fine detail through interviews and street observations, demonstrating that casual conversations, children's play, and other street-based social life tended to be suppressed, particularly as vehicle volumes and speeds increase. Appleyard's findings provided a quantitative case for policy makers to consider the social impacts of current transport policies."

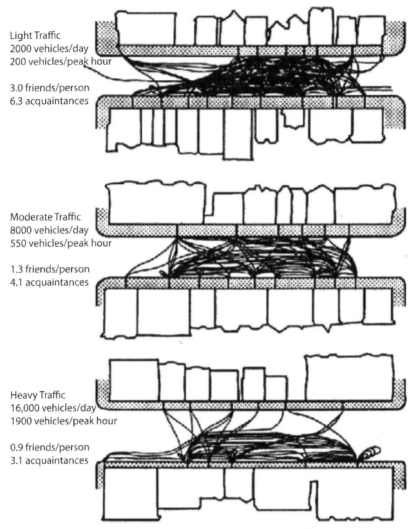

Light Traffic
2000 vehicles/day
200 vehicles/peak hour

3.0 friends/person
6.3 acquaintances

Moderate Traffic
8000 vehicles/day
550 vehicles/peak hour

1.3 friends/person
4.1 acquaintances

Heavy Traffic
16,000 vehicles/day
1900 vehicles/peak hour

0.9 friends/person
3.1 acquaintances

Figure 10.1: Community interaction and personal use of street space on streets
with increasing levels of traffic
Source: Appleyard (1981)

The disruption of social networks and reduction of interactions between neighbours has far reaching effects on quality of life, well-being and health. One study has examined the relationship between social and community ties and longevity (referred to as "lifespan"). This was conducted in Almeda County in the USA and has been summarised by Davis (2012a):

"[It] found that people who lacked social and community ties were more likely to die in the following follow-up period than those with more extensive contacts. The association between social ties and lifespan was found to be independent of self-reported physical health status, socioeconomic status, and lifestyle practices such as smoking, alcohol consumption, obesity, physical activity, and the use of health services.

The researchers examined four social relationships: marriage; contacts with close friends and relatives; church membership; informal and formal group associations. In each instance, people with social ties and relationships had lower death rates than people without such ties. The more intimate ties of marriage and contact with friends and relatives were stronger predictors than were the ties of church and group membership. To assess the cumulative effects and relationships, a Social Network Index was created based on the four sources of contact. For every age group examined, and for both sexes, people with many social contacts had the lowest death rates and people with the fewest contacts had the highest rates. More recent studies have confirmed these findings and added evidence that social activities among older people – that may entail little or no physical activity – have a positive impact on lifespan. Meaningful social activities reduce the harmful effects of stress by enhancing the body's immune response function."

The fundamental findings made by Appleyard and followed up by others have been applied in many of the world's major cities by Jan Gehl, the Danish architect. His recommendations in London, Brisbane, Melbourne and many other cities major heavily on promoting walking and cycling, creating high quality living environments and transforming cities so that they become more civilised, more human scale and rich in social interaction, childrens' play and the enjoyment of street life by all ages and social groups (Gehl, 2010).

Gehl's approach is summarised in ITDP, Gehl and Nyggard (2010) and the authors reduce the complexities of city development, planning and transport to 10 principles all of which underpin the importance of people-centred planning, creating livable cities and demonstrating that successful 21st century cities will be "replete with choices..make heavy use of non-motorised transport and be post fossil fuel." The 10 principles deliver high volumes of social interaction and social use of high quality public places and make a significant contribution to eliminating loneliness and social isolation. They are:

1. Walk the walk; the importance of creating great pedestrian environments.

2. Powered by people; the role of the bicycle in creating livable cities.

3. Get a bus; the bus uses much less space and fuel than cars and frees up valuable space.

4. Cruise control; car sharing and better management of car use make better use of space in cities.

5. Deliver the goods; the importance of moving to cleaner, smaller, quieter and slower delivery vehicles.

6. Mix it up; maximise use of space and human activity by putting retail on the ground floor, offices on the next floor and then housing.

7. Fill it in; build on vacant lots and Brownfield sites.

8. Get real; celebrate place distinctiveness and special places by building on history, geography and nature in urban design.

9. Connect the blocks; make sure that distances are short and that pedestrians and bikes can move easily and safely between origins and destinations.

10. Make it last; in all urban design use high quality materials, create well-designed spaces and employ high standards in the management of spaces.

In Melbourne, Gehl Architects (2004) were commissioned in 1993 and then again in 2004 to advise on what could be done to arrest the decline of Melbourne's central area and create a vibrant place that is heavily used by hundreds of thousands of residents and visitors. Unusually the two commissions provide comparative data on pedestrian activity over this 10 year period. The 1993 commission made many recommendations about creating high quality pedestrian spaces and routes, meeting place, seating areas and café spaces including the very successful "lanes" area where unpleasant back streets were converted into thriving public spaces lined with cafes and shops. The importance of the Melbourne project is that it shows how a city in decline can be turned around by focussing on people, high quality pedestrian activity and opportunities for "lingering" (interestingly there isn't an attractive English word for the very attractive business of spending more time in public spaces to enjoy the city).

In the period 1993-2004 Melbourne pedestrian traffic increased significantly (Table 10.1):

	% change 1993-2004
Pedestrian traffic weekdays (daytime)	+39
Pedestrian traffic weekdays (evening)	+98
Saturday (daytime)	+9
Saturday (evening)	+13

Table 10.1: Changes in the period 1993-2004 in pedestrian traffic in Melbourne
Source: Gehl Architects (2004)

Gehl's detailed work at city street and public space levels clearly demonstrates that cities characterised by high traffic volumes, unpleasant environments and low levels of pedestrian and cycling can be turned around. The Melbourne project update in 2004 recommends the "roll-out" of this approach to suburban areas and the German experience with traffic calming (Verkehrsberuhigung) demonstrates that the majority of residential streets can be re-shaped to be people-friendly and supportive of social interaction. In Freiburg over 90% of city streets benefit from a 30kph speed limit, tree planting, attractive and well maintained walking and cycling routes, local facilities that deliver high quality accessibility and a high quality integrated bus, tram and local rails system that provide an attractive alternative to the car.

The situation in Melbourne away from the CBD is not good. There is very little traffic calming, poor quality walking and cycling routes and a privatised public transport system that does not provide an attractive alternative to the car. In addition

Melbourne is scheduled to receive a major new highway, the East West Link (Morton, 2014) which in terms of traffic generation, air pollution, noise and greenhouse gas emissions wipes out all the gains made through the adoption of Gehl's recommendations in the CBD.

Chapter 11
Freight

B oege (1995) has made a very significant contribution to our understanding of freight in the modern world. The detailed analysis of every component of a container of strawberry yoghurt clearly identifies the freight transport equivalent of the passenger transport explosion of mobility and transformation of distance into a consumer commodity. Just as people have shifted effortlessly into a highly mobile mode of functioning for personal travel so that ever-increasing distances separate homes, shops, work etc so in the world of freight, distance is also exploding. The yoghurt study showed that the distances over which widely available products were sourced amount to 1005 kilometres for a 150g container of strawberry yoghurt. This translates into one pot of yoghurt being responsible for moving one lorry 9.2 metres.

The Boege study reveals a very important characteristic of freight movement. Much of it is useless, by which I mean the time, effort and distances involved were much greater than was necessary. There is no evidence of the long-held human principles and values around the minimisation of time, effort and cost to produce an acceptable outcome whether this is the manufacture of yoghurt or the sourcing of ingredients that go into lunch time sandwiches in a British supermarket or chain specialising in "meal deals"(e.g. Boots, Marks and Spencer). Freight transport behaves as though distance is no longer a constraint. Distance has been eliminated from the decision-making around where to make things, where to sell things and where to source the ingredients or components. Whitelegg (1994a) in his report on "absurd freight movement" discusses many more case studies that challenge the yoghurt achievements in terms of illogicality and distance maximisation.

The discussion so far would not cut any ice at all with the world of freight and logistics. Logistics, by the way, is just a more impressive word for describing the business of moving things around. In the 19th and early 20th centuries some impressive entrepreneurs including Henry Ford, Lord Leverhulme and Lord Ashton sorted out complicated global supply systems to support (respectively) cars, soap and linoleum and just got on with the shipping, forwarding and freight movements without the need to invent a pompous new word.

Freight and logistics in the second decade of the 21st century is a very sophisticated, computer-based, real-time, 100% monitored system for making sure that the flow of goods gets to where it is needed and when it is needed but it is blind to any discussion of sources and the possibility that local sourcing or regional sourcing might be an alternative to the world of yoghurt that Boege measured. The sophistication of logistics is oblivious to the fact that for many goods and materials in the supply chain there are a large number of possible sources that are nearer to the place where they are needed.

Freight is the perfect manifestation of the mobility growth paradigm. The idea that it might be possible to source something within a 100kms radius of where it is needed rather than a 1000km radius has no traction. It is ridiculous. Sourcing and logistics is about serious bargaining over cost, discounts, the exploitation of monopoly positions and the importance of stripping out labour costs. If a large retailer of manufactured kit furniture, based in Sweden, can source the timber from Russia rather than Sweden or from Poland to meet the domestic market in Sweden then it will do so. It does this because it can do it, because logistics is up to the task and because chasing low/very low labour costs is part of the entrepreneurial dynamic in a globalised system obsessed with competition and stripping out costs wherever possible. This is made all the easier because of the low cost of transport. The huge literature on "the internalisation of external cost" (van Essen, 2011) makes it very clear that freight transport is heavily subsidised, does not pay its way and this encourages a kind of distance maximising ethos throughout the supply chain.

Van Essen (2011) estimates that the total of transport externalities in the EU, plus Norway and Switzerland, is more than 500 billion Euros pa. 77% of this is accounted for by passenger transport and 23% by freight transport. Freight transport is effectively underpriced to a total that approximates 23% of 500 billion Euros pa and this underpricing distorts the choices made by those corporations and individuals balancing labour costs, taxes and transport costs when they consider location and distances over which goods can be shipped. Den Boer (2009) estimates that lorries pay through all forms of taxation for 38% of the costs they generate. Conventional undergraduate economics would inform policy makers that this is a powerful inducement to increase road freight transport, contrary to climate change, biodiversity, air pollution and other policy objectives.

The mobility paradigm is very strong in freight transport because of the way it misrepresents economic principles to justify higher levels of freight transport. Almost every new road, airport, seaport or freight distribution centre is justified to some degree on the argument that it will help the economy, create jobs and connect an allegedly remote or disadvantaged region with distant markets and so strengthen the local economy. This was a key argument in the case for the Heysham M6 Link road in Lancaster in the north of England. This new road, it was claimed, would assist the port of Heysham, help the port to grow, create jobs and strengthen the local economy. In the case of Lancaster but also in almost every other case where there is an economic argument for a new road majoring on freight there is no mention of the detailed work by SACTRA (1999) and Whitelegg (1994b). The so-called "2 way road effect" (SACTRA, (1999), paragraph 10, page 16) could not be clearer. A new road justified by reference to connectivity and its importance for freight can just as easily suck jobs out of the local economy as create jobs.

There is no evidential link between new roads, more jobs or local economic gain. The mobility paradigm can be recognised by its deletion of all evidence that points to other outcomes e.g. the loss of jobs as a result of improved connections. The mobility paradigm promotes "truths" that are self evident (more freight transport is good) and makes sure that ideas and evidence that does not fit this story-line are deleted from the discussion.

Freight transport in the European Union of 27 countries in 2012 was "close to" 3.9 trillion tonne kilometres (TKM) of which 45% were by road and 40% by sea (European Commission 2013b). The European Environment Agency (2013) tracks key transport indicators in its annual TERM report and the latest report summarises freight transport trends.

Freight transport in the EU27 has increased significantly in the period 1995-2011. The growth has not been even. There was a high point in 2007 and a small decline since then which is normally attributed to the economic recession. Other points that should be noted include:

- The dominance of road freight. 76% of land based freight is by road and the remainder by rail.
- Land freight movement grew by 72% in the period 2001-2011 but more than doubled in some former Soviet bloc countries e.g. Bulgaria and Poland.
- Road freight tkm in Poland is now bigger than Germany.
- The importance of maritime transport. Shipping still has a large part to play in EU27 goods transport.

The EU has a target to reduce by 30% road freight that travels over 300kms by 2030 and by 50% in 2050.

For many years now there has been a discussion in Europe around "decoupling." Decoupling is the term used to describe a situation where the economy is growing (e.g. GDP per capita) but tkm is falling. This would means that the EU economy has achieved real progress in producing economic growth but at the same time reducing the environmental impact of that growth. De-coupling has not happened.

The lorry or truck has been a serious cause for concern for many decades. This was analysed in some detail in the Armitage report in the UK (Armitage, 1980). Lorries (sometimes referred to as Heavy Goods vehicles or HGVs) have a disproportionately large impact on safety and environment when the size of the impact is compared with the number of lorries. Den Boer (2009) reports that they are a major source of health damaging particulate emissions, they account for 47% of the costs associated with noise and 13% of fatalities in road crashes and they produce 23% of all CO_2 emissions generated on roads. The European Environment Agency (2013) estimates that 42% of all cycle deaths in London are caused by lorries.

Lorries are also inefficient. The European Commission (2013b) estimated that 24% of goods vehicles are running empty, average loading of the rest is 57% and the overall efficiency is 43%. This is a very poor performance and something that has persisted since the time of the Armitage report.

The lorry takes up a great deal of road space, damages the road surface, worsens air and noise pollution, produces greenhouse gases, kills and injures other road users, is subsidised and is inefficient in accomplishing its tasks.

A recent US study estimated that trucks were responsible for 4500 deaths pa (Dong et al, 2013). In the USA trucks account for 4% of all registered vehicles, 11% of all passenger vehicle occupant deaths and 14% of pedestrian and cyclist deaths.

Lorries (trucks) are a key part of the mobility paradigm that feeds on an outdated economic ideology (growth is good) and then supports large scale infrastructure investment. This paradigm and its underlying ideology was succinctly summarised by the UK Minister of Transport, Patrick McLoughlin, in July 2013 (DfT, 2013):

"We need to maximise every one of our economic advantages, and deal with every factor that holds us back if we are to succeed in the global race.

Transport is one of the most important factors in making our country prosper. As a densely-populated island, we should benefit from being better connected and more compact. This government has already committed to a major transformation of the rail network. However roads remain the most heavily used mode of transport for people and businesses and we need to give them the same attention.

Over decades we have learnt more about where we need to improve roads and where other forms of transport work best, and how to manage demand across different modes. We are also preparing for new technology and setting up the UK as a global leader in ultra-low emission vehicles.

In June, we announced in "Investing in Britain's Future" the biggest-ever upgrade of our existing roads, worth up to £50 billion over the next generation. We have approved or advanced 52 national road projects since 2010, and we are addressing some of the most serious problems on our network. We are putting in place studies so we can deliver results on long-standing problems, and funding the maintenance needed to keep the network as a whole in top condition."

The growth of road freight into the future supported by the UK government in "Action for roads" is not sustainable on climate change and land take grounds. Road freight emissions are a fast growing source of greenhouse gases and it would sensible and proportionate to apply a wide range of measures to bring about a reduction in greenhouse gases from this sector of the economy. This is turn would produce a large number of co-benefits linked to human health (reduction of noise, air pollution and death and injury caused by trucks), a reduction in the high public cost of catering for lorries and a boost to walking, cycling and quality of life by reducing the negative impact of lorries on roads and on levels of walking and cycling.

Dalkmann and Brannigan (2007) have provided a very useful framework for dealing with the need to deliver a sustainable transport system and this can be applied to freight transport. The special case of aviation (passenger and freight) will be discussed in chapter 12 and is not dealt with here. The framework is based on a sequential approach (the order in which we do things matters):

- Avoid.
- Shift.
- Improve.

Avoid

The mobility paradigm assumes that tkm of freight transport will grow year on year. There is no discussion about a possible end-point or stabilisation and certainly no discussion about reduction. This is illogical. There is a wide ranging discussion in energy about the ways in which energy demand can be reduced and we can avoid the costs and difficulties associated with new nuclear or coal fired power stations. We can reduce energy demand and this also brings with it increases in quality of life. The German "Passiv Haus" concept, now imported into the UK, is a particularly good example (Bere, 2013). Energy use in the home can be reduced to 10% of what was previously thought to be a good standard of energy performance. The reduction improves quality of life, health and reduces costs and this concept can be adopted in road freight transport. The strength of the mobility paradigm and the seductive persuasiveness of the "more freight-more roads-more jobs" discourse blocks this policy option.

Avoiding freight transport can be achieved by substituting "near" for "far" i.e. taking the Boege yoghurt study as a starting point we can interrogate all the possible sources of components in a manufacturing or assembly process and set up a system that would select "near" rather than "far." "Near" would be the default option.

Whitelegg and Kirkbride (2003) carried out a detailed study of freight transport in the retail food market. They looked at large supermarkets, small shops and an intermediate "regional" supermarket. Examining a small number of selected products they tracked CO_2 emissions throughout the supply chain i.e. supplier to retailer, warehouse, RDC etc. In the case of cheese they found that substituting local sources for more distant sources would reduce emissions by up to 92% but more typically by around 60%. In the case of chicken, the same substitution would reduce emissions by 40-70%.

Holzapfel (1995) has carried out an analysis at the regional level to show that in a defined region (he suggest 250 sq kms) a policy of using local sources across a much wider range of goods than considered in Whitelegg and Kirkbride would reduce lorry kilometres by 67%.

The transition from the current paradigm (distance is not in any way a constraint) to a new paradigm based on geographical logic and distance minimisation is already happening in many parts of Europe. The slow food movement (Petrini, 2007) is based on a number of principles that are discussed in Honore (2005) and whilst concerned mainly with the quality of food, celebration of local foods, local culture and place distinctiveness it also has the effect of minimising distance. It is a real world example of a completely different paradigm to the one that plugs into economic growth, speed and increasingly distant sourcing.

Farmers Own (Bondens egen) in Sweden is an organisation set up specifically to link growers and suppliers of meat, dairy products and vegetables with customers. Its highly innovative approach demonstrates the importance of organisational skills and different models of doing things. Rather than relying on supermarkets and retail chains that run national and international systems of procurement and distribution and extract profits from the overall system, the Swedish model is not for profit, local and run by users. Its main characteristics are:

- It is the world's first fully integrated web system for sales and marketing of locally produced food.
- It has 180 farms supplying the produce to dedicated outlets.
- It runs a "one invoice" system so a purchaser is able to buy as many products as he/she wants without the complexity of dealing with many suppliers.
- The system helps growers and producers to adjust their planning so that supplies can be adjusted to match demand.
- It contains an environmental indicator checker so customers and suppliers can see what environmental damage is caused by this system compared with the larger supermarket system.

The Farmers Own system was used as a model in a report to the Greater London Assembly (Whitelegg, 2005) about how to link producers and consumers and increase the amount of local food consumed by Londoners. In 2005 London's food was predominantly sourced from outside the UK whilst at the same time there were many local sources and large parts of the so-called "home counties" e.g. Hertfordshire, Surrey and Kent were more than capable of producing high quality food.

Much of the work on freight and localisation has been carried out on food. Food in the UK accounts for 41billion tonne-kilometres (btkm) of freight movement which is 28% of the total and produces 19 million tones of CO_2pa. 25% of all HGV activity is food related. Clearly more work is needed to test the contribution of near for far in other sectors of the economy and categories of goods but the principle is clear. It is logical to work towards this substitution and in so doing transfer the current freight transport mobility paradigm so that it operates a much reduced level of activity and still does the job of connecting sources and sinks, origins and destinations.

Shift

Much of the debate in transport is about rather narrowly defined issues that are not well-linked to the generality of sustainability, integration or wider issues about human health and quality of life. In freight transport the sustainability debate tends to revolve around the potential for shifting freight from road to rail or the potential for reducing environmental impacts by moving from diesel engines to alternatively fuelled variants. Both examples fail to grasp the bigger picture and the possibilities for rail freight or waterborne freight will be improved if we have smaller total mass of freight to move around. Reduction or "avoid" must come first.

It is, of course, possible and desirable to move freight from road to rail wherever possible. Travelling in the Freiburg region of southern Germany on local trains one is struck by the large number of freight trains using this main line to Basel in Switzerland and through Switzerland to Italy. The freight trains are very different to UK freight trains. Many of them have whole lorries on specially designed wagons and a coach equipped so that the lorry driver can relax, eat and sleep whilst the whole lorry is transported several hundred kms through Europe. Other trains contain only the rear part of the lorry (the tractor unit or cab is missing) and this also provides a great deal of relief for local communities affected by noise or air pollution. This "piggyback" system of trains carrying lorries does not happen in the UK and yet it has a great deal of potential.

The discussion about shifting freight from road to rail has an economic dimension. Whilst it would be wrong to conclude that a decision about whether or not to ship goods by rail or road is a simple matter of comparing costs it is also the case that the subsidy system can be structured to favour rail over road and, as in the case of Germany and some other countries, it is possible to introduce a tax aimed at lorries as a measure to recoup some of the costs of road damage or make sure that foreign lorries are meeting their share of the costs e.g. an Italian lorry travelling to Denmark and using Germany motorways for the majority of kms will now pay a tax in Germany for that privilege (the Lastkraftwagen Maut). Taxation can also be used as a measure to reduce lorry miles and as part of a climate change policy.

Shifting freight from road to rail is not difficult but will require very careful thought and funding mechanisms to deliver the right infrastructure and the right balance of taxation. It is also possible to shift freight to canals and coastal shipping but this will also require a great deal of coordinated intervention and the abandonment of the transport growth paradigm. As long as we make decisions about transport infrastructure within the mobility growth paradigm this will stack the outcomes in favour of more roads just as we have seen in 2013 in the case of the Heysham M6 Link road that was not evaluated against a rail option.

A rather different kind of "shift" has been introduced in several cities in Europe and Japan and this is known as "urban logistics" or "freight platforms" (Bestufs, 2007). This intervention works on the principle that delivering freight to cities using very large lorries is not compatible with urban planning and amenity and is also inefficient. An example of inefficiency is the 44 tonne lorry making its way through congested streets in a large city to find a delivery address and dropping of a 10kg package. At the same time other large lorries will be doing very similar things with small packages in the same area. It follows that if a very large lorry could leave a motorway and go directly to a transshipment centre on the edge of the city, drop of all its packages and then return to the motorway this would help the haulage company, reduces time and labour costs and reduce lorry activity in the city. The packages that are left in the transshipment centre can then be bundled up by smaller areas or sections of street and delivered in one operation to 10 destinations rather than 10 trips by a large lorry.

The Bestufs report provides information on 32 schemes (described as Urban Freight Platforms or UFPs) including City logistics in Kassel, Germany and Tenjin joint distribution system, Fukuoka, Japan.

The Tenjin project has reported a reduction in the number of trucks by 65% and a reduction in distance travelled by trucks of 28%.

These projects are not problem free and the Bestufs report includes an account of the Leiden (NL) project which was closed down because it failed to perform in the way that was predicted. Holzapfel (2013) has confirmed that the Kassel project has now ended as a result of concerns about the reliability of transshipments and additional costs. Nevertheless the European Environment Agency reports (EEA 2013) that reductions of 60-75% can be achieved through urban logistic solutions:

"Typically, supplier vehicles deliver to the consolidation or transshipment centre on the edge of the central urban area where the goods are prepared for onward delivery. These schemes often use low emission delivery vehicles and have greater flexibility in delivery access. Delivery trips to businesses using a consolidation centre are significantly reduced with examples in Bristol, Heathrow and Stockholm showing reductions of some 65-70%."

Urban Freight Platforms (UFPs) are complex organisational and financial operations and require a high degree of co-operation from the municipality, the businesses using the service and the "neutral carrier." The neutral carrier is the business contracted to run the UFP. This is not intrinsically difficult but in a commercially competitive environment that is nervous about competition and the imposition of extra costs and the loss of control in a time sensitive environment this can go wrong.

The UFP concept is an excellent example of paradigm shift. It provides an alternative organisational and financial model that has a proven track record in reducing mobility measured as fewer trucks, fewer kms travelled and less time spent in cities by trucks. The Kassel and Tenjin case studies have produced an impressive reduction in lorry activity and mobility. The reduction in mobility is associated with an increases in efficiency and a number of co-benefits including greenhouse gas, noise and air pollution reduction.

Improve

There is a very significant conceptual difference between "avoid" and "shift" (taken together) and "improvement." Improvement implies a high degree of satisfaction and acceptance of the status quo that is characterised by year on year growth (with occasional levelling) of tkm of freight. The mobility paradigm emphasises "improvement" and this has the effect of detracting from a more fundamental and inquisitive exploration of what is wrong with the growth of freight transport and how the system as a whole might change. "Improvement" is also interpreted as a technical matter majoring on alternative fuels, driver training, aerodynamic efficiency, GPS tracking, intelligent highways etc. Improvement does not embrace what would be a real improvement e.g. the full internalisation of external costs so that every tkm of freight carried its full and proportionate share of costs. As these costs would include noise, death and injury, the health effects of air pollution, greenhouse gases, courts and policing, the costs of vehicle inspection, road maintenance and much more it is likely that the cost of a tkm of road freight would rise by a considerable amount. The size of the rise is difficult to estimate but based on the figure quoted above that lorries only pay 38% of the costs they generate it would be substantial. This would be an "improvement" because it would send a strong signal to the whole freight transport and retail industry that lower levels of tkm generated makes commercial, "bottom-line" sense. Currently the possibility of a future characterised by much less freight is not on corporate or governmental radar screens because transport is cheap enough for this cost element not to be taken into account. Such a reduction would deliver substantial financial and environmental gains. Cheap transport might sound very attractive indeed but it delivers a very bad deal for society as a whole because at the societal level it is not cheap.

Conclusion

The rapid growth of motorised passenger transport and its impact on increasing distances that we travel for most everyday purposes has an exact parallel in freight. Freight transport by all modes (btkm) has increased by 25% in the period 1995-2010 and road freight by 36% in the same period (European Commission, 2012). The majority of this growth has taken place because we move things over longer distances and not because we eat more food or consume more non-food physical products. The mobility paradigm has shaped freight transport and has ensured that policy delivers growth. These policies include new and often very expensive infrastructure projects, very large subsidies and the determination not to apply the polluter pays principle and avoiding the internalisation of external costs. Ensuring that freight transport is cheap because it does not pay these costs has embedded the mobility paradigm so firmly that it is not possible for decision takers and politicians to contemplate a paradigm shift for freight.

The consequences of such a deep commitment to the mobility paradigm are severe and generate fiscal stress, negative health impacts and a tide of new infrastructure, severely damaging to nature and habitat that is impossible to resist.

There are many alternatives to this spatially exploded freight world. The writings of Boege, Holzapfel, Whitelegg and others clearly show that the substitution of far for near can be reversed. We can begin to strip out excessive distance from current operations. The development of regional models of co-operation or re-localised economies is already underway in the food industry and has produced a remarkable synergy between those seeking to develop local food and regional supply chains, those seeking to promote "slow food" (Petrini, 2007) and those seeking to abandon the mobility paradigm and substitute a regionalised model (Holzapfel, 1995).

The regionalised model, like all examples of paradigm shift, will not appeal to the principal actors in control of the current paradigm. The ideology that spawns the mobility paradigm is strongly connected to economic growth, technical sophistication and rhetoric around competitive pressures in a globalised economy. The regionalized, polluter-pays model offers a clear route to fiscal prudence. It will lower public and private costs at a time when the language of decision-making bodies in Europe is peppered with phrases that refer to debt reduction, austerity and financial stringency. The regionalized model offers a route to achieving these objectives without all the associated pain of severe cuts in education, health, employment and welfare budgets.

The model also offers a route to a relatively new policy objective, resilience. Whitelegg (2012) discussed resilience and its benefits. If we are entering (or have already entered) a world of peak oil, energy crises, climate change disruption and conflict over access to resources then a regionalised model brings more security and resilience than one based on long or very long supply lines. A system organised around a multiplicity of shorter supply chains, with a capacity for modal substitution will not be as susceptible to disruption as the current system. It will be more resilient.

Resilience also applies to people. People living in a region with strong regional connections between producers and consumers will be less likely to panic or worry when things go wrong in the Middle East or there is a blockade of an oil refinery or the motorway system is closed as a result of severe storm damage. Resilience at the population level has not yet entered the vocabulary of decision takers but it delivers a desirable improvement in quality of life and a much higher probability of achieving multiple policy objectives than the stale business as usual models still in everyday use.

Chapter 12
Aviation

Aviation is booming and takes the mobility debate into entirely new realms where thousands of miles can be covered in very small amounts of time. The range over which people can go shopping, enjoy tourism, take part in cultural events, speak at conferences and simply commute is bigger than ever in the history of civilisation and is still growing.

ICAO (2013) has summarised the current aviation situation:

- 3.1 billion passengers flew in 2013.

- The 2013 total is a 5% increase on 2011.

- This total is expected to reach 6.4 billion by 2030.

- 33 million aircraft departures were recorded in 2013.

- The Asia/Pacific Region was the largest market for air travel with 31% of the global total.

- Aircraft manufacturers are expected to have delivered more than 1,500 new commercial aircraft by the end of 2013 and have recorded orders for 2,800 new aircraft.

The growth of aviation comes with a very strong story line with echoes of the freedom and opportunity allegedly associated with owning and using a car. In the case of flying the story line merges seamlessly with very broad generalisations about widening cultural exchanges, encouraging different parts of the world to work together and supporting an increasingly globalised economy. As in ground based mobility, reality is very different. It remains very questionable as to whether or not thousands of tourists enjoying the delights of Bangkok or Majorca are adding very much to cross-cultural understanding and co-operation. It is even more doubtful that aviation benefits the local economies at its origins or destinations. Whitelegg (2003, 2005b) has described in some detail the loss of revenue and jobs associated with UK aviation as a result of transferring millions of tourists out of the UK. The impact of aviation in aggregate is a clear disbenefit and a loss of income and jobs.

The loss of revenue and jobs associated with aviation costs money to fund. In Chapter 5 I presented information on the subsidy of aviation from public funds in the UK and across the EU. There is no clear logic that has been subjected to analysis for this subsidy. Why should we subsidise a mode of transport associated with job loss and severe environmental and negative climate change consequences? Equally there has been no clear analysis of value for money. The Welsh Assembly Government subsidises air services between North and South Wales at approximately £800,000pa and this has not been evaluated in terms of beneficial economic impact or the viability of alternatives. The subsidy is paid because politicians think it is a "good thing" to link North and South Wales with an air service.

The Welsh example illustrates the clear public policy failure to set objectives, scope the options available for achieving those objectives, carry out a wide ranging analysis of the costs (monetary and environmental) of those options, develop alternatives and implement an optimum solution. In the case of North-South links in Wales the Welsh Assembly Government already subsidises one train each weekday each way between Holyhead and Cardiff at an annual cost of £2.8 million (Welsh Assembly Government, 2014).

The large amounts of public subsidy to air and rail services in one small part of the United Kingdom are indicative of the ideological power of the connectivity and mobility discourse. The problem with this ideology is not that connectivity is unwanted or un-needed but that it has to be modulated by an element of rationality and not ideology. A proportion of the "burden" of connectivity can be met by high quality video-conferencing, IT and mobile communications. Physical contact will still happen from time to time but it would not be convincing to argue that out of every 10 meetings in Wales, 10 must be physical face-to-face meetings. Physical travel with its financial and environmental burdens can be reduced and this reduction can bring a number of social and family benefits as lifestyles adjust to a more moderate pace (Honore, 2005).

Aviation is a dramatic example of the "good thing" argument. What matters in the debate is the rhetoric and aviation is a "good thing." It "binds" disparate parts of a given geographical territory together. It encourages tourism to far flung parts of the planet as if this is a public policy objective. It thrives on vague notions of fairness. It argues that it allows relatively poor people to enjoy long distance travel in ways that previously were only available to relatively rich people and it oils the wheels of a spatially exploded, global economy. Interestingly fairness arguments are often deployed in favour of the expansion of aviation but it is also clear that low-income groups, single parent families and those people living modest lifestyles do not make very much use of aircraft. Air passengers are relatively well-heeled compared to those who do not fly and public funds allocated to airport expansion, rail links to airports and the subsidy of aviation is a transfer of resources from the relatively poor to the relatively rich.

Data on the income of air passengers (CAA, 2012) reveal that at Heathrow Airport the mean annual income of business users was £80636 (international) and £65409 (domestic). For leisure passengers the mean annual income was £55780 (international) and £68925 (domestic). Air travellers are relatively wealthy and the mobility ideology, linked misleadingly to fairness, is a very convenient framework for supporting aviation and promoting regressive policies and the growth of inequalities in income and wealth.

The impacts of aviation

The environmental impacts of aviation are well known and have been discussed for many years (RCEP, 1995; Upham et al, 2003). As is often the case in transport and its dominant mobility paradigm the repeated discussion of severe negative impacts has no impact whatsoever on reducing those impacts. The growth of aviation is stimulated and fuelled by large scale subsidies and a co-operative planning system that routinely agrees with proposals for new runways and terminals e.g. Manchester Runway 2 and Heathrow Terminal 5. Information on negative impacts and especially on negative health impacts is not allowed to dampen rates of growth and dent the overblown rhetoric around global competitive performance and the economic success of "UK PLC."

The Royal Commission on Environmental Pollution (RCEP, 1995) was very clear in its report on transport and the environment:

"An unquestioning attitude towards future growth in air travel, and an acceptance that the projected demand for additional facilities and services must be met, are incompatible with the aim of sustainable development, just as acceptance that there will be a continuing growth in demand for energy would be incompatible....the demand for air transport might not be growing at the present rate if airlines and their customers had to face the costs of the damage they are causing to the environment." (RCEP, 1995, Para 5.39).

Whitelegg and Cambridge (2004) summarised the main environmental impacts of aviation as:

- Noise pollution and its effect on human health.
- Local air pollution and its effects on human health.
- Greenhouse gases and climate change.

These impacts are discussed in the original report and this discussion is not repeated here.

A more recent study of health impacts of aviation around Heathrow Airport (Hansell et al, 2013) concluded that exposure to aircraft noise increased the risk of cardiovascular disease:

"High levels of aircraft noise were associated with increased risks of stroke, coronary heart disease and cardiovascular disease for both hospital admissions and mortality in areas near Heathrow airport in London. As well as the possibility of causal associations, alternative explanations such as residual confounding and potential for ecological bias should be considered."

There are also serious concerns about the effects of aircraft noise on the learning and cognitive skills of children (Clark, Head and Stansfield, 2013):

"Research into the impact of noise on children has carried out a new study to follow up a study done between 2001 and 2003 into the impact of noise from road traffic and aircraft on children aged 9 – 10. That was called the RANCH study (Road traffic noise and Aircraft Noise exposure and children's Cognition and Health). The new study, carried out in 2008, wanted to assess the effects of noise over time on cognition. The study did indicate that levels of aircraft noise experienced in primary schools might affect aspects of children's cognition, even several years after they have left the primary school – even taking socio-economic factors into account. The study looked at the same children aged 15-16 years old, who had attended noisier primary schools six years earlier. They found aircraft noise was more disturbing or annoying to these children than to controls, even after accounting for aircraft noise at their current school."

It is clear that aviation has a number of well-documented negative health impacts (Hume and Watson, 2003) and that the evidence base on these impacts continues to accumulate. It is also clear that policy makers are not prepared to intervene in ways that would reduce the scale of these impacts even though the steps that need to be taken are very clearly laid out in the literature on sustainable transport (Vallack et al, 2014).

This refusal to intervene to deal with a public health problem is repeated on a larger scale in the refusal to act in ways that would reduce greenhouse gases from the aviation sector and assist in the urgent need to deal with climate change.

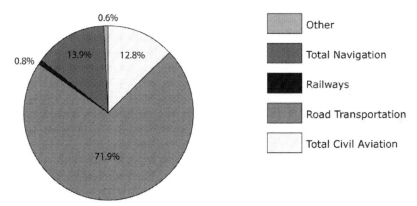

Figure 12.1: Transport emissions of CO2 equivalent by source (percentages) in the EU 28 in 2012
Source: European Commission (2014), section 3.2.5, page 131

Climate Change

Aviation is a fast growing source of greenhouse gases. In the European Union of 28 member states (EU28) the total aviation emissions of greenhouse gases (million tonnes of CO2 equivalent) has grown from 84.1 in 1990 to 150.7 in 2012 (European Commission, 2014). The 150.7 million tonnes of Co2 equivalent emissions in 2012 (EU28) including international bunkers were 12.8% of all transport emissions (figure 12.1).

Total civil aviation emissions of 150.7 million tonnes of CO_2 equivalent were 3.12% of total greenhouse gas emissions (all sources total of 4824.4 million tonnes of CO_2 equivalent). The impact on climate change is estimated using the Radiative Forcing Index (Sausen et al, 1999) which suggests that it would be appropriate to multiply measured CO_2 eq emissions by 1.9 to arrive at an accurate estimate of climate change impact. This is explained in a little more detail in a T&E (2012) briefing document:

"Aviation's impact on climate change is not confined to its carbon emissions alone: aircraft generate significant impacts upon radiative forcing with net additional warming effects over shorter timescales. Taking the CO_2 and non-CO_2 impacts together, aviation accounts for 3.5% of the total warming of the climate attributed to anthropogenic activities, rising to 4.9% if the effect of aviation-induced cirrus cloud formation is included.

Excluding the effects of induced cirrus, the overall radiative forcing by aircraft is a factor of 1.9 times greater than the forcing by aircraft carbon dioxide emissions alone. However, to date, the focus of efforts in the EU and ICAO has been on CO_2, justified by a lower level of scientific certainty surrounding the non-CO_2 effects and an ongoing debate on a suitable metric (although alternative, temperature-based metrics are already emerging). It is essential that the sector's total impact on the atmosphere is reflected in policy decisions, with appropriate measures to tackle CO_2, NOx and contrail impacts taken in parallel."

The history of attempts to bring aviation's contribution to climate change into the debate about mitigation is a troubled and complicated one in which all airports, airlines and representative bodies have worked very hard to exclude this sector from any kind of proportionate responsibility in reducing greenhouse gases.

International aviation emissions were excluded from the Kyoto Protocol and so whilst countries committed themselves to reducing greenhouse gas emissions by 80% of 1990 levels by 2050, aviation has continued to pollute the atmosphere. The global warming potential of all UK flights (domestic and international) is equivalent to 80% of the whole country's road vehicle fleet. Examining this in relation to Kyoto shows why governments are keen to leave out aviation from its commitments. It is now been recognised by the UK Government that it if they take into account aircraft emissions it will not be able to meet its Climate Change Act target of a 80 per cent reduction in CO_2 by 2050.

Aircraft use most fuel and produce greatest emissions during the take-off and landing phases when maximum power is required. Up to 25% of fuel is burned during this phase. On shorter journeys the ratio of fuel used per km to total distance is high, Take-off and landing become less significant as the flight distance increases and emissions become a smaller fraction of the total. A comparison of emissions by different modes is shown in figure 12.2 and clearly demonstrates that short haul flights produce the greatest CO_2 emissions per passenger kilometre (van Essen et al, 2003).

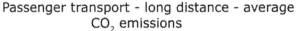

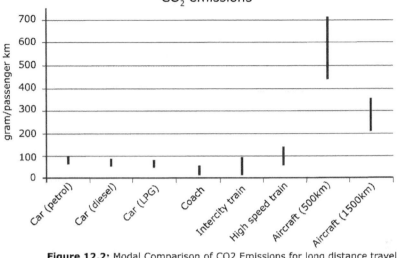

Figure 12.2: Modal Comparison of CO2 Emissions for long distance travel
Source: (van Essen et al, 2003)

The most fuel-efficient flight distance is around 4,300 km (2,300 nautical miles or 2,700 miles) corresponding, for example, to flights from Europe to the east coast of North America? However, nearly three-quarters of all new flight routes in Europe and North America are less than 2000 km meaning aircraft are not operating as efficiently as they should.

There is therefore a clear case for introducing policies that reduce the demand for these less-efficient trips such as shifting to cleaner modes of transport or using technology to substitute trips. The over-riding public policy response is the complete eradication of all subsidies to aviation and the full implementation of the "polluter pays principle" also known as the full internalisation of external costs.

Reducing greenhouse gases in the aviation sector

Vallack et al (2014) carried out a detailed study of the potential for decarbonising the transport sector in the UK by 2050. The research project covered road, rail, aviation and shipping, estimated CO2 emissions that are the responsibility of the UK in 2050 (the Business as usual or BAU scenario) and then demonstrated how this total could be reduced by the implementation of a series of interlinked measures (the maximum impact or MI scenario). The final results are summarised in Figure 12.3 (see next page).

The project concluded that it was feasible to achieve a 100% decarbonisation of road and rail transport but this was not possible for shipping and aviation (Figure 12.3).

The aviation BAU Scenario already included changes expected over the next 40-50 years. The DfT (2009) recognises that, even in the longer-term, the decarbonisation of aviation (and shipping) and the use of alternative fuel sources will be more challenging than for road and rail modes.

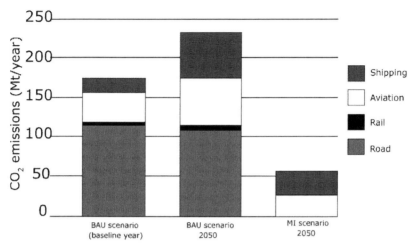

Figure 12.3: Summary of UK transport CO2 emissions for the baseline year (2003-2006/7) depending on sector, and in 2050 for the business as usual (BAU) and maximum Impact (MI) scenarios
Source: Vallack et al (2014)

The International Air Transport Association (IATA) (2009) roadmap towards carbon neutral growth (no increase in emissions as demand continues to grow) includes setting emissions standards, use of biofuel and improvement in air traffic management. By 2020, a 1.5 per cent per annum improvement in fuel efficiency is expected. Within this timeframe, the industry is also expected to achieve carbon neutral growth. By 2050, emissions will have reduced by 50 per cent compared to 2005. The Sustainable Aviation Group (2008) presents a more optimistic future where demand increases threefold by 2050 but emissions from aircraft manage to return to 2000 levels. They suggest that this can be achieved through a combination of new technologies and operational efficiency gains and with ten per cent reduction by using biofuels.

The MI Scenario assumes there will be a reduction in flying activity and distance travelled due to people changing their lifestyles by taking fewer long-haul holidays, international business trips and overall travelling less by air. UK internal flights could be eradicated through substitution of transportation modes that are less GHG intensive than aircraft and by information technology playing a key role in reducing domestic and international air travel in the business sector.

Fiscal measures: In the MI Scenario there will be higher ticket prices due to a rise in the price of oil and with the introduction of some form of carbon tax. Reductions in flying, based on price elasticities (Brons, 2002) for leisure travellers will reduce emissions by 27 per cent.

Behavioural: Aviation growth will continue, albeit at an increasingly slower rate, and a general "greening" of attitudes and behaviour will gradually smooth out growth rates in the latter half of the projection. Improvements in other transport modes will see people substituting air with rail travel, for example, when travelling from the UK to continental Europe. Businesses will replace physical travel with virtual meetings due to improved telecommunication. High speed internet will see video-conferencing and tele-presence systems commonplace in offices. The MI foresees a cultural-change in organisations towards travel through de-incentivising foreign travel and a stronger sense of corporate social responsibility.

Constraining capacity: The BAU Scenario was based on DfT forecasts that included additional capacity at Stansted Airport and a third runway at Heathrow Airport. In the MI Scenario, we assume that the policy that sanctioned these additional runways would be reversed (as subsequently occurred under the 2010 Conservative-Liberal Democrat coalition government with respect to the third runway at Heathrow airport). However, growth at airports in terms of air traffic movements and passenger numbers will continue at expected rates using existing airport capacity. The impact of constrained capacity was modelled in the DfT CO_2 forecasts for 2050 in which CO_2 emissions reduce from 59.9 Mt CO_2 under their 's12s2' scenario to 54 Mt CO_2 under their 'maximum use' (s02) scenario. Therefore, as a consequence of this intervention measure to constrain demand, we assume a 10 per cent reduction in aviation emissions under the MI Scenario.

Technology: The MI Scenario does not foresee a radical shift in aircraft design or a major switch to alternative fuels. It is assumed aircraft manufacturers meet their Advisory Council for Aeronautical Research in Europe (ACARE, 2001) objectives to improve fuel efficiency in new aircraft by 2030. After this, additional improve-ments to the design of existing aircraft, making smaller improvements in efficiency, will be retrofitted in the current fleet. ACARE suggests that from 2021, 0.5 per cent per annum increase in efficiency is feasible with further developments in new lightweight composite materials for turbines and compressors. Whilst the technol-ogy exists conceptually to produce more efficient aircraft, such as use of blended wing bodied aircraft, airlines are assumed to retain their existing aircraft fleets based on current designs. In the MI Scenario by 2050, the oldest and most fuel intensive aircraft will be scrapped or re-engineered. However, it is envisaged that more fuel efficient propfans, a hybrid between a turbofan and a turboprop engine, will be used for short-haul flights.

It is assumed that biofuels will only replace a small proportion of fossil fuel use in aviation due to limited production capacity constrained by the amount of land required to produce feedstock, issues relate to food security and the potential loss of biodiversity that could occur through land-use change. Hydrogen-based propulsion systems for aircraft are not yet technically feasible and would potentially pose a number of problems such as releasing water vapour (a GHG) into the atmosphere. Synthetic kerosene is another potential substitute fuel which could be used. However, its production process could lead to even more GHG emissions (CAEP, 2007). The use of these alternative fuels is not therefore, assumed for the MI Scenario.

As a result of the technological improvements, but not including radical new technology, CO2 emissions from aviation in the MI Scenario are reduced by 14 per cent in 2050. This is consistent with the scale of reduction suggested by the Sustainable Aviation Group (2008).

Other improvements are feasible in areas such as airspace management (NATS, 2008) where there could be a coordinated approach to flight planning (Stollery, 2008) and sharing airspace with military operations (European Commission, 2009) who themselves will have lower levels of activity and with better communication due to technological developments in global positioning satellites and telematics (EUROCONTROL, 2008).

The final results for aviation showed that a 56% reduction in CO2 emissions was possible (Table 12.1).

	Baseline Mt CO2	BAU 2050 Mt CO2	Reduction in CO2 relative to BAU	% reduction in MI relative to BAU
Baseline year	37.5			
BAU total		59.9		
MI (1)		54.0	5.9	-10
MI (2)		51.8	8.1	-14
MI (3)		52.1	7.8	-13
MI (4)		43.5	16.4	-27
MI (5)		55.0	4.9	-8.2
MI (6)		58.2	1.7	-2.8
All 6 MI measures combined		26.3	33.6	-56%

Table 12.1: Summary results for aviation from the interventions in the Maximum Impact (MI) scenario (numerical values are in Million Tonnes of CO2 except for the final column which is a percentage).
Source: Vallack et al (2014)

Conclusion

Aviation is a fast growing global activity associated with the spatial explosion of tourism, shopping, conferencing and business relationships. It is the highest level of development of the mobility paradigm and its supportive ideology. It is associated with a great deal of glamour and excitement notwithstanding the fact that the reality of sterile airports, lengthy queues and delays at over-bearing security controls and a total experience that is anything but glamorous. Aviation has also achieved a great deal in redefining the subject matter of economics. If the careful traveller within the EU would like to use trains to travel from Manchester to Rome (for example) the cost of the return rail trip will be £493.30 per person and the return air trip will be £64 (both costings were obtained on 22.9.14 for the same date 8 weeks ahead; Ryanair provide the air fare and "loco2.com" the rail fare). It is not credible that these two totals accurately reflect the true costs of vehicles, equipment, air traffic control, security, infrastructure, energy/fuel etc. Aviation has succeeded in transferring many costs to third parties as well as receiving subsidies and trains, in spite of receiving subsidies, have failed to achieve the same degree of success as aviation. Most of the discussion about air quality around airports, noise and health and aviation's proportionate responsibility for climate change are meaningless as long as this enormous price gulf separates two competing modes of transport. All those apart from the most ardent members of the Green Party or Greenpeace will be found choosing air travel over the rail option.

In spite of this enormous market failure there is still a lot that can be done to deal with the negative effects of airports and flying and the unresolved questions around public health. Whitelegg and Cambridge (2004) identified a small number of public policy interventions that would bring aviation fully into the climate change and public health frame. These included:

- The full internalisation of external costs.

- The adoption of WHO guidelines on noise levels (WHO, 1999) that should not be exceeded and the enforcement of these limit values around airports. This would imply a ban on night-time flights in the period 2300-0700.

- The requirement to reduce all air pollutant emissions from aircraft, airport activities and road traffic to and from the airport so that full conformity with European air quality guidelines and regulations is achieved.

- Air tickets would be subject to VAT and its equivalent in all 28 EU member states.

- The adoption of a clear strategy supported by appropriate fiscal instruments to shift all passenger journeys over 500kms in length from air to rail.

- The full incorporation of all aviation's greenhouse gas emissions into national and EU strategies to reduce these emissions by at least 80% by 2050.

Chapter 13
China and India

Introduction

One of the remarkable characteristics of the mobility paradigm is its enormous potential for replication. The rapid growth in the number of cars in China and India and the decline in walking, cycling and public transport represent a new and vigorous stage in the evolution of mobility and one that is likely to be repeated in other parts of Asia and throughout Africa. The growth of mobility is a global phenomenon that is re-shaping cities, regions and nations to support the next wave of growth. Its ability to mop up enormous budgets and transfer resources from the poor to the rich contributes to lack of progress in eradicating poverty and to severe, negative health effects that bear down disproportionately on billions of low income citizens.

The growth of motorised mobility in China and India is the result of the vigour and aggressiveness of the mobility paradigm. As a paradigm at the heart of public policy it had its origins in 19th century European countries and the USA and has been adopted globally. It has commandeered widespread support from the decision-making elites in countries with large numbers of relatively poor citizens. It has commandeered budgets when these are desperately needed for education, health care, rural accessibility, water and sanitation and it has been adopted with enthusiasm and determination in ways that other possible technological innovations have failed to match.

A comparison between mobility and some other possibilities for similar applications of budgets, vigour and determination is revealing. If the proponents of higher levels of mobility could have been reallocated to the provision of clean drinking water and sanitation the world would have eliminated the twin scourges of lack access to these basic components of a healthy life.

Europeans started sorting out clean, safe drinking water and sanitation around the same time that mobility took off via an extended programme of spending on canals, railways and roads. The canal era in the UK was well underway by the early 1800s to be followed by railways in the period 1840-1890 and significant improvements in road conditions and length as the 19th century progressed. On any measure we have been very successful in populating the world with railways, including China and India and this goes on. China is now embarking on a huge programme of high speed rail investment. Water is, however, a very different matter and our success with railways has not been replicated in the ways we deal with other major infrastructure networks e.g. clean drinking water and mains sewerage.

The United Nations (UN, 2014) has estimated that 748 million people "still draw their water from unimproved sources" and one billion people "still resort to open defecation." Our global success in spreading the opportunity to travel much longer distances with much faster modes of transport requiring much higher budgets has raced ahead of our ability to provide clean drinking water and sanitation to hundreds of millions. It very much looks like the ability to travel as far and as fast as possible lubricated by eye-wateringly large subsidies (see Chapter 5) and producing seriously damaging environmental consequences, including climate change, has a much higher priority than clean drinking water and sanitation.

China and India are developing very fast in terms of GDP per capita, military capability, road building, high speed trains, aviation and other areas of spending that feed the mobility paradigm. There has been progress with reducing poverty though nothing like the progress that is needed and nothing like the degree of progress that would be achieved if those responsible for increasing mobility could switch their mind-set and efforts and budgets to reducing poverty.

The United Nations (UN, 2014) estimates that 1.2 billion people live in extreme poverty (living on less than $1.25 per day). 32.9% of this total lives in India and 12.8% live in China. These are two countries currently experiencing an explosion in mobility and spending on the kind of transport infrastructure which can only benefit the richest groups of the population. Our lack of ability to intervene in a serious way to eliminate poverty and propagate the innovations that contribute to this goal is seriously lacking in the effort and determination devoted to mobility. There is also a direct link between the differential performance of these two innovation waves. If we spend huge amounts on mobility we have less to spend on clean drinking water and sanitation and less to spend on rural education and agriculture and these areas of spending can play a large part in eradicating poverty. We have chosen mobility and demoted the alternatives.

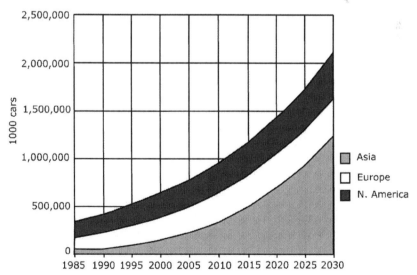

Figure 13.1: World vehicle populations
Source: Teufel (1995)

Global Trends

Teufel (1995) has drawn attention to some global trends that reveal the dramatic nature of the mobility explosion. The main prediction is an increase in the global vehicle fleet from 500 million in the mid-1990s to 2.3 billion in 2030. Figure 13.1 (previous page) and Figure 13.2 (below) show the global total of vehicles and the number of vehicles per 1000 people in the period 1985-2030.

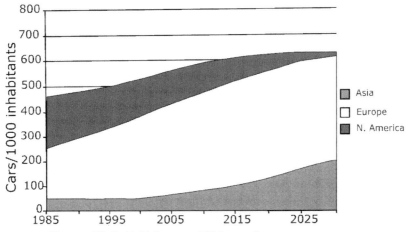

Figure 13.2: Vehicles per 1000 people
Source: Teufel (1995)

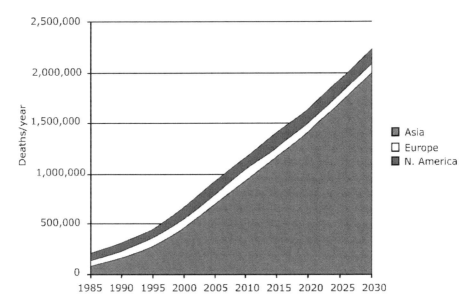

Figure 13.3: Deaths in the road traffic environment
Source: Teufel (1995)

The forecast figure of 2.3 billion by 2030 could well be an under-estimate given the total reported by the World Health Organisation of 1.6 billion (WHO, 2013).

Figure 13.3 (previous page) shows the very steep rise globally in deaths in the road traffic environment. The vertical scale is deaths per annum and the large shaded area describes Asia. By 2030 approximately 1.5 million citizens in Asia will be killed in road crashes. Teufel (1995) does not calculate the proportion of these that will take place in China or India but on a simple pro rata population basis China and India will account for more than half of these 1.5 million deaths.

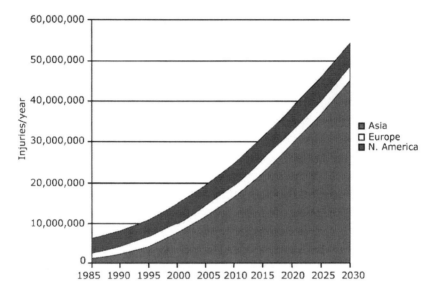

Figure 13.4: Traffic accidents (cars) globally: numbers of injured
Source: Teufel (1995)

In figure 13.4 the vertical scale is the number of injured citizens per annum. By 2030 there will be approximately 60 million injuries each year. The large shaded area on the graph describes Asia which will account for approximately 30 million injuries by 2030. Over half of these (on a population pro rata basis) will be in China and India.

Figure 13.5 (next page) is probably more relevant to China than it is to India, simply because of the huge scale of China's infrastructure programme and budgets to support new road, rail and airport construction. It is also relevant to trends in India e.g. the major urban extensions in the Salt Lake area of Kolkata and associated new roads, all of which take up valuable food growing land that previously supplied over 16 million people with food products. Competition for land for agriculture, transport infrastructure and urban development is severe in China. Transport infrastructure is also very demanding in land take. Figure 13.5 shows that Asia will require approximately 80,000 kms sq. of land for transport infrastructure to cope with car numbers by 2030. This is land for road building and parking. In the case of China and India this is land that would otherwise be available for food production, for afforestation, biodiversity and carbon sequestration.

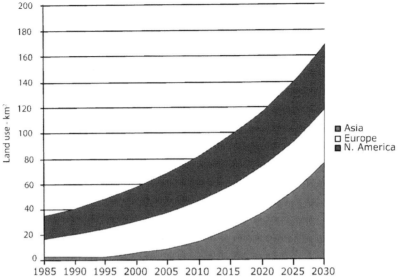

Figure 13.5: Land use demands of the private car (global figures)
Source: Teufel (1995)

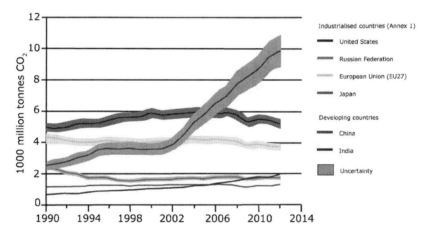

Fig 13.6: CO2 emissions from fossil fuel use and cement production in the top 6 emitting countries and the EU
Source: PBL and JRC (2013)

CO2 and climate change

"Comparing regional CO2 emission trends reveals large differences in underlying causes, which complicates the evaluation of the robustness of observed trends. For 2012, remarkable trends were seen in the top 3 emitting countries/regions, which accounted for 55% of total global CO2 emissions. Of these three, China (29% share) increased its CO2 emissions by 3%, which is low compared with annual increases of about 10% over the last decade. In the United States (16% share) and the European Union (11% share) CO2 emissions decreased by 4% and 1.6%, respectively. In addition, in India and Japan, emissions increased by 7% and 6%, and the Russian Federation noted a 1% decrease. Although China's CO2 emissions per capita are comparable to those in the EU and almost half of US emissions per capita, its CO2 emissions per USD in Gross Domestic Product (GDP) are almost double those of the EU and United States and similar to those of the Russian Federation" (PBL and JRC, 2013).

In terms of the actual quantities of CO2 emissions (not per capita) China is currently the largest emitter on the planet followed by the USA and then India. The country breakdown and trend can be seen in Figure 13.6 (previous page).

Per capita emissions tell a very different story (Table 13.1).

	2012	Change 1990-2012 (%)
USA	16.4	-17
EU	7.4	-19
China	7.1	233
India	1.6	110

Table 13.1: Per capita CO2 emissions in tonnes per person per annum
Source: PBL and JRC (2013)

The USA is still the world leader in per capita CO2 emissions just as it is in car ownership and annual car mileage. This sends a clear message to China and India in the sense that the political will to reduce CO2 emissions is dampened by the very high numbers from the USA and the association of that high level of emissions with economic and political success and global leadership. Put very crudely it is not an attractive proposition to reduce CO2 emissions in China and India when the USA is top of the list of CO2 emitters, has benefitted from 100 years or more of unrestrained fossil fuel burning and its associated emissions and shows very little sign of moving in the low carbon direction. The situation is even worse in Australia where a very high quality of life is routinely associated with very high CO2 emissions and a rapid withdrawal from any vestige of greenhouse gas mitigation.

China and India have a strong case for pursuing economic growth, increased mobility and higher CO2 emissions even though this trajectory will push the planet further and faster towards a point of catastrophe and no return (Rockstrom et al, 2009).

China is now "level-pegging" with the EU so there is no excuse for not implementing serious climate change mitigation strategies especially in transport. India is still very low indeed in terms of per capita CO2 emissions which give it a huge window of opportunity to indulge in some "leap frogging." Leap frogging means that India would not have to follow the same tedious year on year growth in mobility fuelled by huge subsidies and road building but could fast forward to a situation where all its cities were equipped with world best walking, cycling and public transport infrastructure and the multi-billion road building programme was switched off. This is possible and would be the single most significant step that could be taken to improve the quality of life of the bottom 50% of India's wage earners.

Fulton and Replogle (2014) have focused attention on the mobility explosion in China and India and its consequences for CO2 and on the availability of interventions that will reduce these emissions from the transport sector. In the case of China they predict that transport emissions will grow from 200 megatons pa today to 1200 megatons (1.2 gigatons) in 2050. In the case of India transport emissions are expected to grow from 70 megatons today to c500 megatons by 2050. In both countries the authors suggest a programme of increased investment in public transport to reduce the predicted totals of CO2 emissions.

The Fulton and Replogle report is methodologically very similar to the Vallack et al (2014) discussion of business as usual compared to the "maximum impact scenario." Just as we can totally decarbonise road and rail transport in the UK we can adopt similar interventions in China and India to reduce carbon emissions. Clearly there will be major differences in exactly what is done in each of these three countries. Any intervention has to mesh very closely with patterns of urban development and with wider social objectives e.g. poverty eradication in India and with the reality of vast areas of deeply rural India where walking, cycling, rickshaws and other forms of transport not seen in the developed world will have a large role to play. Public transport is part of the solution but for rural China and India there will have to be much more attention to a huge increase in locally based health care provision and very safe, secure walking and cycling facilities to tackle the twin problem of poor access and high levels of death and injury on the roads.

Mobility in China and India

Pucher et al (2007) have catalogued the most important transport trends in China and India. These are summarised in Figures 13.7, 13.8, 13.9 and 13.10.

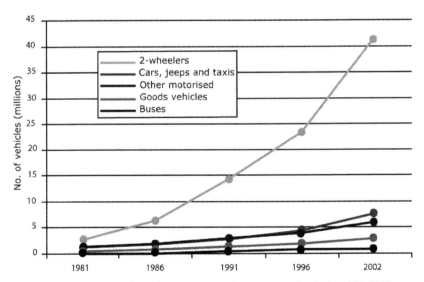

Figure 13.7: Growth of India's motor vehicle fleet by type of vehicle, 1981-2002 (in millions). The category "others" includes tractors, trailers motorised 3-wheelers such as auto rickshaws and other miscellaneous vehicles
Source: Pucher et al (2007)

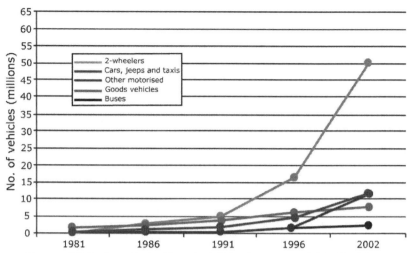

Figure 13.8: Growth (millions) of China's motor vehicle fleet by type of vehicle, 1981-2002
Source: Pucher et al (2007)

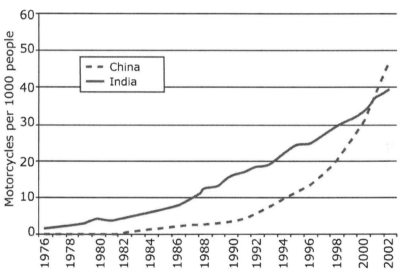

Figure 13.9: Rising motorcycle ownership in India and China, 1976-2002
Source: Pucher et al (2007)

The same article (Pucher et al, 2007) catalogues the very serious impacts of these rising levels of private motorised transport on air quality, death and injury in road crashes, noise and congestion. Of special interest and unusually in the transport literature the authors also explore the impact of these negative trends on the urban poor, highlighting the very severe consequences for the poor and the most vulnerable of the rising tide of motorised mobility.

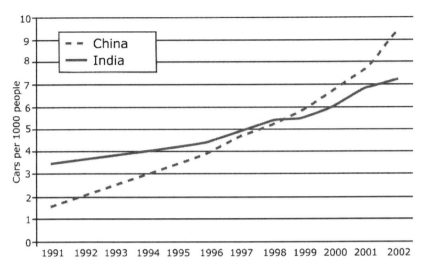

Figure 13.10: Rising car ownership in India and China, 1991-2002
Source: Pucher et al (2007)

Their conclusion emphasises one of the fundamental characteristics of the mobility explosion and its global impact. It has been deliberately designed and implemented. The severe negative consequences in China and India are not unintended consequences. They represent deliberate policy choices:

"Governments in both countries have strongly supported increased motorisation to stimulate their economies, to modernise their transport systems, and to meet the growing demand for cars and motorcycles among the middle and upper classes. It seems highly unlikely that the strong trend toward increased motorization can be stopped, let alone reversed, although perhaps it can be slowed" (Pucher et al 2007).

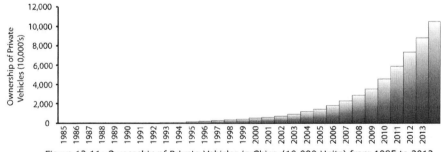

Figure 13.11: Ownership of Private Vehicles in China (10,000 Units) from 1985 to 2013
Source: Gao et al (2014)

Car ownership and use has seen a dramatic increase in China in the period 1985-2013 (Figure 13.11).

The growth in ownership of private vehicles is reflected in modal split data (Figure 13.12, next page), albeit for the capital city only.

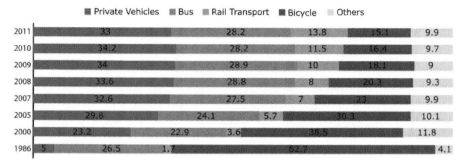

Figure 13.12: Travel Modes of Beijing Residents' Daily Trips (%) (1986-2011)
Source: Gao et al (2014)

The increase from 5% to 33% in the percentage of trips made by private vehicles is a remarkable transformation in a 25 year period and together with the collapse of bicycle use (62.7% to 15.1%) is a reminder of how quickly transportation choices can change. It is of course quite possible that the change can be in the other direction but the possibility of an "explosion" in walking, cycling and public transport use is rarely admitted in the urban transport debate. What appears to be acceptable in the direction so clearly demonstrated in China is not so acceptable the other way round.

Mani et al (nd) have discussed the mobility explosion in India. The mains points emerging from the study are:

- India's private motor vehicle market (motorised 2-wheelers and cars) grew by more than 85% between 2003 (around 59 million vehicles) and 2009-10 (around 110 million vehicles) at an average annual growth rate of 11%.

- Public transport mode share declined in Indian cities between 1994 and 2007.

- Modal share for non-motorised transport (walking and cycling) declined in all Indian cities. Cycling modal share has come down from an average of 30% in 1994 to less than 11% in 2007, attributable to an increase in trip length as a result of urban sprawl, inadequate facilities for cycling and growth in private motor vehicle ownership and use.

Consequences

The global burden of disease associated with road transport is much larger than normally assumed and is summarized in Table 13.2 (next page) (WHO, 2014).

The total of just over 1.5 million deaths and just under 80 million DALYS (Disability Adjusted Life Years) represents a significant amount of human misery, grief, tragedy, burden on health budgets and economic loss in low and middle income countries struggling with large demands on budgets.

China and India have been very successful indeed in transforming their respective life styles and economies in the direction pioneered by North America and European countries. Higher levels of car ownership and use and a reduction in walking, cycling and public transport use are deliberate outcomes of fiscal, economic growth

Rank	Cause	Deaths	DALYs
1	Ischaemic heart disease	90639	1,909,563
2	Stroke	58827	1,148,699
3	COPD	17266	346376
4	Lower respiratory infections	5670	489540
5	Lung cancer	11395	232646
6			
7			
8	Road injury	1,328,536	75,487,104
9			
10			
Total		1,512,333	79,613,928

Table 13.2: Leading causes of death worldwide, associated Disability Adjusted Life Years (DALYs), and burden attributable to motorised road transport, 2010
Source: WHO (2014)

and infrastructure investment policies that fail to take account of the appalling air quality, road deaths and injuries consequences. There are, of course , many other negative consequences but these dimensions tell their own powerful story about the unacceptable and damaging consequences of policies to promote private motorised transport.

Air pollution from vehicle exhaust emissions is a significant contributor to the burden of disease. Pollution from vehicles is the cause of 184,000 deaths globally, including 91,000 deaths from ischaemic heart disease, 59,000 deaths from stroke and 34,000 deaths from lower respiratory infections, chronic obstructive pulmonary disease and lung cancer" (World Bank, 2014).

WHO data for ambient (i.e. outdoor) air pollution deaths for China and India are summarised in Table 13.3.

	2004	2008
China	356,664	470,669
India	140,937	168,601

Table 13.3: Mortality associated with outdoor air pollution in China and India
Source: http://apps.who.int/gho/data/view.main.100320

Death and injury in the road traffic environment is also a very significant contributor to the burden of disease and premature mortality. There is also a lack of agreement on the statistics of death and injury. The WHO (2013) status report on road crash fatalities reports a figure of 70,134 deaths for China and 130,037 for India. The Chinese fatality rate is 20.5 per 100,000 population and India is 18.9 per 100,000 population. These numbers are very high indeed but the WHO reports death rates per 100,000 population that are much higher e.g. Dominican Republic (41.7), Iran (34.1), Iraq (31.5) and Nigeria (33.7). At the other end of the scale Sweden is 3.0, the UK is 3.7 and The Netherlands is 3.9.

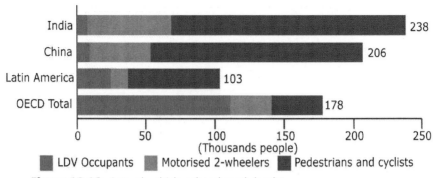

Figure 13.13: Annual vehicle related road deaths
Source: WBCSD Mobility 2030: Meeting the Challenges to Sustainability (2004)

Figure 13.13 summaries the death toll in road crashes.

The World Bank (2014) takes the view that road crash fatality numbers underestimate the true situation:

"Official government statistics substantially underreport road injuries. Estimates based on Global Burden of Disease 2010 data suggest, for example, that road injury deaths are more than twice the official statistics in India, four times those in China and more than six times the official numbers in parts of Africa" (World Bank, 2014).

More detail is provided in table 13.4.

	China	India
Official National Statistics	65,225	130,037
Global Burden of Disease Estimate	283,000	274,000
% Under-reporting	334	111

Table 13.4: Under-reporting in official statistics of road traffic deaths in China and India, 2010
Source: World Bank (2014)

Breaking out of the mobility paradigm: recommendations

According to Gang Hu (2003) Chinese cities are the most congested and polluted of all cities in the UITP database of urban transport (Kenworthy and Laube, 2001). This situation exists at relatively low levels of car ownership and use. The report "Urbanisation, energy and air pollution in China" (Chinese Academy of Engineering and Chinese Academy of Sciences, 2004) predicts that car ownership will increase from c 7.5 million in 2005 to 28.5 million in 2020 (at an 8% pa growth in GDP). Increased levels of income and wealth and urbanisation will fuel this increase in motor vehicles, most of which will be located in urban China.

The consequences for Chinese cities are severe:

- Increased levels of congestion.

- Increased levels of deaths and injuries from road traffic crashes.

- Loss of land to car-based infrastructure.

- Increased financial demands as a result of purchasing oil and increased insecurity resulting from oil depletion and geopolitical uncertainty over oil supplies.

These consequences apply with equal force to Indian cities and these are now examined and linked with very clear recommendations that will reduce risks, reduce uncertainties, improve environmental quality, improve the functioning of cities and improve the quality of life of all those living in urban areas in both countries.

Congestion

The problem

Congestion is the inevitable result of over-reliance on a space consuming technology (the car) in a geographical situation where space is in short supply. Cars need a great deal of space in which to drive, manoeuvre and park and the result of providing that space (or attempting to supply that space) is always inefficient and costly and underpriced to the user. Low and Gleeson (2003) put this very succinctly when comparing the number of people that can be moved by different modes of transport in an equivalent amount of space. Highways can carry 2500 people per hour per single lane of traffic; bus lanes can carry 7000 per hour in the same space and rail based transport 50,000 people per hour in the same space. Trying to accommodate the car demands significant areas of extra land and this land could otherwise be made available for housing, green space, nature, historic buildings, trees, public space or food production.

Pucher et al (2007) highlight the congestion problems of both countries. In Mumbai average traffic speeds fell by half in the period 1962-1993. In Delhi average speeds went down from 20-27kph in 1997 to 15kph in 2002. Speeds have also fallen in Chines cities. Average speeds in Beijing fell from 45kph in 1994 to 12kph in 2003. The average speed for buses declined to 9kph. 20% of Beijing's inner roads are completely gridlocked, with a traffic speed of less than 5kph (Pucher et al, 2007).

The UITP Millennium Cities Database (Kenworthy and Laube, 2001) shows Beijing to be one of the most congested cities in the world with average traffic speeds of 18kph. This can be compared with Singapore at 35kph or Hong Kong at 28kph. Only Bangkok experiences worse congestion than Beijing at an average speed of 15kph.

Traffic congestion at these serious levels causes extra pollution from slow moving or stationery vehicles. It also causes large economic losses. Congestion costs in London are estimated to be £37 million per week or over £1 billion per annum (Whitelegg, 2011).

Unless solutions are found to congestion problems in Beijing, Delhi, Shanghai and Mumbai, the economy of these cities will suffer serious loss of productivity and competitive advantage and will cease to be an attractive proposition for inward investment. Congestion is a problem that can be managed and the model for effective intervention is London.

The Recommendation

That Beijing and Delhi adopt a London-style congesting charging regime as soon as possible and that this be then rolled out to the largest 5 cities in each country.

The Rationale

Congestion is largely the result of an increase in demand for an underpriced resource. In this case the resource is road space. It is also the result of public policy that produces large allocations of public finance for road space, e.g. Beijing's 5 ring roads. A congestion charge or road pricing regime acts as a price signal to encourage a different pattern of use of road space. In many urban areas of the world (including Beijing) average trip length is less than 10km and can easily be achieved by public transport and, in some case, by walking and cycling. All these alternatives to the car are much more efficient in terms of space use and it is desirable to encourage the more efficient space users and at the same time discourage the less efficient. This can be done by introducing a congestion charge.

London introduced congestion charging in February 2003. It was introduced against a background of considerable controversy and media opposition by a strong mayor (Ken Livingstone) supported by an election victory in the mayoral race where congestion charging was a declared aim. It is now regarded as a great success and is currently being implemented in Stockholm. The recently published three-year review of the congestion charge provides evidence of the main results:

- Congestion levels are down by 30% when the 2004/5 situation is compared with 2002.
- Bus service reliability is up.
- Bus patronage is up 14%.
- The charge produced net revenue of £90 million most of which has been spent on improving bus services.
- There has been a reduction in road traffic accidents.
- There has been a reduction in NOx air pollution.
- There has been an increase in cycling.

The charge produces an income of over £0.5 million per day (110,000 vehicles each paying £5 or 75 RMB). This has now increased to £8 or 120 RMB. This income stream gives politicians a great deal of flexibility to develop sustainable transport initiatives (Whitelegg, 2011).

Increased levels of deaths and injuries from road traffic accidents

The problem

These data have already been reviewed in an earlier section of this paper and are not repeated here. Pucher et al (2007) identify road safety as a major problem in both countries:

"There has been an alarming increase in traffic fatalities in both China and India over the past three decades. Even controlling for population growth, the traffic fatality rate per million inhabitants has roughly quintupled in China and tripled in India."

Deaths and injuries in road crashes are closely associated with urbanisation. As more people live in cities and average income rise then motor vehicle numbers go up and road infrastructure is enlarged. More vehicles and more infrastructure increases the level of risk as pedestrians and bus users are faced with busy roads that sever their communities and have to be crossed. Increased levels of vehicle-pedestrian conflict will increase the number of deaths and serious injuries in Chinese and Indian cities as urbanisation levels increase.

The Recommendation

China and India should adopt the recommendations of the WHO review of road safety (2004) and set binding targets for death and injury reduction of at least 50% in deaths on a 2002 base to be achieved as quickly as possible. This should be implemented on the basis of international best practice reported in WHO (2004) and in the rationale (below).

Rationale

Deaths and injuries in road crashes are predictable and preventable. They are, moreover, not a transport issue but a public health issue linked fundamentally to the quality of life and welfare of citizens. Deaths and injuries can be reduced by detailed attention to the design of all aspects of the highway system and by detailed attention to behavioural modification e.g. driving at excessive speed, under the influence of drugs and alcohol etc.

Considerable progress has been made in reducing deaths and injuries in the UK, Sweden and Australia.

In the UK a 40% reduction in deaths and seriously injured to be achieved by 2010 has been agreed (the reduction for children is 50%).

In Sweden a road safety policy known as "Vision Zero" was passed by Parliament in 1997 which established an ethical dimension for road safety based on the principle that it is not acceptable for anyone to be killed in a road crash. This "Vision" is associated with detailed measures and targets e.g. a 50% reduction in deaths in the period 1996-2007.

In the state of Victoria (Australia) the state government has introduced an innovative road safety strategy to reduce deaths by 20% in 5 years.

In the case of middle and low income countries including China and India the highly coordinated Vision Zero approach may not be feasible. In these countries there is a much more urgent need for immediate action to remedy the infrastructure deficit for pedestrians, cyclists and bus users. A walk around Delhi or Kolkata rapidly reveals the urgent need for a major upgrade of pedestrian and cycling infrastructure. At the very minimum this should include:

- Widened pavements so that large volumes of pedestrians do not have to wander into the road.

- Safe, secure road crossing arrangements at frequent intervals so that pedestrians do not have to deal with large volumes of traffic as they struggle to cross a road.

- Segregated cycling facilities so that lorries and buses cannot enter the reserved bike lane.

- Special arrangements for bus users so that they can enter and exit the bus without wandering into the stream of traffic.

Chinese cities also need attention but the concentration of large volumes of the urban poor in the street environment of Indian cities makes the need more urgent in that country.

A good starting point for both Chinese and Indian cities is the guide to footpaths produced by ITDP (2013).

Loss of land to car-based infrastructure

The problem

Urbanisation consumes land. The dominant characteristic of urbanisation in many countries is urban sprawl or suburbanisation, which extends the spread of the city, increases the length of journeys that have to be made and increases automobile dependency as accessibility declines in response to spatial dispersion. As a rough "rule of thumb" a city becomes more unsustainable as the expansion of its land area grows faster than its growth in population. The process is not a simple cause and effect system. As cities grow in wealth its residents want larger homes and purchase cars. As car numbers increase so public bodies build more road infrastructure and lock the city into car dependency as it becomes increasingly difficult to satisfy trip purposes by walking, cycling and public transport. These sustainable modes then decline in importance, sometimes assisted by public policy that takes away space or discriminates in other ways against the pedestrian and the cyclist. Denser cities (compact cities) are more likely to be accessible and pedestrian friendly than dispersed cities. Denser cities will use less energy, produce less pollution and greenhouse gases and will be less demanding in terms of new transport infrastructure (highways, ring roads and parking spaces. This relationship is graphed in Figure 13.14.

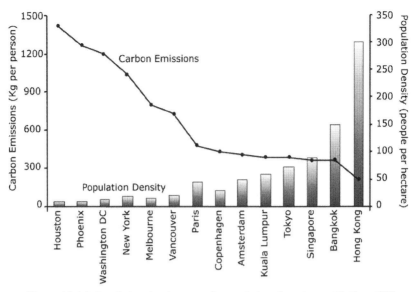

Figure 13.14: Population density vs. carbon emissions from transportation, 1990
Source: http://www.worldwatch.org/press/news/2002/06/28/

It is clearly the case that density has a bearing on trip length, modal choice and emissions but as Mees (2009) has shown "density is not destiny" and relatively low density urban areas are capable of shifting from car dependency to high levels of public transport use and a smaller modal share for cars. Equally the relatively high density and mixed use charcateristics of many German towns and cities can support very high levels of walking, cycling and public transport. The density debate in recent years (Burke and Dodson, 2014) has created a rather artificial oppositional character which is not necessary. We can have very attractive cities planned at higher densities but density in itself, unconnected with an intelligent, coordinated, account-able public transport design is not enough to produce desirable change. Mees (2009) shows very clearly that high quality public transport delivered within an accountable, coordinated city region governance model is a fundamental necessity for success.

Low density regardless of the excellence of its public transport system is associated with loss of land and there are many reasons why this loss should be resisted not least of which is the importance of "green lungs", nature, forest, ecology, outdoor recreational opportunities and food production for local markets. Land take for transport is particularly damaging.

Land take also impacts on agricultural output. Lester Brown (Brown, 2009) has made the link between land conversion and food production:

"Farmers are losing cropland and irrigation water to nonfarm uses. The conversion of cropland to other uses looms large in China, India, and the United States. China, with its massive industrial and residential construction and its paving of roads, highways, and parking lots for a fast-growing automobile fleet, may be the world leader in cropland loss. In the United States, suburban sprawl is consuming large tracts of farmland." He also makes the link between food for people and food for cars:

"Beyond this, the owners of the world's 910 million automobiles want to maintain their mobility, and most are not particularly concerned about whether their fuel comes from an oil well or a corn field. The orgy of investment in ethanol fuel distilleries that followed the 2005 surge in U.S. gas prices to $3 a gallon after Hurricane Katrina raised the annual growth in world grain consumption from roughly 20 million tons per year to more than 40 million tons in both 2007 and 2008, creating an epic competition between cars and people for grain."

Increasingly China and India will have to choose whether land is used to produce one final crop of tarmac and concrete or whether it can be permitted to grow food year on year. As in the case of oil dependency the loss of food output puts these two very large populations increasingly at the mercy of rising prices, volatile markets and vulnerability to international crises and wars over resource availability. The loss of land to highways and parking brings very significant consequences in terms of security, food production and fiscal demands.

Lester Brown again:

"In addition to losing cropland to severe soil erosion and desert expansion, the world is also losing cropland to various nonfarm uses, including residential construction, industrial construction, the paving of roads and parking lots, and airports, as well as to recreational uses, such as tennis courts and golf courses. If for every million people added to the world's population, 40,000 hectares of land are needed for nonfarm uses, adding more than 70 million people each year claims nearly 3 million hectares, part of which is agricultural land. The cropland share of land converted to nonfarm uses varies widely both within and among countries, but since cities are typically located on the most fertile land, it is often high— sometimes 100 percent.

China is currently working to create 100 million jobs in the manufacturing sector. With the average factory in China employing 100 workers, China needs to build 1 million factories—many of which will be sited on former cropland. India, with the annual addition of 18 million people and with accelerating economic growth, is facing similar pressures to convert cropland to other uses.

Residential building claims on cropland are also heavy. If we assume each dwelling houses on average five people, then adding 70 million or more people to world population each year means building 14 million houses or apartments annually.

While population growth spurs housing demand, rising incomes spur automobile ownership. The world automobile fleet is expanding by roughly 9 million per year. Each car requires the paving of some land, with the amount paved ranging from a high of 0.07 hectares per vehicle in sparsely populated countries such as the United States, Canada, or Brazil to a low of 0.02 hectares in densely populated areas such as Europe, Japan, China, and India.

As long as a fleet is growing, the country has no choice but to pave more land if it wants to avoid gridlock. In India, a country of only 8 million cars, each new million cars require the paving of roughly 20,000 hectares of land. If it is cropland, and of average productivity, this translates into roughly 50,000 tons of grain, enough to feed 250,000 people at the country's current meagre food consumption level. A country that will need to feed an additional 515 million people by 2050 cannot afford to cover scarce cropland with asphalt for roads and parking lots."

On the basis of Lester Brown's calculations it is likely that the land take for transport uses alone in China implied by the growth forecasts for car numbers to 2020 will take enough land away from food production that could otherwise have fed 70 million people. This is a severe challenge to sustainability.

Recommendation

That Chinese and Indian cities implement rigorous land use and transport plans that can minimise land take, maximise accessibility on foot, by bicycle and public transport, minimise land take for highways and parking. These plans can be modelled on the cities of Portland (Oregon), Copenhagen (Denmark) and Curitiba (Brazil). This can be modelled on the UK transport and land use policy known as "PPG13." Planning Policy Guidance Note 13 was published in 2006 and was official UK government policy on transport (DCLG, 2006). The objectives of PPG13 are:

"To integrate planning and transport at the national, regional, strategic and local level to:

- Promote more sustainable transport choices for both people and for moving freight;
- Promote accessibility to jobs, shopping, leisure facilities and services by public transport, walking and cycling, and
- Reduce the need to travel, especially by car."

Rationale

Spatially dispersed, car dependent cities are expensive to build and maintain, require large amounts of energy to sustain normal life, produce large amounts of pollution and greenhouse gases and increase vulnerability to energy shocks and food availability. Cities should be managed to achieve high densities, transit-oriented development, high modal share for walk and cycle and low levels of car ownership and use.

The consequences of urban sprawl are financially ruinous. Sheehan has summarised some work in this area:

"A number of studies in the US have quantified the extra infrastructure costs required by unfocussed development....if 25 million units of new housing in the US were to be accommodated between 2000-2025 in a more space efficient way, the nation would preserve more than 1.2 million hectares of land, require 3000 fewer miles of state roads and need 4.7 million fewer water and sewer "laterals." The result would be a saving of $250 billion" (Sheehan, 2001).

Facilitating a process of sustainable urbanisation will require clear and positive attention to land use, density, compact city ideas and sustainable transport. This is also economically attractive:

"Cities in which density is high and journeys are made mostly on foot, by bicycle and on public transport are the ones that spend the least on ensuring the mobility of city dwellers. In cities in developing countries, when walking, cycling and public transport are dominant, the total cost of journeys to the community is in the order of 6-8% of GDP, whereas it can exceed 14% in sprawling cities where 90% of journeys are made by car" (Vivier,2006).

It is clear that densely populated cities with high quality, safe access by relatively inexpensive modes of transport to all destinations actually cost less to run and leave more scarce cash available for education, health care, walking and sanitation.

Conclusion

China and India have embraced the mobility paradigm with vigour and enthusiasm. Car ownership rates are exploding, road traffic deaths and injuries have reached epidemic levels, air quality linked to vehicle exhaust emissions is a killer and the urban and rural poor struggle with the full weight of these negatives and very little improvement in basic walking and cycling conditions and very little improvement to public transport. Cities in both countries are drowning in gridlocked traffic and billions of dollars are thrown at new roads, flyovers and subsidies to vehicle manufacturing, all of which disproportionately benefit the rich and have nothing to offer to the poor. Cities are sprawling into the countryside and replacing productive food growing land with tarmac and concrete. The loss of local food growing potential will add to the burdens on the poor. Food products shipped in from distant origins will be more expensive and beyond the reach of the poor who currently consume local food available in local markets. They will also be deprived of their livelihood as small food producing units on land at the edge of these cities is taken away from them and often in very brutal circumstances. The loss of land, loss of an income and deprivation of human rights are all part of the price paid for the onward march of mobility.

There is some good news. China and India have demonstrated that they can mobilise funds and political initiative for sustainable transport projects and projects that genuinely improve conditions for those not owning or using cars. After describing 3 strategies in China for encouraging motorised transport Gao et al (2014) discuss measures that are intended to restrain car use:

"More strictly, strategies restricting purchase and use of private vehicles are now emerging in the megacities of China. For instance, the Beijing municipal govern-ment initiated the rationing of road space for the 2008 Olympics. Car use was curtailed according to the number on the license plates. Another example is limiting quota of new car registration in an attempt to curb unsustainable levels of automobile ownership (Song, 2013). This has since been further tightened by 37.5% to 150,000 per year in 2017. Up until the end of March 2014, Beijing, Shanghai,

Guiyang, Guangzhou, Shijiazhuang, Tianjin and Guangzhou had already joined in similar efforts to restrain car ownership. Shanghai has adopted the Singapore-style Certificate of Entitlement for new car purchase, which means bidding at an auction for the right to buy a new car."

In addition to measures to restrict car use there are measures to improve urban public transport:

"On the other hand, priority has now been transferred towards developing Urban Public Transport (UPT) at the national strategy level, especially Rapid Mass Transit (RMT) through the Twelfth Five-Year Plan. RMT, which includes Subway/Metro, Bus Rapid Transit (BRT) within cities, as well as inter-city High-Speed Rail (HSR), is now undergoing massive growth (Newman, Kenworthy and Glazebrook, 2013). Take the Chinese urban rail transport as an example. It was initially established in 1969 in Beijing, 106 years after the London Underground/Tube was first constructed in London (Strickfaden and Devlieger, 2011). Although developing urban rail transport was primarily embraced in the Tenth Five-Year Plan in China (2001-2005), Chinese investment in urban rail transport mushroomed from RMB 12 billion (2001) to RMB 260 billion (2012), with a 32.3% compound annual growth rate (2012-2013 China Urban Rail Transport Development Report). By the end of 2013, there were 87 urban rail lines in service among nineteen Chinese cities, with a total network length of 2,539 km."

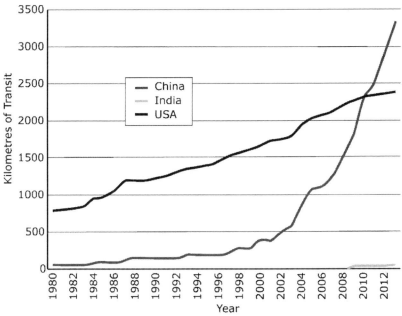

Fig 13.15: Growth of Rapid Transit by Country, 1980-2013
Source: Gadpelli (2014)

Both China and India have made progress with bus rapid transit systems (Gadpelli, 2014). These systems offer a significant improvement in the quality of bus services with segregated road space for the buses, modern low floor vehicles and safe infrastructure for passengers to board and alight. These are a considerable improvement on the familiar buses to be seen in cities like Kolkata (Calcutta) which are old, dirty, stuck in traffic and expose passengers to road traffic danger as they board and alight. India has several BRT projects in place including Ahmedabad, Delhi, Indore, Jaipur, Rajkot and Surat. China has over 30 BRT systems in place or under construction including Beijing and Guangzhou. Figure 13.15 shows the growth of BRT systems by country in the period 1980-2013.

The existence of some impressive vehicle restraint policies and high quality public transport projects does not alleviate the overwhelming dominance of negative effects of the rising tide of mobility on the 2.5 billion citizens in China and India. The scale of death and injury in crashes, the air quality problems and the enormous imbalance between spending on the rich and the poor all point to a serious deterioration in social justice, equity and quality of life in both countries and there is no sign of fundamental societal change in the direction of fairness, equity and sustainability.

Chapter 14
Conclusion

" In system change literature Donella Meadows defined a paradigm as the shared idea in the minds of society, the great big unstated assumptions, constitute that society's paradigm, or deepest set of beliefs about how the world works. These beliefs are unstated because it is unnecessary to state them – everyone already knows them" (Goepel, 2014).

This book is intended to promote the abandonment of the mobility paradigm and its replacement by something that maximises benefits to all sections of society locally and globally and minimises disbenefits. For convenience this is referred to as the accessibility paradigm.

The developed world has adopted the mobility paradigm as a core component of what a modern nation state must do. It is hard-wired into most aspects of public decision-taking, budgets and public opinion. Every country has its own wish list of projects and investments that are intended to increase mobility. This includes more road space, more airports, more high speed rail and strong financial incentives through investment and subsidy to support the fundamental objective of more mobility. Mobility has captured the ideological high ground. More mobility just sounds "good." Its list of associations is very impressive indeed; we can all have more freedom, more destinations to visit, more flexibility to live and work in widely separated locations and greater choice over schools and hospitals and where we live, regardless of the distances involved.

Challenging more mobility will never be easy but most of the chapters in this book have identified extremely serious negative consequences that flow from more mobility and the degree to which the growth of mobility is supported by huge public spending and a total disregard for social justice or spending that is in some way mediated by reference to fairness. For many in all societies (the poor, the old, the young, the disabled) spending is inadequate to meet basic needs. Spending is heavily skewed towards those who use cars a lot, those who want to travel very fast and very expensively by high speed rail lines and those who fly a lot. This bias excludes those who would like to walk or cycle to a local destination or those who want to live in circumstances not polluted by poor air quality, noise and the risk of death and serious injury.

There are many alternatives to the high mobility world currently on offer. The main thrust of this book has been to identify accessibility as a complete replacement for mobility but the alternatives have been captured through other perspectives including architecture (Gehl, 2010), social commentary and analysis (Illich, 1974 and Honore, 2005) and in politics (Sachs, 1993). The alternatives to mobility do not simply reduce or eliminate the negative consequences of year-on-year increases in mobility. They change the whole political, economic and social system so that it is kinder, more supportive of community life and values people far more than it values the ability to move around a lot in a vehicle. The essence of this fundamental shift in societal perspective has been concentrated by Sachs (1993) into "the 4 Lessens", described as a "new pathway for good living":

- In time: less speed, meaning more slowly and more reliably.

- In space: less distance, meaning closer and clearer.

- In the material world: less clutter meaning simpler and fewer.

- In the economy: less market, meaning providing and making for oneself.

This is the essence of the much needed and now overdue paradigm shift.

The mobility paradigm should be deleted and replaced by an accessibility paradigm that guarantees high quality walking, cycling, public transport and public health for all income groups, social groups and geographies. The accessibility paradigm requires a shift in thinking and willing, a shift in budgets and a strong social justice impulse that is lacking in most countries. It would produce more destinations that can be easily accessed by more people than a mobility paradigm. It recognises that distance is not a consumer commodity that we should set about increasing year-on-year and that the amount of distance we consume has no bearing on quality of life, satisfaction, happiness, community viability or health. We can all live much more satisfying and productive lives in supportive communities at lower levels of distances consumed and this is the objective of deleting mobility (i.e. more distance travelled) and replacing it with accessibility (many more things can be reached at a lower time, financial and environmental cost).

Politically an argument in favour of reducing mobility has a lot in common with an argument in late 18th century Liverpool, Bristol and Lancaster for abolishing the slave trade. Why would any right-minded person want to abolish something that played such a large part in national life, in the ideology of the British Empire and in the economic viability of several cities? Those that argued for abolition of the slave trade and then slavery itself had a tough time but they succeeded (Hague, 2008).

History is littered with dramatic examples of paradigm shift and there is no reason to suppose that the mobility paradigm will not follow slavery, children working down coal mines, the denial of voting rights to women and other ridiculous examples of 19th and early 20th century norms and be consigned to the dustbin.

Interestingly a major paradigm shift is already underway in Germany (Lechtenboehmer and Samadi, 2013) and has more than a passing relevance to mobility. The conceptual links between energy policy and transport policy are strong. Both have been dominated for decades by an unquestioned assumption that more is good and should be supported by heavy investment in new infrastructure. In the case of electricity generation this meant more power stations should be built and in the case of transport more roads, airports and high speed rail must be built. In both cases the subject of demand management was often talked about but not rigorously implemented. In both cases it was recognised that there are sound arguments for reducing the need to travel and reducing the amount of electricity used but this did not alter the fundamental trajectory of more is better.

In energy the paradigm has clearly shifted and in transport it has not. It is now quite normal to talk about energy efficiency in the home, workplace and other buildings and thereby find ways to reduce consumption. This is also associated with a strong policy emphasis on renewable energy to shift the mode of production from fossil-fuel rich and dangerous technologies (e.g. nuclear) to zero-carbon and benign technologies e.g. wind, wave and solar. In transport none of this shift has occurred. Politicians and other decision-takers have learned the language of demand management and the many advantages that flow from increasing the use of walking, cycling and public transport but the dominant paradigm is still about economic growth and the need for additional infrastructure that promotes the maximum consumption of time (speed) and space (distance).

Germany has now taken the energy debate to the stage of a fundamental paradigm shift (Lechtenboehmer and Samadi, 2013):

- Renewable energy will fully replace nuclear power by 2050.
- 8 nuclear power stations were ordered to shut down 3 days after Fukushima.
- The remaining 17 nuclear stations will close by 2022.
- Germany will not need to import electricity and can phase out 100% of fossil fuel generation.
- There will be reductions in demand to assist this transformation.
- The loss of nuclear power will be more than compensated for by more renewables, reduced net exports and reduced demand.
- CO_2 from German power stations will be 50% lower in 2020 compared to 1990.

The German government set up an Ethics Commission for a safe energy supply in March 2011 and this Commission supported the end of nuclear power because Germany has "less risky alternatives" (Ethics Commission for Safe Energy Supply, 2011).

The "Energiewende" has been summarised by Graubner (2013):

"In a nutshell, it describes the country's politically supervised shift in direction from nuclear and fossil fuels to renewable sources of energy. This idea of a changing power path helps explain the literal translation: "energy turn." The government says this transition will reduce security hazards and ensure Germany creates a greater share of its own power in future."

All of these changes in the German energy system map perfectly onto what is possible in the transport system. They have not yet been implemented in the German transport system but the debate is well in advance of that in any other EU country and the EU is well in advance of the debate in the USA.

Walking, cycling and public transport are the conceptual equivalents of renewable energy. The paradigm shift in mobility will be achieved by these "transport renewables" together with demand management (i.e. reducing the need to travel and the need to transport large amounts of freight over long distances). Put at its simplest we can manage perfectly well at much lower levels of distance consumption and we can re-balance cities, regions and neighbourhoods in cities so that accessibility is drastically improved and there are many more "things" to access that are nearer than they are in a high mobility world with its high fossil-fuel and highly subsidised evolution.

Importantly from a transport perspective Lechtenboehmer and Samadi (2013) conclude:

"The incompatibility between nuclear power and high shares of renewable energy is mainly due to the inability of the former (technically as well as economically) to provide the operational flexibility that the integration of high levels of fluctuating renewable energy sources requires."

On one level this is a very technical point about the way the electricity grid works but the point also applies at the policy and conceptual levels. We cannot achieve success in a transport transformation if we continue to design, build and fund the seriously non-sustainable alternatives. It is clear in attempts to increase the amount of cycling that, like solar energy, we can make some progress but fall short of a significant shift in favour of cycling. Just as nuclear and coal-fired power stations dominate the market for electricity, determine the shape of the grid and control the market so large amounts of additional road space and car parking determine the shape of our transport system and block the progress of attempts to increase cycling.

In terms of my general thesis that we are all locked into a mobility paradigm with strong ideological roots in progress, status and economic growth this is unsurprising. The growth of mobility is promoted with such a strong sense of will, determination, vigour and a complete lack of the same budgetary constraints applied to health care, drinking water and sanitation that there should be no surprise. It is the inevitable result of a determined effort by millions of professionals, academics, politicians, banks and manufacturers. What is surprising is that those countries with a strong reputation for ecological awareness and environmental policy at home are the same countries pursuing the reckless mobility agenda in China and India.

Germany has a well-deserved reputation for its high quality public transport, high modal share for bikes, the abolition of nuclear power, the energy transformation towards 100% renewable electricity, the complete decarbonisation of the Germany economy, the complete decarbonisation of the national rail system, car-free residential areas and a high quality of life in delightful cities. At the same time it is the power house of social, environmental and public health deterioration in China.

The Financial Times (22nd October 2014) reported that premium car sales in China are currently 1.3 million pa but confidently predicted to reach 2.5m-3m by 2020. German manufacturers supply about 80% of these vehicles. Table 14.1 summarises the scale of the involvement of German car manufacturers in China.

	Number of cars sold	Annual growth rate
Audi (Volkswagen)	490,000	20%
BMW	380,000	21%
Mercedes-Benz (Daimler)	215,000	11%

Table 14.1: Number of cars sold by German car companies in China
Source: 'JLR looks to turn a corner with new China plant', Financial Times, 22nd October 2014, Companies, page 15

In India the main Japanese Development Agency (JICA) has funded the construction of totally useless, expensive flyovers in Kolkata (Calcutta) on the discredited logic that they will help to ease congestion. They do not help to ease congestion but they help to perpetuate the illusion that we can build our way out of congestion and support higher levels of car manufacturing, car ownership and car use.

Transformational Change

The task that now has to be completed is a total transformation of the mobility paradigm and its replacement by something much healthier and with strong social justice, climate change and quality of life dimensions. Fortunately there are precedents for a transformational change (TC) approach (Mersmann et al 2014; Goepel, 2014).

TC is defined as follows:

"In this guidebook we broadly follow a definition given by the Sustainable Transitions Research Network, which talks about trans- formative change at the systems level, including major changes in production, consumption, and definitions given by some of its members who refer to radical, structural change of a societal (sub) system or a fundamental change in structure, culture and practices" (Mersmann et al 2014).

In order to adequately address the issue of climate change, a paradigm shift both in mitigation and adaptation activities is necessary. From global experiences of supporting sustainable development we know that despite all advances, persistent problems remain that time and again lead to set-backs in sustainable development pathways. Addressing these problems requires a critical, and sometimes radical, questioning of fundamental paradigms.

Achieving a major paradigm shift or transformational change will require a number of concrete changes that multiply the chances of overall success and release the virtuous virus of different models of thinking. Once we start to do things in a different way we will see that other things have to change as well and the many changes that become manifest will merge into a wider, deeper societal change that can be described as a paradigm shift. This is what happened with the German "Energiewende" described above. There was no single source of intelligence to work out that Germany could shift the whole energy system into 100% renewable, a shutdown of the nuclear option and a phase out of coal fired power stations. The steady growth of energy efficiency and demand management e.g. the PassivHaus movement, the spread of solar energy production encouraged by a generous feed-in tariff and the solid, best practice examples of places like Freiburg-im-Breisgau with its huge solar-PV industry, widespread adoption of PVs and iconic buildings also helped. Freiburg is widely recognised as a splendid place to live, work and invest in because it looks so good and works so well and has a reputation for innovation and boldness which maps onto different models of thinking very well indeed.

We now need a "Verkehrswende" (a transport transformation or turning point equivalent to the "Energiewende"). This is already underway though with very poor levels of awareness and a stubborn attitude of resistance to anything new and a fond attachment to the old model. Should anyone be in any doubt about the old model and its persistence they can look at a special issue of the journal "World Transport Policy and Practice" (Whitelegg, 2014) and its survey of some major British road schemes, all of which are justified by reference to discredited notions of job creation, time savings, congestion relief and economic regeneration. This is the mind-set that will now change and there are 10 specific tangible interventions that will promote and nurture the overall paradigm shift that will now take place.

The "Energiewende" morphs into the "Verkehrswende" in 10 easy steps:

1. Complete abolition of the concept of time savings in transport decision-making, cost benefit analysis, transport appraisal and all related methodologies and advice. This is discussed in Whitelegg (2012).

Expenditure on transport projects is usually justified on the basis of time savings and the monetarisation of that time saving is then set against the costs of the project to justify the project itself. This is the traditional cost benefit analysis that is now very old (Harrison and Quarmby, 1972). It is my contention here that this logic is fundamentally flawed and has created a world in which time savings are highly valued and can then be inserted into a project for a new motorway, bypass or high speed train to justify very large expenditures on the grounds that the benefits are much bigger than the costs.

There are several interrelated problems with the valuation of time as a key input into transport decision-taking and budget allocation. These problems have been explored in some detail in the literature (Whitelegg, 1993). The first and most important problem is the relationship originally identified by Marchetti (1994) and taken up by Metz (2008) that describes some very important constants in travel behaviour. Most of us will spend approximately one hour per day travelling and make approximately 3 trips per day. As technology changes over time and modes of transport become faster we substitute space for time. Put in very simple terms we consume the advantages and gains that are potentially available from saving time by increasing distance so that we maintain our "target" level of 1.1 hours of travel per day. In empirical terms this means that time savings have the effect of increasing distance travelled, space required for that travel, costs and the consumption of landscape by new transport infrastructure. The whole time saving logic and argument is based on the fiction that time savings provide individual and societal gains when they do not. They are consumed by extra distance.

2. Abolition of all subsidies to transport unless directly linked to climate change mitigation, reducing social exclusion and improving accessibility.

The European Environment Agency (2007) has estimated that the total annual subsidy to all transport modes in the EU is 270-290 billion Euros pa. Of this total 125 billion Euros goes to road transport, 73 billion to rail and 27-35 billion to aviation. These numbers are very large indeed and larger than many of the numbers currently under discussion within Eurozone finance ministries for bailing out Greece or other EU member states struggling with fiscal crises. It is not at all clear what gains are generated to European citizens by such largesse with public money beyond the rather obvious one that we are all encouraged to travel more, travel over longer distances and incur substantial personal and private costs to feed that level of mobility.

The removal of subsidies should be carried out at the same time as the full internalisation of external costs especially for aviation and lorries. Careful attention would be applied to the avoidance of double-counting. The objective is not to penalise airlines or passengers or road freight but to make sure that the activity is paying its way in routine operational mode and not being subsidized in addition. This is the very old "polluter pays principle" which is widely ignored as a basis for public policy.

The removal of subsidies and the full internalisation of external costs should be carried out at the same time as a full independent audit of all transport spending from public funds to identify which income group and geographies are gaining and which are losing. Are we spending more of our scarce public funds per capita on London than we are on Liverpool and why? Are we spending more of our scarce public spending on the wealthiest 10% of the population than on the poorest 10% and why?

3. The adoption of "service level agreements" for bus and rail services so that a high level of provision is maintained for a large number of origins and destinations at a frequency that corresponds with behavioural change towards these modes. This currently happens in Zurich and Basle and in rural areas in Switzerland and should be widely copied. It is also essential that buses and trains are integrated so that they can be used interchangeably on individual journeys and be designed in such a way to be cycle-friendly.

There are many examples of very high quality, integrated public transport systems e.g. the urban systems in Vienna and Zurich and rural public transport in Switzerland. The connectivity and ease of use associated with bus, tram and heavy rail in the Basle region of Switzerland puts the UK and many parts of the world to shame. The small town of Dornach (population 6468) is well connected to Basle by tram and train. The small settlement of Gempen (population 854) has 14 buses each day to the high quality bus station in Dornach. This level of connectivity simply does not exist in the UK and it is not difficult or expensive to upgrade to Swiss service levels.

4. Adopt the Vision Zero Swedish road safety policy (Whitelegg and Haq, 2006) and the zero carbon policy for road and rail transport (Vallack et al, 2014). It is very clear that the current approach to road safety globally (with some important exceptions e.g. Sweden) is defective and that there should be a presumption of zero death and zero serious injuries underpinning all our thinking and interventions (Johnston et al, 2014). It is a major stain on a so-called civilised society that we accept over 3000 deaths every day globally and refuse to embrace a total safe-system designed, vision zero policy.

It is very clear that climate change is a very serious threat globally and locally and that reducing greenhouse gases from all sources as quickly as possible, is a sensible, precautionary, economic and public health strategy to protect life and maximnsied the chances that all of us in every country can live a reasonably healthy, satisfying, crisis-free existence. Currently we are failing to reduce these emissions. Transport is responsible for 25-30% of these emissions and these must be reduced. There are no technical or financial problems to prevent the reduction in transport emissions and Vallack et al (2014) have shown exactly how this could be done. It is not being done and it must be done.

5. Eighty percent of the world population lives in cities. Cities are failing to deliver a high quality of life for their residents. Traffic danger, noise, pollution, death and injury on the roads and the loss of community vitality, social support and social interaction contribute to poor quality urban environments. Jan Gehl has shown how this decline can be reversed (Gehl, 2010). The full list of Gehl's recommendations should be implemented in all cities, globally.

Gehl recommends corrective measures to create or restore high quality city living:

"Acknowledging the importance of an inviting public realm, gradually reconquering the public spaces taken over by cars in the past 5 decades has become a key priority in cities throughout the world. Reconquering means gradually shifting portions of the surface space currently used for cars to people activities. This shift should go together with a greater awareness of the public realm and its importance for the social fabric of the citizens. Reconquered cities apply a holistic approach to their public realm in which the total experience of being present in and moving through public space is cared for with a new sensitivity."

Gehl coins the terms "reconquering cities" and "reconquered cities" to describe the process and the desirable end point of policies that improve the built environment, restores quality places and celebrate people rather than cars. He lists 11 cities that are being "reconquered" (Portland, USA; Curitiba, Brazil; Copenhagen, Denmark; Lyon, France; Melbourne, Australia; Bogota, Colombia; Strasbourg, France; Freiburg, Germany; Cordoba, Spain).

None are in the UK.

Gehl's work is central to the task of transformational change and abandoning the mobility paradigm. It has already happened in one place so all those involved with transport, quality of life, policy and urban planning can go to Freiburg-im-Breisgau and see the "real thing."

In Freiburg im Breisgau in southern Germany the street has been reclaimed for ordinary, everyday use by residents and all age groups. Freiburg has a very distinctive transport, public realm, spatial planning and green space policy that restore the role of the street in community life (Stadt Freiburg, 2010).

The elements that feed into a high quality living environment with streets for people are clear, effective and transferable and include:

- General 30kph/20mph speed limits on all residential roads (the largest roads are excluded). 90% of Freiburg's 240,000 residents live on streets that are limited to 30kph/20mph.

- Cycling infrastructure and cycling promotion are high on the political agenda and have produced the environmental and safety/security conditions that encourage cycling with the result that 26% of all trips every day are by bike. The same can be said for walking with a 23% modal share. For the year 2020 Freiburg plans to increase cycling to 28% and walking 24% modal shares and produce a 20% share for public transport leaving 28% for the car.

- The spatial planning policy is organised to maintain and intensify the compact city idea (Newman et al, 2009). The city resists attempts to expand the suburbs and blocks plans for out of town shopping centres and retail parks to maintain strong urban centre retailing and services and strong local shopping centres that can supply everyday needs (Salomon, 2010).

- High quality public transport especially trams and buses that are fully integrated with both interchange and ticketing and integrated with the development of new car-reduced areas in Vauban and Rieselfeld. The number of trips by public transport pa in Freiburg has increased from 27.3 million in 1980 to 72.8 million in 2009.

- Vauban and Rieselfeld. Vauban is a new residential area in Freiburg on the site of a former French barracks with a population of 5000 and Rieselfeld is a still expanding new residential area with 10,500 residents (Stadt Freiburg, 2010). Both areas are served by tram, both have exceptionally high energy efficient homes and photo voltaic installations and both are car-reduced in the sense that car free living is encouraged and "Aufenthaltsqualitaet in öffentlichen Raum" is a design principle that is actually implemented. The English translation of this concept would be "the quality of the public realm that encourages residents to spend time in that realm." As noted earlier the concept has very little resonance with thinking in the UK.

- The centre of Freiburg is almost totally car-free and in a way that is significantly different to the pedestrian areas of York or Lancaster or Oxford where cars and lorries frequently invade the pedestrian areas and destroy the "Aufenthaltsqual-itaet."

- Freiburg attaches a very high importance to the quality of the public realm generally including parks and green spaces, urban ecology, tree planting and the famous small streams that run through the city centre, the "Baechle" (Stadt Freiburg,2009). Freiburg has planted 22,000 trees on streets, has 3,800 small garden allotments and 160 play areas.

6. Prioritise accessibility and geography in the provision of health care, education, libraries, swimming pools and post offices so that decisions about location and size are scrutinised for their impact on journey distances and the availability of public transport for those trips. There shall be an "access presumption" so that, for example, decisions do not disadvantage those without a car or those for whatever reason choosing to use public transport to use these services.

7. Thirty kilometres per hour to be set as a default, system wide speed limit on all residential roads including roads and highways that go through small villages. This will follow the model of similar wide-area treatments in the UK and in major German cities. The planning assumption will be that major cultural change (very much like drink driving attitudes) will deliver the change in speeds and will not require extra police enforcement. In that small number of cases where drivers do not obey the limit there shall be enforcement of a traditional policing nature but with a large input from innovative enforcement measures e.g. "community speedwatch" (Community Speedwatch, 2014).

8. Demolish large capacity urban highways that bring huge volumes of traffic into cities and send a very clear signal that the city is designed for cars. The implementation of an accessibility paradigm and the abandonment of the mobility paradigm are not likely to happen when such strong symbols are left in place. This has already happened in Seoul in Korea and needs to happen in Bremen, Liverpool, Manchester and Birmingham and most other places. The demolition must be associated with a transformation of time, space and opportunity. It delivers an opportunity to promote the slow modes with all the benefits that flow from higher percentages of trips made on foot and by bike (Honore, 2005). It redefines spatial form, awareness and sensitivity to provide spaces that are nourishing, spiritual and bring nature into the city and it will contribute to improved access via high quality spaces to destinations. This is the much needed "Verkehrswende."

9. We need to develop and implement new forms of democratic participation. At the moment families living on heavily trafficked streets, with children and with friends on the other side of the street have no rights at all. The mobility paradigm with all its promise of freedom has denied substantial segments of the population of very important freedoms. Residents on busy streets must be given the power to redefine the street. This need not be a complete ban on cars though that has to be discussed. It can be much wider pavements (sidewalks), tree planting, outdoor sitting areas and 5mph speed limits. The discussion and decisions would be led by the residents who would also listen to the traditional viewpoints of the planners and

the engineers but the presumption would be in favour of "streets for people" and not streets for cars.

10. On a larger geographical scale it is important to recognise the very special situations in China and India. In these countries there is an absolute, over-riding requirement for a complete re-engineering of pedestrian and cycling space. All 2.5 billion residents in these countries need segregated, high quality walking and cycling facilities connecting all residential areas with all destinations. It is unacceptable to have an expert-led discussion of "infrastructure" which usually means roads and high speed rail whilst at the same time basic infrastructure that can be used by everyone is airbrushed out of the picture. It is not even on the agenda. It is abundantly clear that in China and India and throughout all low and middle income countries the nation state and global organisations must prioritise clean drinking water, sanitation and walking/cycling facilities for everyone.

The evidence pointing to the need for a major paradigm shift is large, credible and persuasive. The steps that have to be taken to get there (1-10 above) are not difficult to adopt so will it happen?

The answer is probably "no" when looked at from the perspective of 2016 in a country (the UK) still enraptured by the mobility ideology and redefining it in terms of reducing deficits, boosting jobs, and promoting very expensive infrastructure. This is not a problem. There is no need for a full "frontal assault" on the mobility paradigm and it would not be helpful to adopt such an all-embracing and overwhelming policy change. The paradigm shift will happen. It is inevitable and like the Energiewende in Germany it will happen as a result of synergistic, cumulative change in several closely related areas that are already underway. The changes already underway are:

- A fundamental shift in road safety policy to move towards the Swedish Vision Zero approach.

- The acceleration of zero carbon transport alternatives so that we will be able to make many more routine choices about modes of transport that are calm, zero polluting, supportive of healthy people and healthy communities and child friendly.

- The realisation that we have a major public health challenge in front of us. Sometimes this emerges as deaths from poor air quality, sometimes as obesity and Type 2 diabetes and sometimes as death and serious injury. All of these are part of the same love affair with the car and mobility and all require the promotion of so-called "active travel" which is gaining public health support globally.

Like all major examples of social change, inevitability goes with the requirement for constant repetition, persuasion, reinforcement and engagement. Britain did not abolish the slave trade and then slavery itself because it woke up one morning and decided it was the right thing to. Abolition followed serious, sustained effort to bring about that change. The British Empire did not wake up one morning and suddenly agree with the "Quit India" campaign. The decision to abandon "the jewel in the crown" was the result of sustained effort and by major political changes that made it inevitable. A similar story can be told about the Berlin Wall in 1989 and the reunification of Germany.

Sorting out mobility, transport, urban design and public health may not be as momentous as slavery, India and Berlin but it is up there with a list of major social changes and paradigm shifts that have happened or are waiting to happen and it will happen.

The End

References

ACARE (2001) European Aeronautics: Vision for 2020. Advisory Council for Aeronautics Research in Europe, Brussels, Belgium.

Agren, A (2013) Air pollution causes 210,000 deaths each year, Acid News, Number 3, October 2013, page 14, reporting on the MIT study "Air Pollution and early deaths in the United States. Part 1 Quantifying the impact of major sectors in 2005, MIT News, 29 August 2013.

Appleyard, D (1981) Livable Streets, Berkeley, University of California Press.

Appleyard, D and Lintell, M (1971) The environmental quality of city streets: the residents view point, Journal of the American Institute of Planners, Volume 38, 84-101.

Armitage, A (1980) Lorries, people and the environment, Department of Transport, UK.

Ausubel, J H and Marchetti, C (2001) The evolution of transport, The Industrial Physicist, April/May 2001, American Institute of Physics, 20-24.

Ausubel, J H, Marchetti, C and Meyer P (2005) Towards green mobility: the evolution of transport, Programme for the Human Environment, The Rockefeller University, New York.

Baer, P, Athanasiou, T, Kartha, S, Kemp-Benedict, E (2008), The Greenhouse Development Rights Framework. The right to development in a climate constrained world, Heinrich Boell Stiftung, Berlin.

Bassett Jr, D R, Pucher, J, Buehler, R, Thompson, D L, & Crouter, S E (2008). Walking, cycling, and obesity rates in Europe, North America, and Australia. Journal of Physical Activity & Health, 5(6) 795-814.

BBC (2009) Are women cyclists in more danger than men? Article by Sarah Bell, 9 October 2009.

Bere, J (2013) An introduction to Passive House, Royal Institute of British Architects, London.

Bestufs (2007) Best Practice Update 2007, Part 1. Road pricing and urban freight transport. Urban freight platforms.

Boege, S (1995) The well-travelled yoghurt pot: lessons for new freight transport policies and regional production, World Transport Policy and Practice, Volume 1, Number 1, 7-11.

Brons, M, Pels, E, Nijkamp, P and Rietveld, P (2002) Price elasticities of demand for passenger air travel: a meta-analysis. Journal of Air Transport Management 8, 165-175.

Brown, L (2009) Plan B 4.0. Mobilizing to save civilization, Earth Policy Institute, W W Norton and Company.

Burke, M and Dodson, J (2014) Suburban density: disrupting the density debate in Gleeson, B and Beza, B (2014) The Public City. Essays in honour of Paul Mees, Melbourne University Press, 132-148.

CAA (2012) Passenger Survey Report, Civil Aviation Authority, Table 14.7.

CAEP (2007) The potential use of alternative fuels for aviation.

Campbell, I (2011) Analysis of Portsmouth 20mph Road Casualty Data with Allowance for Random Variation, IC Statistical Services.

Chinese Academy of Engineering, Chinese Academy of Sciences, National Academy of Engineering, National Research Council (2004) Urbanisation, energy and air pollution in China: the challenges ahead. Proceedings of a Symposium. The National Academies Press, Washington DC, USA.

Civitas (2008) 'Graz application for 2008 "City of the Year" award', Civitas Project.

Civitas (2009) 'Nantes application for 2009 "City of the Year" award', Civitas Project.

Civitas (2010) Evaluation Report on Bremen Civitas Projects

Clark, C, Head J and Stansfield, S A (2013) Longitudinal effects of aircraft noise exposure on children's health and cognition: A six-year follow-up of the UK RANCH cohort. Journal of Environmental Psychology.
35: 1-9. DOI: 10.1016/j.jenvp.2013.03.002.

Clean Air London (2013) Quick guide to air pollution and the "year of air" in 2013.

Clifton, J (2011) Social isolation among older Londoners, Institute for Public Policy Research (IPPR), London.

Community Speedwatch (2014) (www.communityspeedwatch.co.uk)

Cramer, M (2014) Presentation to a European Parliament meeting in Brussels on 12th February 2014,"Low carbon transport: lost on the political agenda.

Dalkmann, H and Brannigan, C (2007) Transport and Climate Change. Module 5e: sustainable transport: a sourcebook for policy makers in developing cities, Deutsche Gesellschaft fuer Technische Zusammenarbeit (GTZ), Eschborn

Daily Telegraph (2015) Greece will leave euro, predicts Greenspan, Business Section, 9th February 2015.

Davis, A (2010a) Essential Evidence Number 58, Car use, weight gain and climate change, Bristol City Council, UK.

Davis, A (2010b) Essential Evidence Number 57, Community Severance, Bristol City Council, UK.

Davis, A (2012a) Essential Evidence Number 82, Severance, social networks and health, Bristol City Council, UK.

Davis, A (2012b) Essential Evidence Number 91, The impact of free older persons' bus pass on active travel in England, Bristol City Council, UK.

Davis, A (2013) Essential Evidence Number 110, Blaming children for child pedestrian injuries, Bristol City Council, UK.

Davis, A, Valsecchi, C, and Fergusson M (2007) Unfit for purpose: how car use fuels climate change and obesity, Institute for European Environment Policy, London.

DCLG (2006) Planning Policy Guidance Note 13: Transport, Department of Communities and Local Government, UK.

Dean, J S (1947) Murder most foul. A study of the road deaths problem, First printed in Great Britain by Watford Printers Ltd, Watford. Re-printed by RoadPeace, London, 2007.

Den Boer (2009) Are trucks taking their toll? The environmental, safety and congestion impacts of lorries in the EU, CE Delft, The Netherlands.

DfT (2006) Visioning and Backcasting for UK transport policy (VIBAT), Stage 3 report, Policy Packaging and Pathways, The Bartlett School of Planning and Halcrow Group.

DfT (2009) UK Air Passenger Demand and CO2 Forecasts. Department for Transport, London.

DfT (2010) Interim Evaluation of the Implementation of 20mph Speed Limits in Portsmouth: final report, September 2010, Department for Transport, London.

DfT (2013) Action for roads. A network for the 21st century Department for Transport, London, July 201.

Dodson, J and Sipe, N (2008) Shocking the suburbs: oil vulnerability in the Australian City, Sydney, University of New South Wales Press.

Dong, C, Stephen H, Richards, G, Baoshan, H & Ximiao Jiang, (2013) Identifying the factors contributing to the severity of truck-involved crashes, International Journal of Injury Control and Safety Promotion, Published online 18th October 2013.

Douthwaite, R (1992) The Growth Illusion: how economic growth has enriched the few, impoverished the many and endangered the planet, Gabriola Island BC, Canada, New Society Publishers, re-issued and updated in 1999.

Douthwaite, R (1996) Short Circuit. Strengthening local economies for security in an unstable world, Green Books, Totnes Devon.

Dyos, H J and D H Aldcroft (1969) British Transport. An economic survey from the seventeenth century to the twentieth, Leicester University Press, UK.

Elvebakk, B and Steiro, T (2009) First principles, second hand: perceptions and interpretations of vision zero in Norway, Safety Science, 47, 2009, 958-966.

Elvik, R, (1999) Can injury prevention efforts go too far? Reflections on some possible implications of Vision Zero for road accident fatalities. Accident Analysis and Prevention 31, 265–286.

Elvik, R, (2003) How would setting policy priorities according to cost-benefit analyses affect the provision of road safety? Accident Analysis and Prevention 35, 557–570.

Elvik, R (2008) Road safety management by objectives: a critical analysis of the Norwegian approach, Accident Analysis and Prevention 40 (2008), 1115-1122.

Elvik, R and Amundsen A H (2000) Improving road safety in Sweden. Main report. TOI Report 490, Oslo Institute of Transport Economics.

Ethics Commission for a Safe Energy Supply (2011), Germany's Energy Transition: A Collective Endeavour for the Future, German Federal Government, Berlin, 30 May 2011.

EUROCONTROL (2008) Long-Term Forecast Flight Movements 2010 – 2030.

European Commission (1999) EU focus on clean air.

European Commission (2009) European Air Traffic Management Master Plan. European Commission, SESAR and EUROCONTROL.

European Commission (2012) EU transport in figures. Statistical pocketbook.

European Commission (2013a) Smart, green and integrated transport, Horizon 2020 Work Package 2014-2015, H2020-MG-2014/2015, Draft 18th October 2013.

European Commission (2013b) Council decision establishing the specific programme implementing Horizon 2020, the framework programme for research and innovation (2014-2020), Version 8, October 2013, Work Programme 2014-2015, 10. Energy Challenge.

European Commission (2013c) Infrastructure- TEN-T News, 19.11.13 "Parliament backs new EU infrastructure policy".

European Commission (2015) Transport in Figures. Statistical Pocket Book http://ec.europa.eu/transport/facts-fundings/statistics/doc/2015/pocketbook2015.pdf

European Environment Agency (2007) Size, structure and distribution of transport subsidy in Europe, EEA Technical Report No 3/2007 Copenhagen.

European Environment Agency (2008) Success stories within the road transport sector on reducing greenhouse gas emissions and producing ancillary benefits, European Environment Agency, Copenhagen, Denmark, Technical Report No2/2008.

European Environment Agency (2009) Ensuring Quality of Life in Europe's Cities and Towns: tackling the environmental challenges driven by European and global change. Technical Report 5/2009, Copenhagen: EEA.

European Environment Agency (2013) A close look at urban transport. TERM 20132: transport indicators tracking progress towards environmental targets in Europe, EEA Report 11/2013, Copenhagen.

European Environment Agency (2015) Air Quality in Europe-2015, EEA Report 5/2015, Copenhagen

Foletta, N and Field, S (2011) Europe's vibrant low car (bon) communities, ITDP, New York

Fahlquist, J N (2006) Responsibility ascriptions and Vision Zero, Accident Analysis and Prevention, 38 (2006), 1113-1118.

Frank, L, Andresen, M and Schmidt, T (2004) Obesity relationships with community design, physical activity and time spent in cars, Am J Prev Med 27:87-96.

Freie Hansestadt Bremen (2008) Aktionsprogramm Klimaschutz 2010, 5th September 2008.

Fulton, L M and Replogle, M (2014) A global high shift scenario: impacts and potential for more public transport, walking and cycling with lower car use, ITDP, New York.

Gao, Y, Kenworthy, J and Newman, P (2014) Growth of a Giant: A Historical and Current Perspective on the Chinese Automobile Industry Paper presented to the European Transport Conference, Frankfurt, September 29 to October 1, 2014.

Gadpelli, S (2014) Bus Rapid Transit for Indian Cities, ITDP, New York.

Garrard, J. (2008) Safe Speed: promoting safe walking and cycling by reducing traffic speed, Melbourne: Heart Foundation.

Gate, D (2014) The Heysham M6 Link Road, World Transport Policy and Practice, volume 20, number 2/3, 33-42.

Gehl Architects (2004) Melbourne: places for people.

Gehl, J (2010) Cities for People, Island Press, Canada.

Glotz-Richter, M. (2010) To bring it all together in the real world. Walking, cycling, public transport and the role of car sharing, Paper presented at the World Car-Free City Conference, York, UK, July 2010.

Goepel, M (2014) Navigating a new agenda. Questions and answers on paradigm shift and transformational change, Wuppertal Institute, Germany.

Graupner, H (2013) What exactly is Germany's "Energiewende", Deutsche Welle, 22.1.13.

Grayling, T, Hallam, D, Andersen, R and Glaister, S (2002) Streets ahead. Safe and liveable streets for children, Institute for Public Policy Research, London.

Gruen, A, (1992) The insanity of normality: realism as sickness, towards understanding human destructiveness. Grove Weidenfeld, New York.

Hague, W (2008) William Wilberforce. The life of the great anti-slave trade campaigner, Harper Perennial.

Hansell, A et al (2013) Aircraft noise and cardiovascular disease near Heathrow airport in London: small area study.

Haq, G and Whitelegg, J (2014) The insanity of normality, World Transport Policy and Practice, volume 20, number 2/3, 114-126.

Hart, J and Parkhurst, J (2011) Driven to excess: impact of motor vehicles on the quality of life of residents in three streets in Bristol, World Transport Policy and Practice, volume 17, number 2, 12-30.

Harrison, A J and Quarmby, D A (1972), The value of time in Layard, R (ed) Cost benefit analysis: selected readings, Penguin Books.

Heaps, C, Erikson, P, Kartha, S and Eric Kemp-Benedict (2009) Europe's share of the climate challenges. Domestic actions and international obligations to protect the planet, Stockholm Environment Institute, Boston, USA.

Herrstedt, L. (1992) 'Traffic calming design—a speed management method: Danish experiences on environmentally adapted through roads', Accident Analysis and Prevention, 24:3–16.

Hickman, R and D Banister (2005) Towards a 60% reduction in UK transport CO2 emissions: a scenario building and backcasting approach.

Hillman, M, Adams, J and Whitelegg, J (1990) One false move. A study of children's independent mobility, Policy Studies Institute, London.

Hokstad, P and Vatn, J (2008) Ethical dilemmas in traffic safety work, Safety Science 46 (2008) 1435-1449.

Holzapfel, H (1995) Violence and the car. World Transport Policy and Practice, Volume 1, Number 1, 41-44.

Holzapfel, H (1995) Potential forms of regional economic co-operation to reduce goods transport, World Transport Policy and Practice, Volume 1, Number 2, 34-39.

Holzapfel, H (2012) Some remarks about mobility, World Transport Policy and Practice, Volume 18, Number 1, 7-11.

Holzapfel, H (2013) Personal communication, 7th December 2013.

Holzapfel, H (2014) Urbanism and Transport, Routledge, New York and Abingdon.

Honore, C (2005) In praise of slow: how a worldwide movement is challenging the cult of speed, Harper Collins, New York.

House of Commons (2011) Air Quality: a follow-up report, Environmental Audit Committee, 14th November 2011.

House of Commons (2015) Lessons from major rail infrastructure programmes, Committee of Public Accounts, 12th January 2015.

Hu, G (2003) Transport and land use in Chinese cities: International comparisons in Low, N and Gleeson, B Making urban transport sustainable, Palgrave Macmillan, Basingstoke, UK, 184-200.

Hume, K and Watson, A (2003) The human health impacts of aviation in Upham, P, Maughan, J, Raper, D, and Thomas, C (2003) Towards Sustainable Aviation, Earthscan, London, 48-76.

Illich, I (1974) Energy and equity, Marion Boyars, London.

IARC (2012) Monographs on the evaluation of carcinogenic risks to humans, volume 105, Diesel and gasoline engine exhausts and some nitroarenes, International Agency for Research on Cancer, World Health Organisation.

IARC (2013) Outdoor air pollution a leading cause of cancer deaths, International Agency for Research on Cancer, World Health Organisation, Press Release No 221, 17th October 2013.

IATA (2009) Aviation and Climate Change: pathway to carbon neutral growth in 2020. International Air Transport Association.

ICAO (2013) ICAO Air Transport results confirm robust passenger demand, sluggish cargo demand.

IPCC (2013) 5th Assessment Report, Climate Change 2014: Mitigation of Climate Change, Chapter 8, Transport.

Independent Newspaper (2013), London cycling deaths: woman killed in lorry crash becomes 4th fatality in 8 days on streets of capital, 13th November 2013.

ITDP (2008) 2009 Sustainable Transport Award Nominees, Sustainable transport, Winter 2008, No 20, page 29, Institute for Transportation and Development, New York.

ITDP (2013) Footpath design. A guide to creating footpaths that are safe, comfortable and easy to use, ITDP, New York.

ITDP, Gehl Architects and Nelson Nyggard (2010) Our cities ourselves, 10 principles for transport in urban life, ITDP, New York.

Jacobs, J (1961) The Death and Life of Great American Cities. The failure of town planning, Random House, USA.

James, A (2014) The death of the habitats directive, World Transport Policy and Practice, volume 20, number 2/3, 97-107.

Jerrett, M, McConnell, R, Chang, C, Wolch, J, Reynolds, K, Lurman, F, Gilliland, F and Berhane, K (2010) Automobile traffic around the home and attained body mass index: a longitudinal cohort study of children aged 10-18 years, Prev Med 50: S50-8.

Johnston, I R, Muir, C and Howard, E W (2014) Eliminating serious injury and death from road transport. A crisis of complacency, CRC Press, Taylor and Francis Group.

Kenyon, K, Lyons, G and Rafferty, J (2003) Transport and social exclusion: investigating the possibility of promoting social exclusion through virtual mobility. Journal of Transport Geography, 10, 207-219.

Kenworthy, J (2014) Total Daily Mobility Patterns and their Policy Implications for 43 Global Cities in 1995 and 2005, World Transport Policy and Practice, volume 20, number 1, 41-55.

Kenworthy, J and Laube, F (2001) The Millennium Cities Database for Sustainable Transport, Brussels: UITP and Perth: ISTP, Murdoch University.

Kinnersley, P (2014) The return of the Zombie road, World Transport Policy and Practice, volume 20, number 2/3.

Klein, N (2014) This changes everything. Capitalism v the climate, Simon and Schuster, New York.

Koornstra, M et al (2002) SUNflower: a comparative study of the development of road safety in Sweden, The United Kingdom and the Netherlands, SWOV, Leidschendam, the Netherlands.

Lancaster City Council (2013) Clearing the air. The Air Quality Strategy for Lancaster District.

Layard, R (2005) Happiness, Penguin Books, London.

Lechtenboehmer, S and Samadi, S (2013) Blown by the wind. Replacing nuclear power in German electricity generation, Environmental Science and Policy 25, 234-241.

Living Streets (2009) Inquiry into Active Travel: submission from Living Streets, Scotland.

London Assembly (2014) Feet First. Improving road safety in London. Transport Committee.

Low, N and Gleeson, B (2003) "Making urban transport sustainable", Palgrave Macmillan, Basingstoke, UK.

Lucas, K (2012) Transport and Social Exclusion: where are we now? Transport Policy, 20, 105-113.

Maddison, D, Pearce, D, Johansson, O, Calthrop, E, Littman, T, Verhoef, E (1996) The true costs of road transport, Earthscan, Blueprint 5.

Mani, A, Pai, M, and Aggarwal, R (nd) Sustainable Urban Transport in India, EMBARQ and the World Resources Institute.

Marchetti, C (1993) On Mobility, Final Status Report, International Institute for Applied Systems Analysis, Laxenburg, Austria, Contract Number 4672-92-03 ED ISP A.

Marchetti, C (1994) Anthropological invariants in travel behaviour, Technological Forecasting and Social Change, 47, 75-88.

Mees, P (2009) How dense are we? Another look at urban density and transport patterns in Australia, Canada and the USA, Road and Transport Research, volume 18, number 4, 58-67.

Mersmann, F and Wehnert, T (2014) Shifting Paradigms. Unpacking transformation for climate change, Wuppertal Institute, Germany.

Metz, D (2008) The myth of travel time savings, Transport Reviews, 28, 3,321-336.

Momo (2010) The State of European Car-Sharing: final report D2.4 work package 2, Berlin: Momo Car-Sharing, Intelligent Energy Europe (IEE).

Morton, A (2014) The East-West Link, World Transport Policy and Practice, volume 20, number 2/3.

NATS (2009), Flight Plan to cut 10% of CO2 from UK air traffic control, News Release, 10.3.09, NATS, Fareham, UK.

Newman, P and Kenworthy, J (1999) Sustainability and cities: overcoming automobile dependence, Island Press, Washington DC.

Newman, P, Kenworthy, J and Glazebrook, G (2013) Peak car use and the rise of global rail: why this is happening and what it means for large and small cities, Journal of Transportation Technologies, 3(4) 272-287.

NICE (2008) Physical activity and the environment, Public Health Guidance, 8 (PH8), National Institute for Health and Clinical Excellence.

OECD (1999) Environmentally Sustainable Transport. Final report on Phase II of the OECD EST Project. Volume 1 Synthesis Report Organisation for Economic Co-operation and Development, Paris, France, ENV/EPOC/PPC/T(97)1/FINAL.

OECD (1995) Urban travel and sustainable development, European Conference of Ministers of Transport (ECMT), OECD, Paris, France.

OECD (2002a) OECD Guidelines towards EST, Organisation for Economic Co-operation and Development, Paris, France.

OECD (2002b) Policy Instruments for achieving EST, Report
Organisation for Economic Co-operation and Development, Paris, France.
OECD (2006) Decoupling the Environmental Impacts of Transport from
Economic Growth), OECD, Paris, France.
Pape, R (2014) A fair share of climate responsibility, Acid News, Number
3, October 2014.
PBL and JRC (2013) Trends in Global CO2 emissions, 2013 Report,
Background Studies, PBL Netherlands Environmental Assessment
Agency and European Commission Joint Research Centre.
Petersen, R (2002) Land use planning and urban transport, Module 2a.
Deutsche Gesellschaft fuer Technische Zusammenarbeit, Eschborn,
Germany.
Petrini, C (2007) Slow Food Nation. Why our food should be good, clean
and fair, Rizzoli International Publications, New York.
Potočnik, J (2012), Speech by the European Commissioner for
Environment
24th September 2012.
Pucher, J, Peng, Z-R, Mittal, N, Zhu, Y, and Korattyswaroopam, N
(2007), Urban Transport Trends and Policies in China and India: impacts
of rapid economic growth, Transport Reviews, volume 27, no.4, 379-410,
July 2007.
Pucher, J and Buehler, R (2012) Cycling Cities, Massachusetts Institute of
Technology, USA.
RCEP (1995) Transport and the Environment, Royal Commission on
Environmental Pollution, 18th Report, Presented to Parliament, October
1994, Oxford University Press.
Rechnitzer, G and Grzebieta, R H (1999) Crashworthiness systems- a
paradigm shift in road safety systems, Transport Engineering in Australia,
Volume 5, Number 2, 74-82.
Roberts, I, Coggan, C (1994) Blaming children for child pedestrian
injuries, Social Science & Medicine,38(5),749-753.
Roberts, I (2010) (with Phil Edwards) The energy glut. The politics of
fatness in an overheating world, Zed Books, London.
Rockstrom, J [plus 28 additional authors] (2009) Planetary boundaries:
exploring the safe operating space for humanity, Ecology and Society, 14
(2).
Rosencrantz, H, Edvardsson, K and Hansson, S, (2007). Vision Zero-is it
rational? Transportation Research A, 41, 559-567.
Sachs, W (1993) Die vier E's: Merkposten fuer einen massvollen
Wirtschaftsstil. In Politische Oekologie 11 (33), Munich; quoted in
Schneidewind, U and Zahrnt, A (2014), Oekom Verlag, Munich.

SACTRA (1994) New roads generate new traffic, Department of the Environment, Transport and Regions, UK Government, Standing Advisory Committee on Trunk Road Assessment.

SACTRA (1999) Transport and the economy, Department of the Environment, Transport and Regions, UK Government, Standing Advisory Committee on Trunk Road Assessment.

Sausen R, Isaksen I, Grewe V, Hauglustaine D, Lee D S, Myhre G, Kohler M O, Pitari G, Schumann U, Stordal F and Zerefos C (2005) Aviation radiative forcing in 2000: an update on IPCC (1999). Meteorologische Zeitschrift 114, 555 * 561.

Schaefer, A (2005) Global Passenger Mobility Data Set, version 1.0, University of Cambridge, September 2005.

Schaefer, A and Victor, D G (2000) The future mobility of the world population. Transportation Research A, 34, 171-205.

Schneidewind, U and Zahrnt, A (2014) The Politics of Sufficiency, Oekem Verlag, Munich, Germany.

SEU (2003) Making the connections: final report on transport and social exclusion, Social Exclusion Unit, Office of the Deputy Prime Minister, UK.

Sewill, B (2003) The Hidden Costs of Flying, Aviation Environment Federation, London.

Shaw, B, Watson, B, Frauendienst, B, Redecker, A, Jones, T with Hillman, M (2013) Children's independent mobility: a comparative study in England and Germany (1971-2010), Policy Studies Institute, London.

Sheehan, M (2001) City Limits: putting the brakes on sprawl, Worldwatch Paper 156, Worldwatch Institute, Washington DC, page 22.

Shoup, D (2005) The high cost of free parking, American Planning Association, Chicago, USA.

SNRA (2003) Vision Zero: from concept to action, Swedish National Road Administration, Borlange, Sweden.

Song, Z Q (2013) Transition to a Transit City. Case of Beijing, Transportation Research Record: Journal of the Transportation Research Board, 2394 38–44.

Spitzner, M A (2008) The need for gendered approaches to transport policy. Results from case studies in industrialised and developing countries, Wuppertal Institute, Germany.

Stadt Freiburg (2010) Umweltpolitik in Freiburg, Dezernat fuer Umwelt, Schule, Bildung und Gebaudemanagement, Stadt Freiburg im Breisgau.

Steptoe, A, Shankar, A, Demakakos, P and Wardle, J (2013) Social isolation, loneliness and all cause mortality in older men and women,

Proceedings of the National Academy of Sciences (PNAS), Open Access edition, February 15th 2013, Reference number 1219686110.

Stollery, P (2008) ATM Global Environment Efficiency Goals for 2050. CANSO.

Strickfaden, M and Devlieger, P (2011) Empathy through Accumulating Techné: Designing an Accessible Metro, The Design Journal, 14(2), 207-229.

Surridge, M, Green, C, Kaluba, D and Simfukwe, V (2014) Filling a gap in the referral system: linking communities to quality maternal health care via an emergency transport system in six districts of Zambia, World Transport Policy and Practice, volume 20, Number 1, 7-26.

Sustainable Aviation Group (2008) Sustainable Aviation Group CO2 Road Map. http://sustainableaviation.co.uk/wp-content/uploads/sa-road-map-final-dec-08.pdf

Teufel, D (1995) Folgen einer globalen Motorisierung, Umwelt und Prognose Institute, Heidelberg, Germany.

Tingvall, C (1997) The Zero Vision. A road transport system free from serious health losses, in Holst, von H, Nygren, A, Thord, R (eds) Transportation, Traffic Safety and Health, Springer Verlag, Berlin.

Tingvall, C and Haworth, N (1999) Vision Zero: an ethical approach to safety and mobility. Paper presented to the 6th International Conference on Road Safety and Traffic Enforcement Beyond 2000, Melbourne, Australia, 6-7 September 1999.

TNO (1992) EC Policy measures aiming to reduce CO2 emissions in the transport sector. Final Report. INRO-LOG-1992-15, TNO Institute of Spatial Organisation, Delft, The Netherlands, December 1992, 92/NL/037.

Townsend, T and Lake, A (2009) Obesogenic urban form: theory, policy and practice, Health and Place 15(4) 909-16.

Transport and Environment (2011) Car free Milan after PM Pollution, Bulletin, 202, October 2011.

Transport and Environment (2012) A new flightplan: getting global aviation climate measures off the ground. Background report for the conference held in Brussels on 7.2.14.

Transport for London (TfL) (2008) London Low Emission Zone Impacts Monitoring, London: TfL.

Transport for London (TfL) (2011) Pedal cyclist collisions and casualties, Greater London, Fact Sheet 2011-1.

Tuong, N T C (2014) Determinants of private mode choice in Ho Chi Minh City, Vietnam: from the individual perspective, World Transport Policy and Practice, volume 20, number 1, 56-69.

UITP (2009) Public Transport and CO2 emissions, International Association of Public Transport, Brussels.

UKERC (2009) Making the transition to a secure and low carbon energy system: synthesis report, United Kingdom Energy Research Centre.

Unger, N et al (2010) Attribution of climate forcing to economic sectors, Proceedings of the National Academy of Sciences, early edition, February 2010.

United Nations (2012) The Millenium Development Goals Report, 2012, United Nations, New York.

United Nations (2013) Planning and design for sustainable urban mobility. Global report on human settlements 2013. UN Human Settlements Programme.

Upham, P, Maughan, J, Raper, D, and Thomas, C (2003) Towards Sustainable Aviation, Earthscan, London.

Vallack, H, Haq, G, Whitelegg, J and Cambridge, H (2014) Policy pathways towards achieving a zero carbon transport sector in the UK to 2050, World Transport Policy and Practice, Volume 20, Number 4, 28-42.

Van Essen (plus 4 others) (2003) To shift or not to shift, that's the question, CE Delft, The Netherlands.

Van Essen (plus 7 others) (2011) External costs of transport in Europe. Update study for 2008, CE Delft, The Netherlands.

Victoria Transport Policy Institute (VTPI) (2011) Road Pricing, Victoria Transport Policy Institute, Canada.

Vivier, J (2006) Mobility in Cities Database. Better mobility for people worldwide. Analysis and Recommendations, UITP (Union Internationale Transports Publique), Brussels.

Wadhwa, L C (2001) Vision Zero requires 5 star road safety systems, paper presented at 2001 road safety, policing and education conference, 19-21 November 2001, Melbourne, Australia.

Walton, W (2014), The Aberdeen Western Peripheral Route, World Transport Policy and Practice, volume 20, number 2/3.

WBCSD (nd) Mobility for development, World Business Council for Sustainable Development.

Welsh Assembly Government (2014) personal communication from James Ardern, 19th August 2014.

Whitelegg, J (1982) Inequalities in health care. Problems of access and provision, Straw Barnes Press, Retford, UK.

Whitelegg, J, (1983) Road safety: defeat, complicity and the bankruptcy of science. Accident Analysis and Prevention, 15, 2, 153-160.

Whitelegg, J (1993) Time Pollution, Ecologist, 23 (4), 132-134.

Whitelegg, J (1994a) Driven to destruction. Absurd freight movement and European road building, Eco-Logica Ltd.

Whitelegg, J (1994b) Roads, jobs and the economy, Eco-Logica Ltd.

Whitelegg, J (2003) The economics of aviation: a NW England perspective. A report for CPRE North West, Eco-Logica Ltd, Lancaster.

Whitelegg, J (2005a) London Sustainable Food Hub: opportunities for a sustainable food logistics centre in London, London Development Agency and Mayor of London.

Whitelegg, J (2005b) The economic impact of Bristol International Airport. A report for the Parish Councils Airport Association.

Whitelegg, J (2011) Pay as you go: managing traffic impacts in a world-class city, Greater London Authority.

Whitelegg, J (2012) How much transport can landscape tolerate: new ways of thinking about traffic, landscape and nature in Koerner, S, Holzapfel, H and Bellin-Harder, F (eds) Landschaft und Verkehr, University of Kassel, 93-114.

Whitelegg, J (2013a) Quality of Life and public management, Routledge.

Whitelegg, J (2013b) Report on transport and sustainability implications of the planning application to build 42 new homes in Grange over Sands, Cumbria, South Lakeland District Council, planning applications SL/2013/069/, Land between Allithwaite Rd and Carter Rd, also known as the R89 site.

Whitelegg, J (2014) Editor, World Transport Policy and Practice, volume 20, number 2 and 3.

Whitelegg, J and Cambridge H (2004) Aviation and Sustainability: a policy paper, Stockholm Environment Institute, University of York, UK.

Whitelegg, J, Haq, G, Vallack, H and Cambridge, H (2010) Towards a zero carbon vision for UK Transport, Stockholm Environment Institute, University of York, UK.

Whitelegg, J and Haq, G (2004) Intelligent Travel: personalised travel planning in the City of York, Stockholm Environment Institute, University of York, UK.

Whitelegg, J and Haq G (2006) Vision Zero: adopting a target of zero for road traffic fatalities and serious injuries, Stockholm Environment Institute, York, UK.

Whitelegg, J and Kirkbride, A (2003) Wise moves: the potential to reduce greenhouse gas emissions through localisation and co-operation. A report for the Transport 2000 Trust, London.

Whitelegg, J and Pye, W (2009) Traffic and transport evidence presented to the public inquiry into the Centros proposals for a major new shopping centre on Lancaster Canal Corridor North Centros evidence.

Whizman, C and Pike, L (2007) From battery-reared to free range children. Institutional barriers and enablers to children's independent mobility in Victoria, Australia, GAMUT, University of Melbourne.

WHO (1999) Guidelines on Community Noise, World Health Organisation, Geneva.

WHO (2004) World report on road traffic injury prevention, World Health Organisation, Geneva.

WHO (2010) Global recommendations on physical activity for health, World Health Organisation, Geneva.

WHO (2013a) Global Status Report on Road Safety, World Health Organisation, Geneva.

WHO (2013b) Fact sheet 311, Obesity and overweight, World Health Organisation, Geneva.

WHO, (2014a) Air quality deteriorating in many of the world's cities. News Release, 7th May 2014, World Health Organisation, Geneva.

WHO (2014b) Obesity and Overweight. Fact sheet Number 311, May 2014, World Health Organisation, Geneva.

Wilkinson, R and Pickett, K (2009) The Spirit Level: why equality is better for everyone, Penguin Books, Harmondsworth.

Woodcock, J and 17 others (2009) Public health benefits of strategies to reduce greenhouse gas emissions: urban land transport, Lancet 374:1930-43.

World Bank (2014) Transport for health. The global burden of disease from motorised road transport, Report 86304.

Yorkshire and Humber Regional Assembly (2008) Achieving low carbon and sustainable transport systems in Yorkshire and Humber, JMP consultants (Leeds) and Stockholm Environment Institute (York).

Yunita, R (2008) TransJakarta: putting on lipstick while running to catch the bus, Sustainable Transport, Winter, 2008, No 20, ITDP, New York, USA.

Zahavi, Y (1979) The UMOT project, US Department of Transportation Report Number DOT-RSRA-DPD-20-79-3, Washington DC.

List of Figures and Tables

Figures

Tables

About the author

John Whitelegg was born in Oldham in Lancashire in 1949 and went to school in Manchester, then a Geography degree in Aberystwyth, followed by doctoral studies in the same place. After 6 years of living in "Aber" he went to Cardiff to work on a freight transport project, looking in detail at the export of steel products from the South Wales steel industry to the Great Lakes in North America.

This was followed by a spell as an economic development and transport officer in the Outer Hebrides, and then over 20 years in the Geography department at Lancaster University, finishing there as Professor of Geography and Head of Department.

He then set up his own transport consultancy company, Eco-Logica Ltd, working mainly with local and central government and the private sector on sustainable transport. At the same time, he was appointed to a professorship of sustainable transport at Liverpool John Moores University and of sustainable development at York University, and worked for 10 years with the Stockholm Environment Institute at its UK base in York.

John has worked in most European countries, including a professorship at Roskilde University in Denmark and Essen University in Germany, and over two years in the Ministry of City Development, Housing and Traffic of the state of North Rhine Westphalia in Dusseldorf.

He has also worked in Australia on speaking tours and on sustainable transport issues in Melbourne, Sydney, Perth and Brisbane. More recently he worked in Beijing on a sustainable urbanisation project and in Kolkata (formerly Calcutta) on a sustainable transport plan for that city.

He edits the journal *World Transport Policy and Practice*, now in its 24th year (www.worldtransportjournal.com).

John enjoys lots of walking in the Shropshire Hills, community campaigns, growing food on an allotment, talking to grandchildren and living in other countries.

Printed in Great Britain
by Amazon